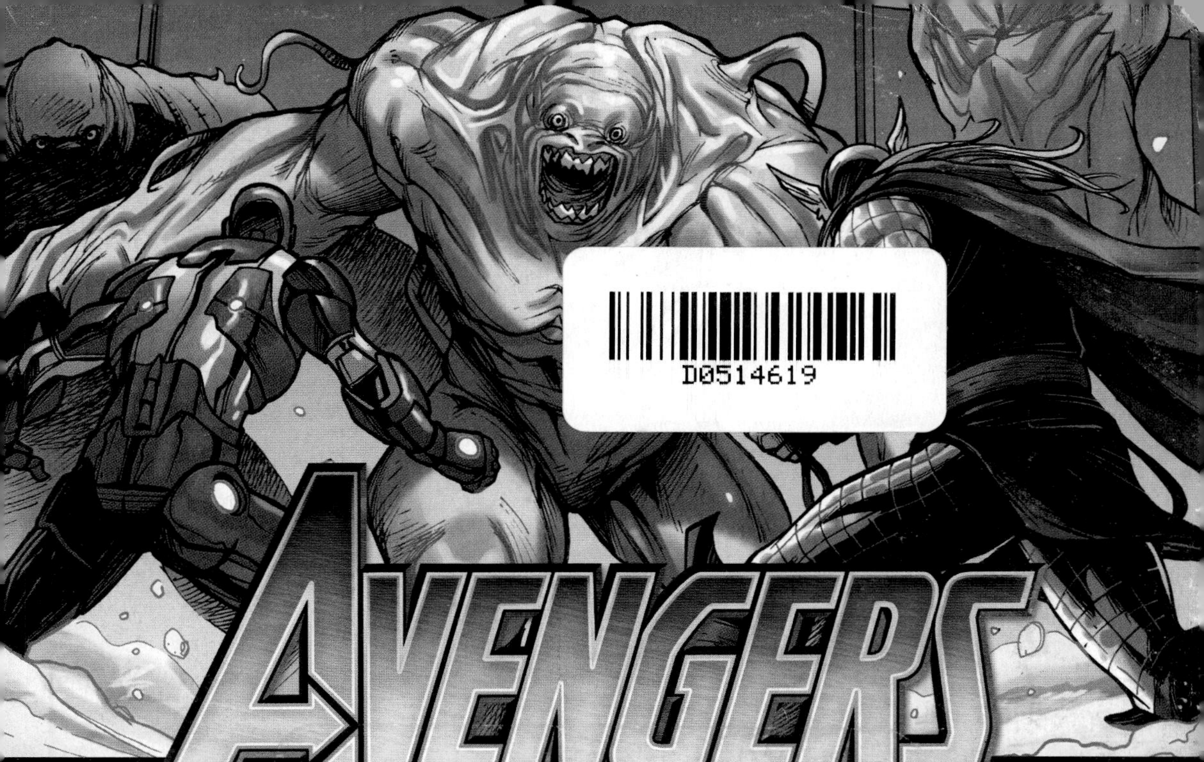

AVENGERS ASSEMBLE

SCIENCE BROS

WRITER
KELLY SUE DeCONNICK

ARTIST (#9-11)
STEFANO CASELLI

PENCILER (#12-13)
PETE WOODS

INKER & FINISHES (#12-13)
SCOTT HANNA

WITH **MARK BAGLEY** (BREAKDOWNS, #13)

COLOR ARTIST
RAIN BEREDO

ANNUAL #1

WRITER
CHRISTOS GAGE

ARTISTS
TOMM COKER
WITH **MIKE MAYHEW**, **MIKE DEODATO**, **LUKE ROSS**
& **VALENTINE DE LANDRO**

COLOR ARTIST
DANIEL FREEDMAN

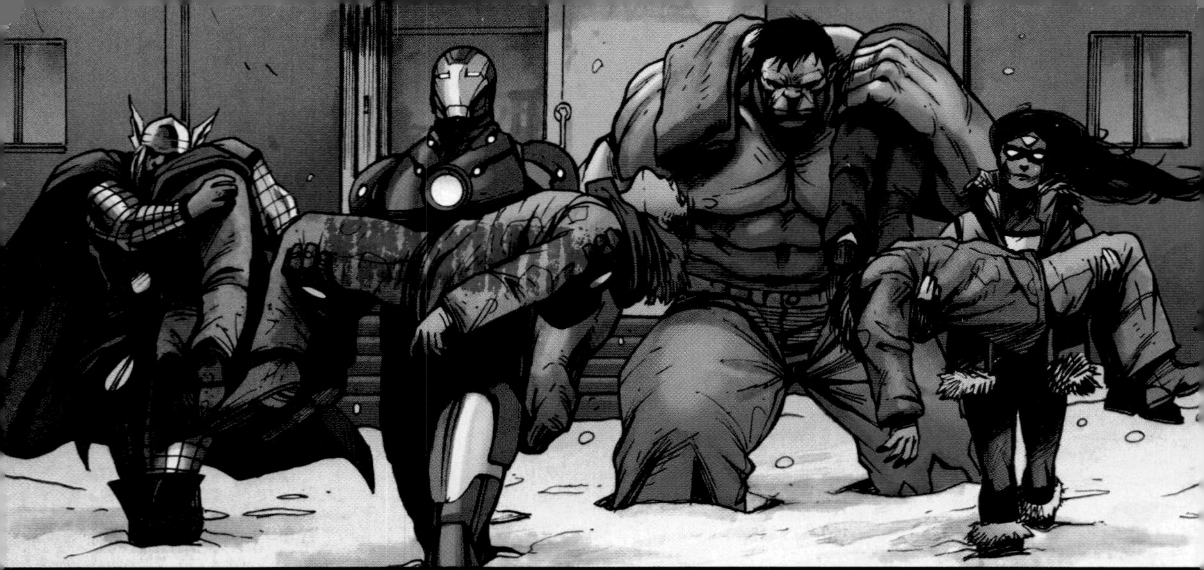

LETTERER
VC'S CLAYTON COWLES

COVER ARTISTS
STEVE McNIVEN & ***JASON KEITH*** (#9),
GREG LAND & ***FRANK D'ARMATA*** (#10),
MICO SUAYAN & ***JESUS ABURTOV*** (#11), ***NIC KLEIN*** (#12-13)
AND ***TOMM COKER*** & ***DANIEL FREEDMAN*** (ANNUAL #1)

ASSISTANT EDITOR
JAKE THOMAS

EDITORS
TOM BREVOORT WITH ***LAUREN SANKOVITCH***

Collection Editor: Cory Levine
Assistant Editors: Alex Starbuck & Nelson Ribeiro
Editors, Special Projects: Jennifer Grünwald & Mark D. Beazley
Senior Editor, Special Projects: Jeff Youngquist
SVP of Print & Digital Publishing Sales: David Gabriel
Book Design: Jeff Powell

Editor in Chief: Axel Alonso
Chief Creative Officer: Joe Quesada
Publisher: Dan Buckley
Executive Producer: Alan Fine

AVENGERS ASSEMBLE: SCIENCE BROS. Contains material originally published in magazine form as AVENGERS ASSEMBLE #9-13 and ANNUAL #1. First printing 2013. ISBN# 978-0-7851-6797- Published by MARVEL WORLDWIDE, INC., a subsidiary of MARVEL ENTERTAINMENT, LLC. OFFICE OF PUBLICATION: 135 West 50th Street, New York, NY 10020. Copyright © 2012 and 2013 Marvel Characters Inc. All rights reserved. All characters featured in this issue and the distinctive names and likenesses thereof, and all related indicia are trademarks of Marvel Characters, Inc. No similarity between any of the names, characters, persons, and/or institutions in this magazine with those of any living or dead person or institution is intended, and any such similarity which may exist is purely coincidental. **Printed in the U.S.A.** ALAN FINE, EVP - Office of the President, Marvel Worldwide, Inc. and EVP & CMO Marvel Characters B.V.; DAN BUCKLEY, Publisher & President - Print, Animation & Digital Divisions; JOE QUESADA, Chief Creative Officer; TOM BREVOORT, SVP of Publishing; DAVID BOGART, SVP of Operations & Procurement, Publishing; C.B. CEBULSKI, SVP of Creator & Content Development; DAVID GABRIEL, SVP of Print & Digital Publishing Sales; JIM O'KEEFE, VP of Operations & Logistics; DAN CARR, Executive Director of Publishing Technology; SUSAN CRESPI, Editorial Operations Manager; ALEX MORALES, Publishing Operations Manager; STAN LEE, Chairman Emeritus. For information regarding advertising in Marvel Comics or on Marvel.com, please contact Niza Disla, Director of Marvel Partnerships at ndisla@marvel.com. For M[illegible] subscription inquiries, please call 800-217-9158. **Manufactured between 6/21/2013 and 7/29/2013 by QUAD/GRAPHICS ST. CLOUD, ST. CLOUD, MN, USA.**

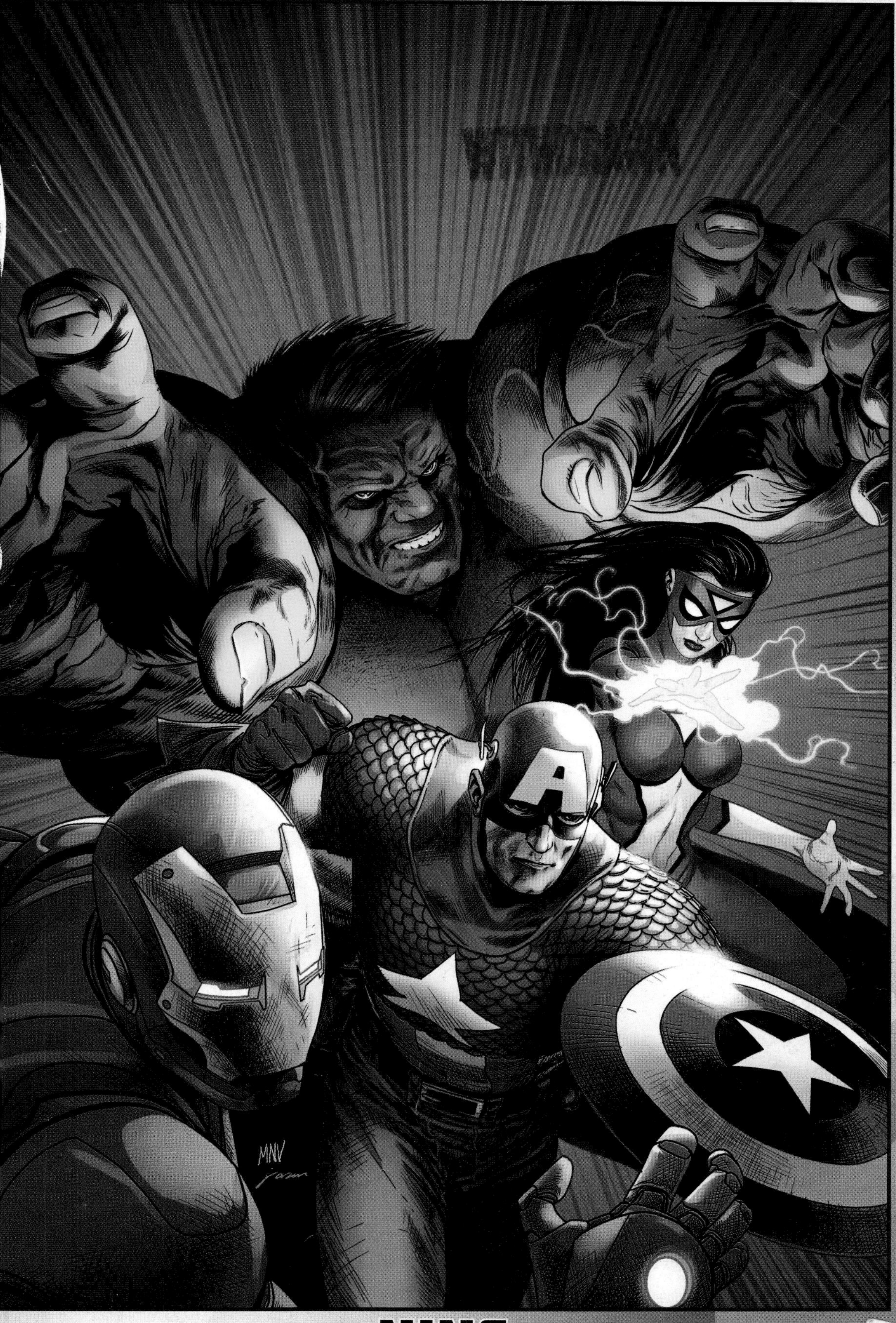

NINE

AND THERE CAME A DAY, A DAY UNLIKE ANY OTHER, WHEN EARTH'S MIGHTIEST HEROES FOUND THEMSELVES UNITED AGAINST A COMMON THREAT! ON THAT DAY, THE AVENGERS WERE BORN, TO FIGHT THE FOES NO SINGLE SUPER HERO COULD WITHSTAND!

AVENGERS ASSEMBLE

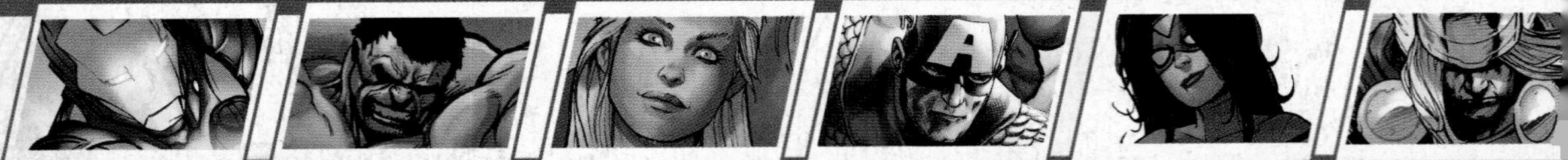

IRON MAN
TONY STARK
BILLIONAIRE TECHNOLOGIST, HIGH-TECH ARMOR

THE HULK
BRUCE BANNER
BRILLIANT MAN, GAMMA-CHARGED MONSTER

CAPTAIN MARVEL
CAROL DANVERS
FIGHTER PILOT, FLIES, ZAPS, PUNCHES

CAPTAIN AMERICA
STEVE ROGERS
SUPER-SOLDIER

SPIDER-WOMAN
JESSICA DREW
SPIDER-POWERED SECRET AGENT

THOR
GOD OF THUNDER

FILE: ASSEMBLE_009

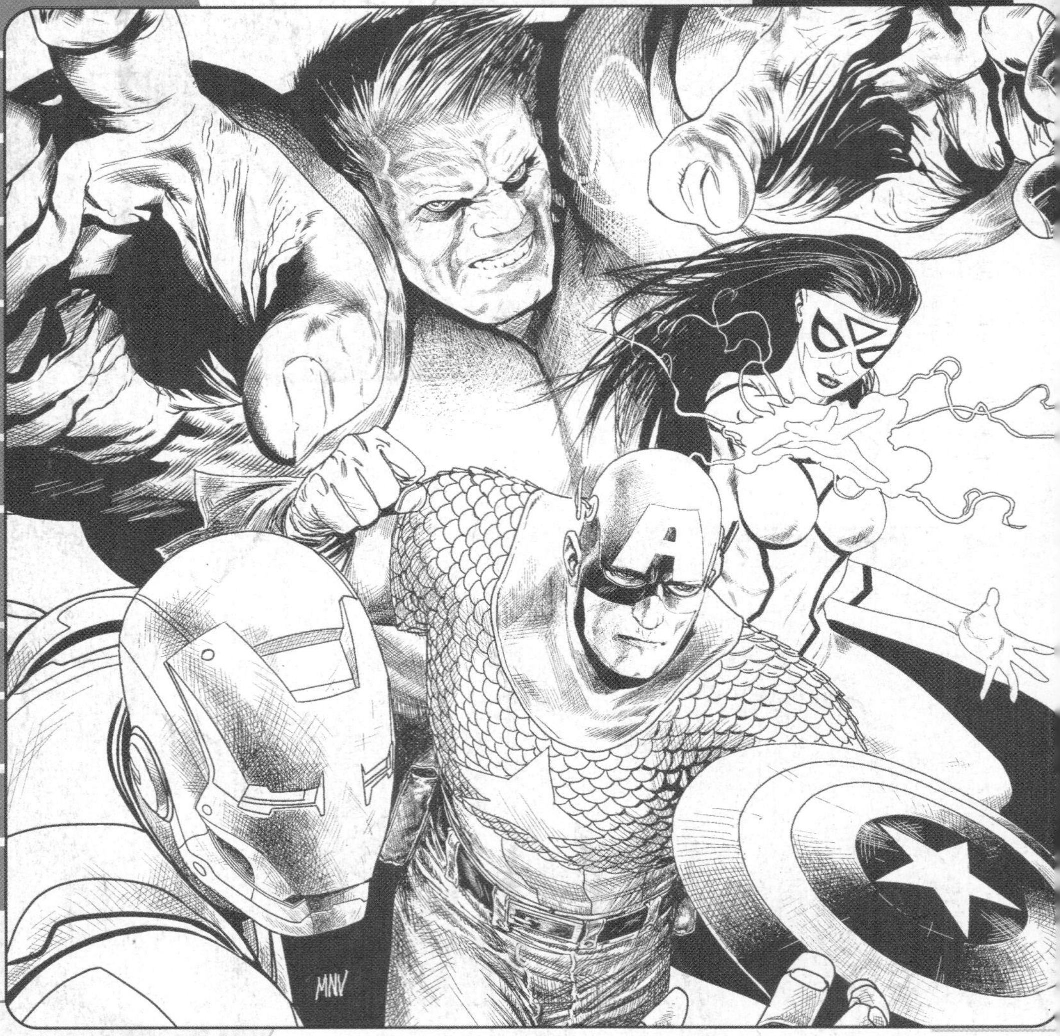
MNV

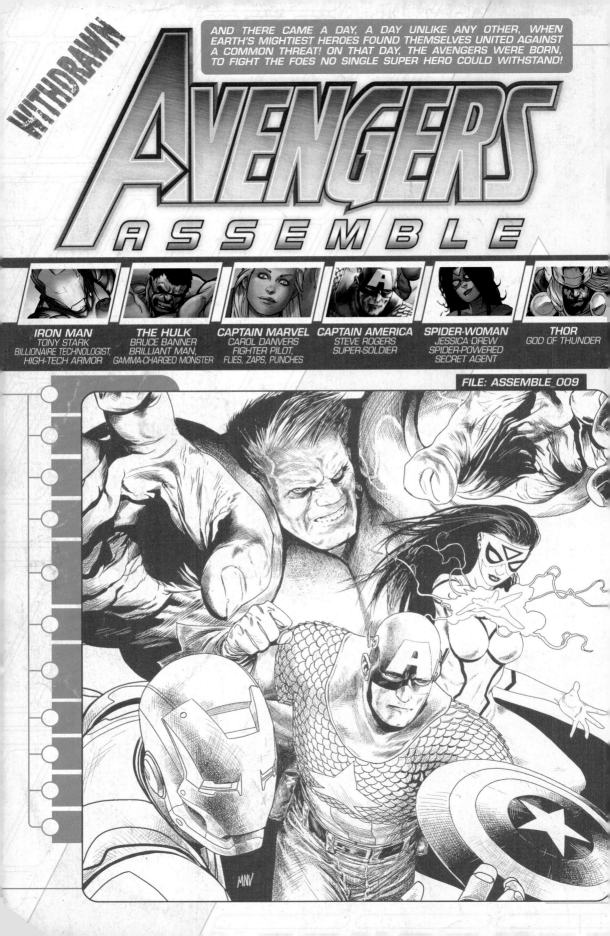

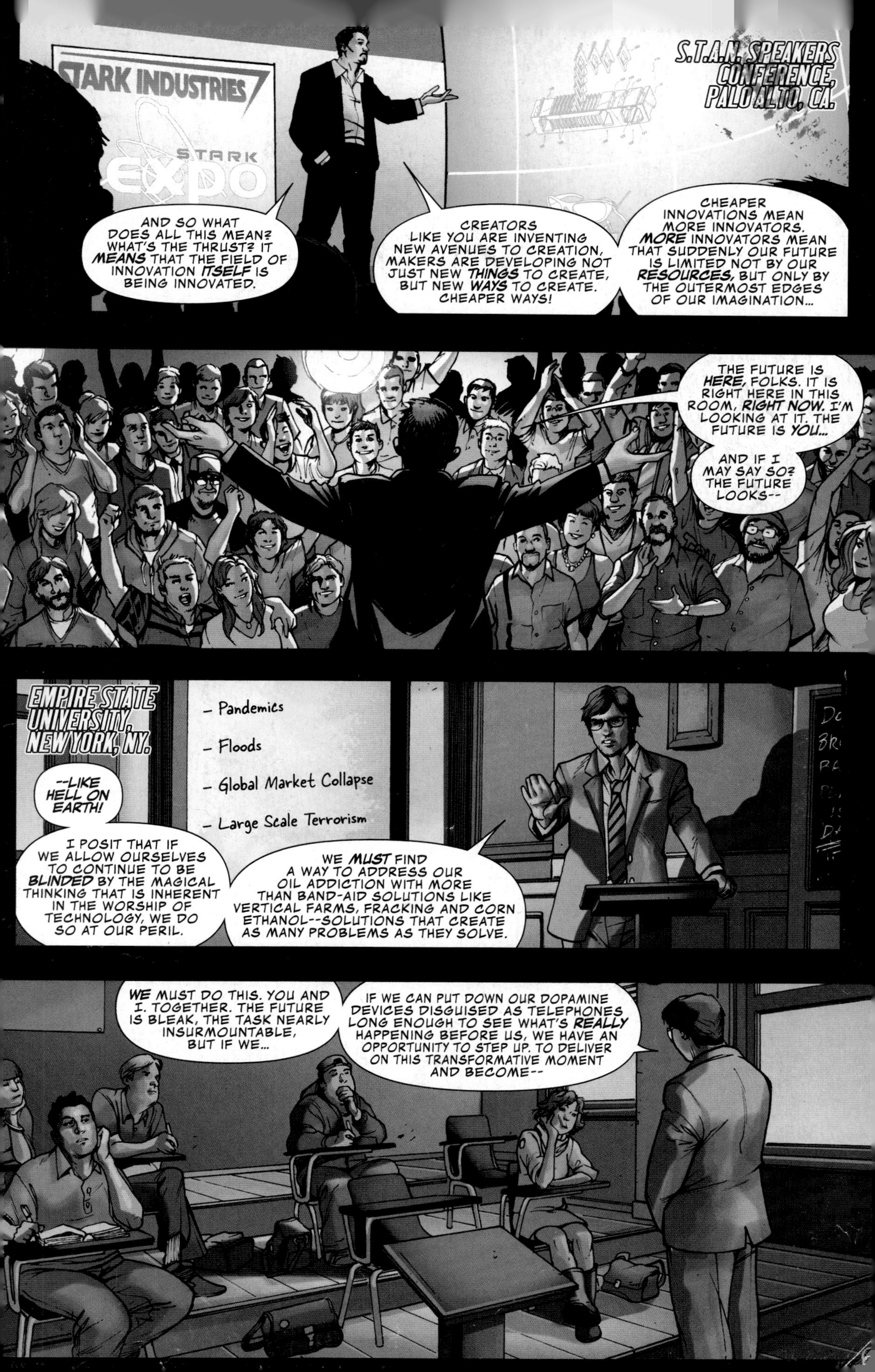
S.T.A.N. SPEAKERS CONFERENCE, PALO ALTO, CA.
STARK INDUSTRIES
STARK EXPO
AND SO WHAT DOES ALL THIS MEAN? WHAT'S THE THRUST? IT MEANS THAT THE FIELD OF INNOVATION ITSELF IS BEING INNOVATED.
CREATORS LIKE YOU ARE INVENTING NEW AVENUES TO CREATION, MAKERS ARE DEVELOPING NOT JUST NEW THINGS TO CREATE, BUT NEW WAYS TO CREATE. CHEAPER WAYS!
CHEAPER INNOVATIONS MEAN MORE INNOVATORS. MORE INNOVATORS MEAN THAT SUDDENLY OUR FUTURE IS LIMITED NOT BY OUR RESOURCES, BUT ONLY BY THE OUTERMOST EDGES OF OUR IMAGINATION...
THE FUTURE IS HERE, FOLKS. IT IS RIGHT HERE IN THIS ROOM, RIGHT NOW. I'M LOOKING AT IT. THE FUTURE IS YOU...
AND IF I MAY SAY SO? THE FUTURE LOOKS--
EMPIRE STATE UNIVERSITY, NEW YORK, NY.
- Pandemics
- Floods
- Global Market Collapse
- Large Scale Terrorism
--LIKE HELL ON EARTH!
I POSIT THAT IF WE ALLOW OURSELVES TO CONTINUE TO BE BLINDED BY THE MAGICAL THINKING THAT IS INHERENT IN THE WORSHIP OF TECHNOLOGY, WE DO SO AT OUR PERIL.
WE MUST FIND A WAY TO ADDRESS OUR OIL ADDICTION WITH MORE THAN BAND-AID SOLUTIONS LIKE VERTICAL FARMS, FRACKING AND CORN ETHANOL--SOLUTIONS THAT CREATE AS MANY PROBLEMS AS THEY SOLVE.
WE MUST DO THIS. YOU AND I. TOGETHER. THE FUTURE IS BLEAK, THE TASK NEARLY INSURMOUNTABLE, BUT IF WE...
IF WE CAN PUT DOWN OUR DOPAMINE DEVICES DISGUISED AS TELEPHONES LONG ENOUGH TO SEE WHAT'S REALLY HAPPENING BEFORE US, WE HAVE AN OPPORTUNITY TO STEP UP. TO DELIVER ON THIS TRANSFORMATIVE MOMENT AND BECOME--

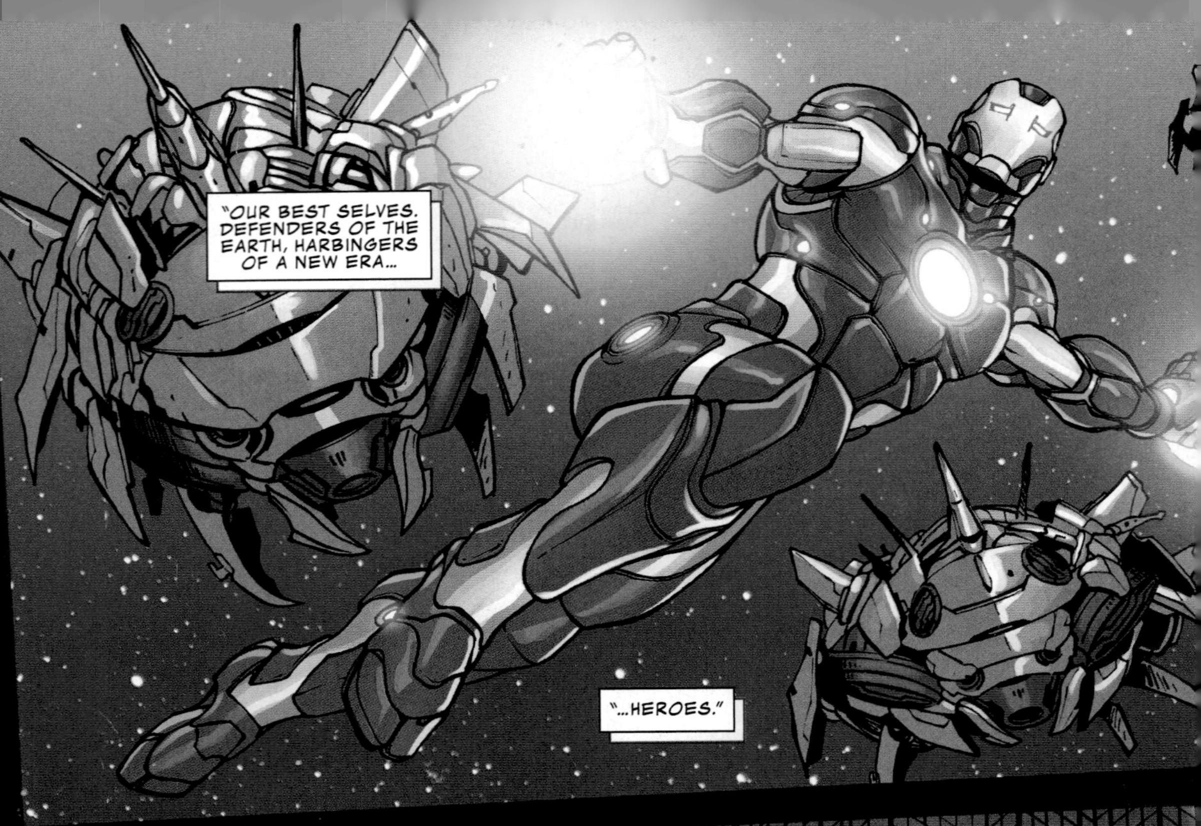
"OUR BEST SELVES. DEFENDERS OF THE EARTH, HARBINGERS OF A NEW ERA...
"...HEROES."

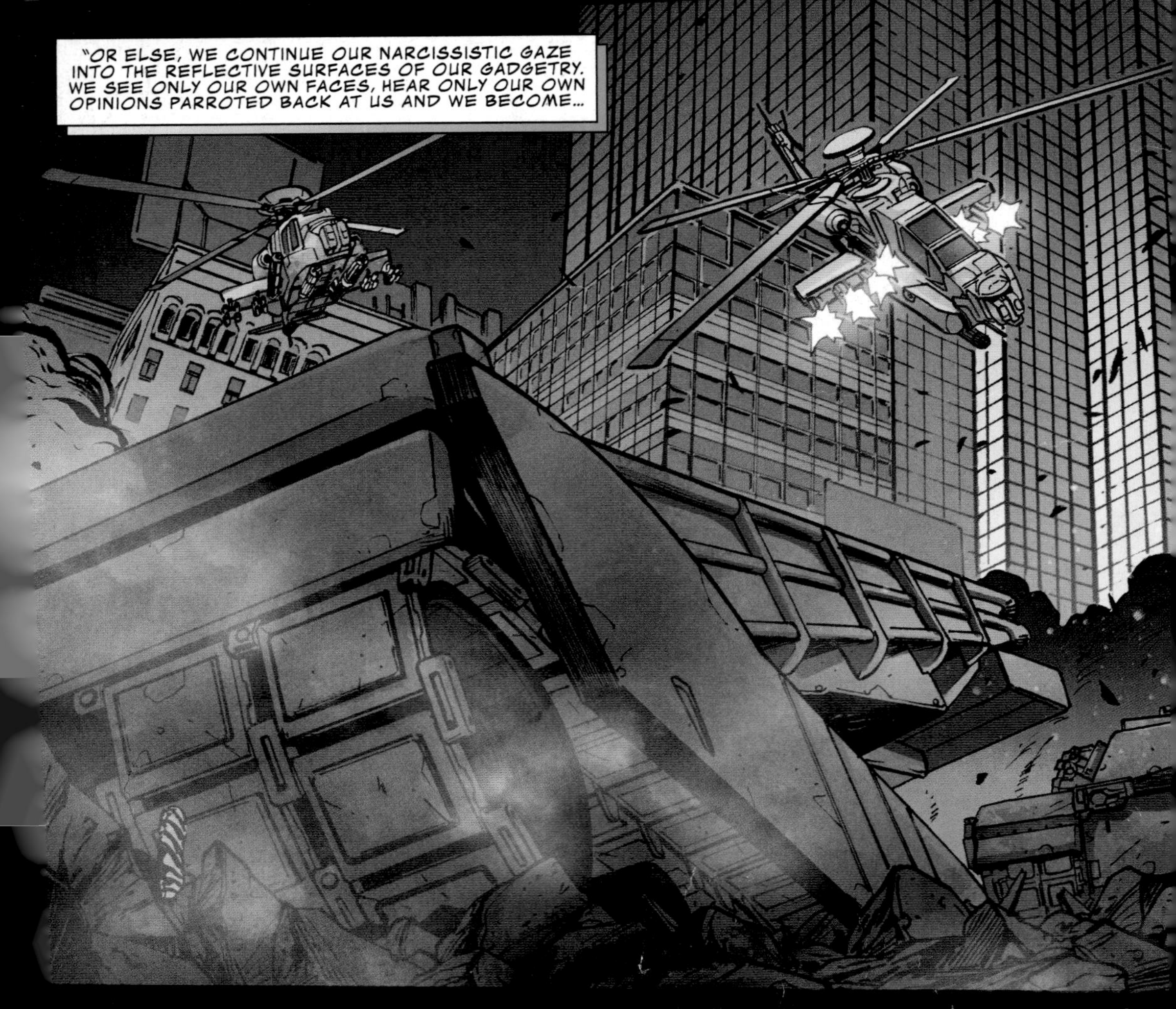
"OR ELSE, WE CONTINUE OUR NARCISSISTIC GAZE INTO THE REFLECTIVE SURFACES OF OUR GADGETRY. WE SEE ONLY OUR OWN FACES, HEAR ONLY OUR OWN OPINIONS PARROTED BACK AT US AND WE BECOME...

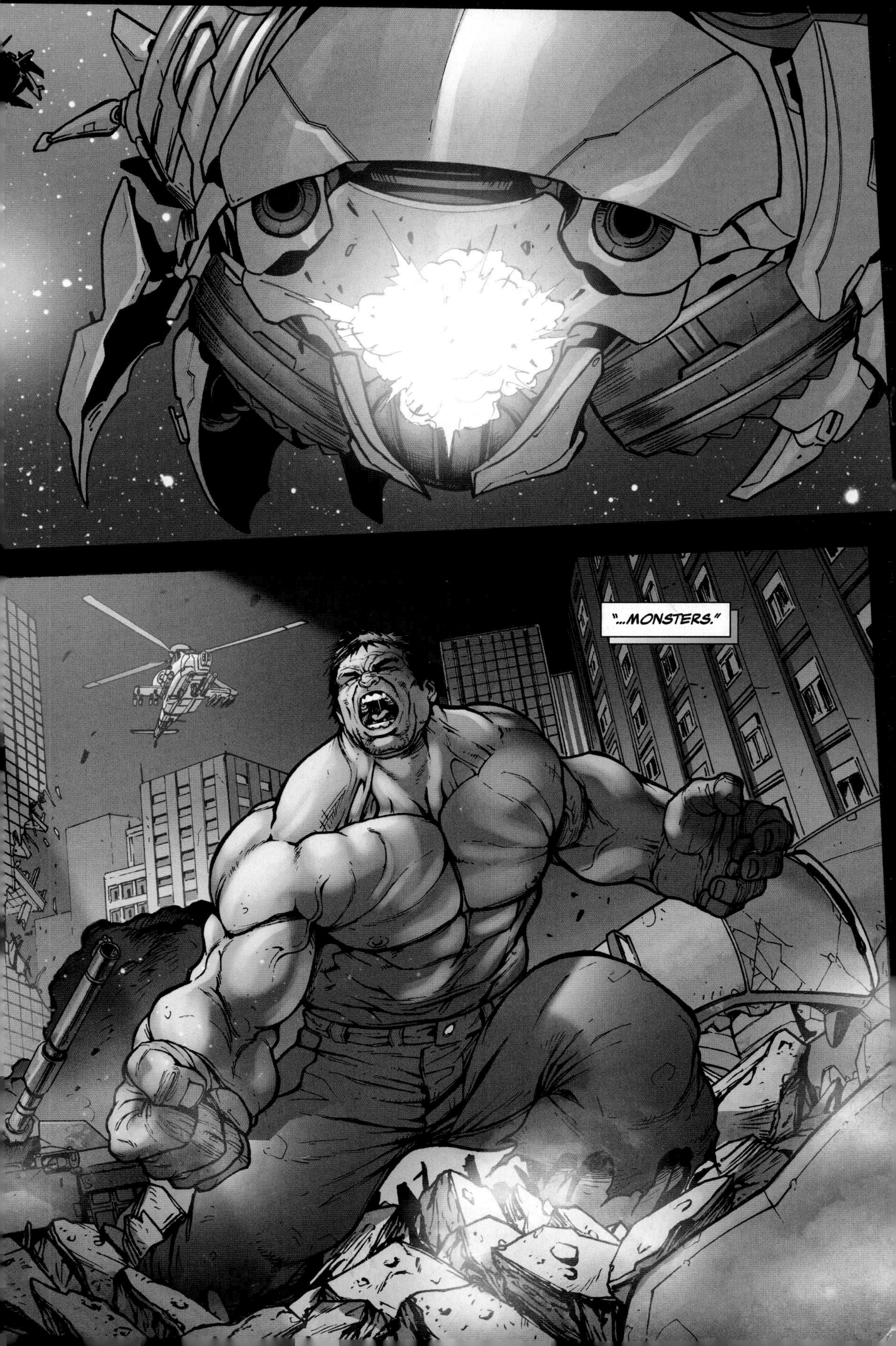
"...MONSTERS."

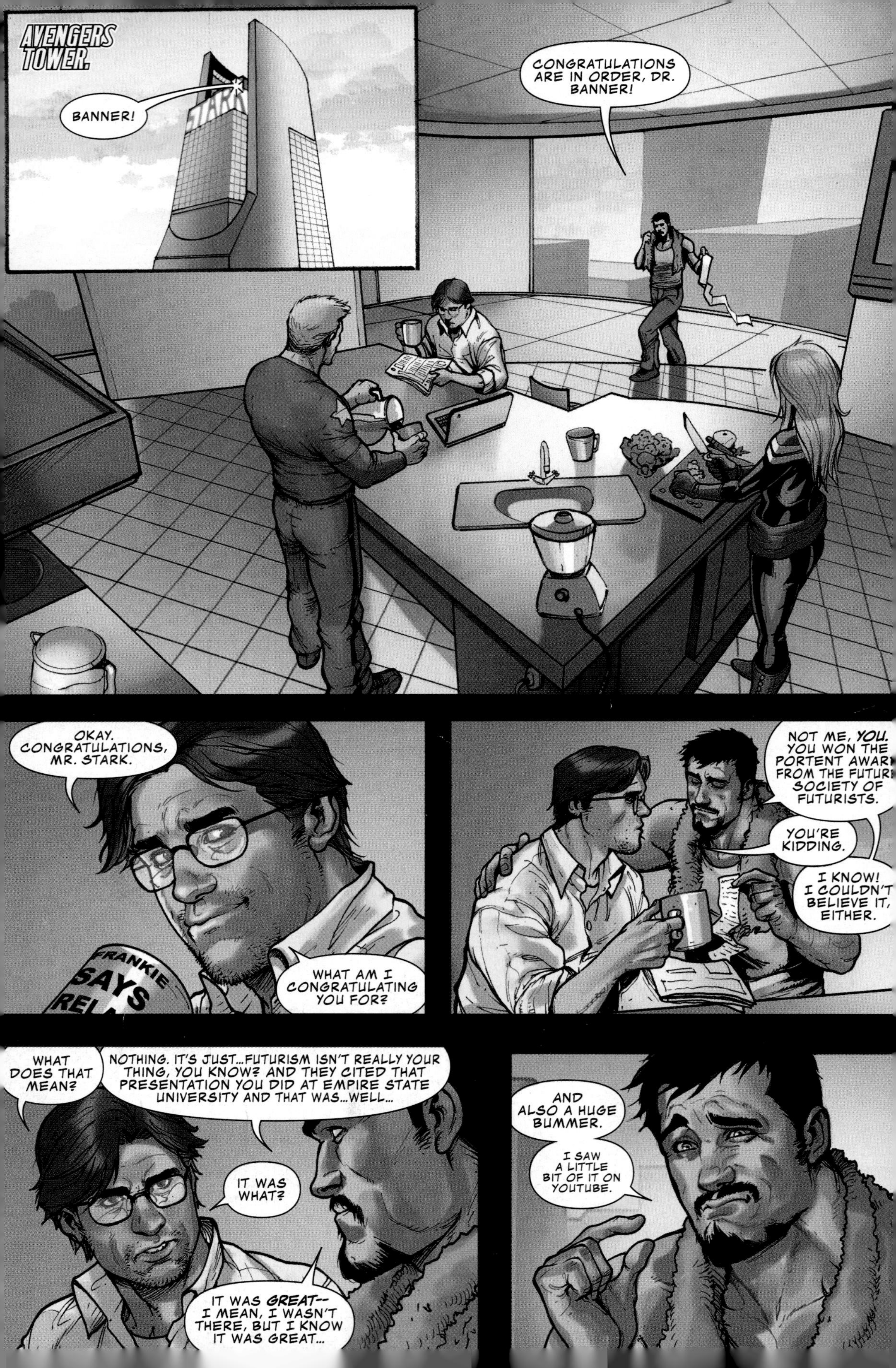
AVENGERS TOWER.
BANNER!
CONGRATULATIONS ARE IN ORDER, DR. BANNER!
OKAY. CONGRATULATIONS, MR. STARK.
WHAT AM I CONGRATULATING YOU FOR?
NOT ME, YOU. YOU WON THE PORTENT AWAR
FROM THE FUTUR
SOCIETY OF FUTURISTS.
YOU'RE KIDDING.
I KNOW! I COULDN'T BELIEVE IT, EITHER.
WHAT DOES THAT MEAN?
NOTHING. IT'S JUST...FUTURISM ISN'T REALLY YOUR THING, YOU KNOW? AND THEY CITED THAT PRESENTATION YOU DID AT EMPIRE STATE UNIVERSITY AND THAT WAS...WELL...
IT WAS WHAT?
IT WAS GREAT-- I MEAN, I WASN'T THERE, BUT I KNOW IT WAS GREAT...
AND ALSO A HUGE BUMMER.
I SAW A LITTLE BIT OF IT ON YOUTUBE.

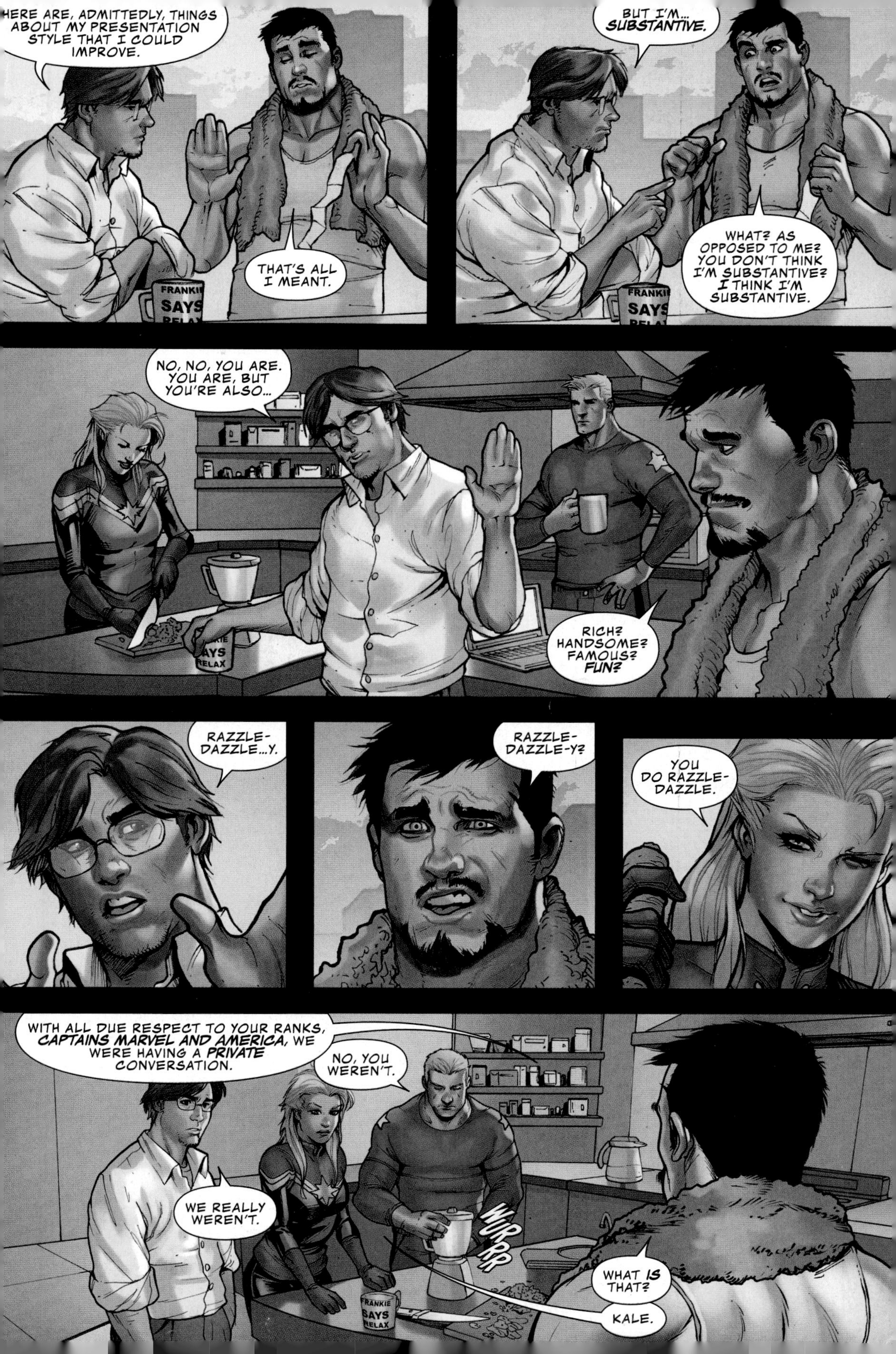

HERE ARE, ADMITTEDLY, THINGS ABOUT MY PRESENTATION STYLE THAT I COULD IMPROVE.
THAT'S ALL I MEANT.
FRANKIE SAYS
BUT I'M... SUBSTANTIVE.
WHAT? AS OPPOSED TO ME? YOU DON'T THINK I'M SUBSTANTIVE? I THINK I'M SUBSTANTIVE.
FRANKIE SAYS
NO, NO, YOU ARE. YOU ARE, BUT YOU'RE ALSO...
RICH? HANDSOME? FAMOUS? FUN?
RAZZLE-DAZZLE...Y.
RAZZLE-DAZZLE-Y?
YOU DO RAZZLE-DAZZLE.
WITH ALL DUE RESPECT TO YOUR RANKS, CAPTAINS MARVEL AND AMERICA, WE WERE HAVING A PRIVATE CONVERSATION.
NO, YOU WEREN'T.
WE REALLY WEREN'T.
WURRR
WHAT IS THAT?
KALE.
FRANKIE SAYS RELAX

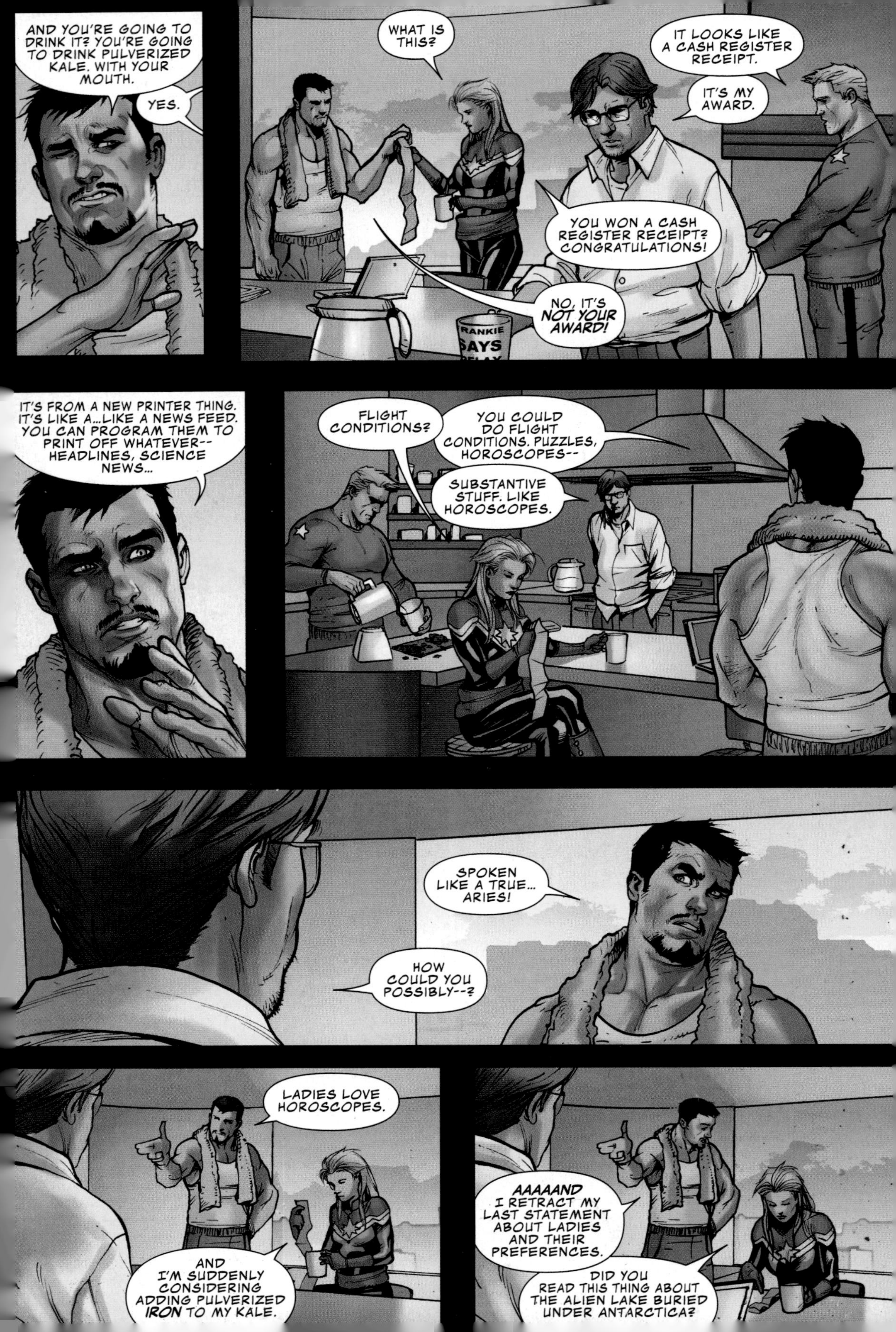
AND YOU'RE GOING TO DRINK IT? YOU'RE GOING TO DRINK PULVERIZED KALE. WITH YOUR MOUTH.
YES.
WHAT IS THIS?
IT LOOKS LIKE A CASH REGISTER RECEIPT.
IT'S MY AWARD.
YOU WON A CASH REGISTER RECEIPT? CONGRATULATIONS!
NO, IT'S NOT YOUR AWARD!
FRANKIE SAYS
IT'S FROM A NEW PRINTER THING. IT'S LIKE A...LIKE A NEWS FEED. YOU CAN PROGRAM THEM TO PRINT OFF WHATEVER-- HEADLINES, SCIENCE NEWS...
FLIGHT CONDITIONS?
YOU COULD DO FLIGHT CONDITIONS. PUZZLES, HOROSCOPES--
SUBSTANTIVE STUFF. LIKE HOROSCOPES.
SPOKEN LIKE A TRUE... ARIES!
HOW COULD YOU POSSIBLY--?
LADIES LOVE HOROSCOPES.
AND I'M SUDDENLY CONSIDERING ADDING PULVERIZED IRON TO MY KALE.
AAAAAND I RETRACT MY LAST STATEMENT ABOUT LADIES AND THEIR PREFERENCES.
DID YOU READ THIS THING ABOUT THE ALIEN LAKE BURIED UNDER ANTARCTICA?

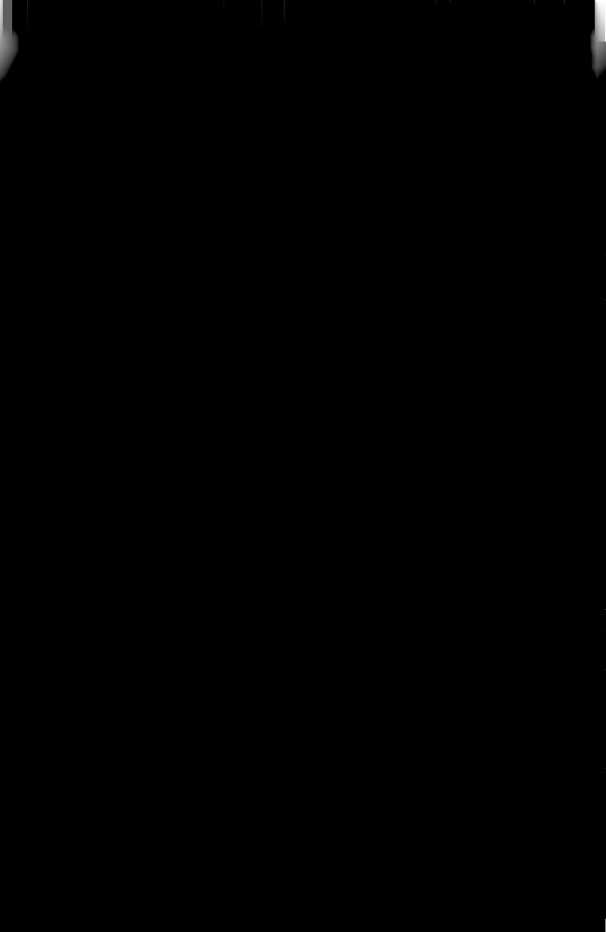

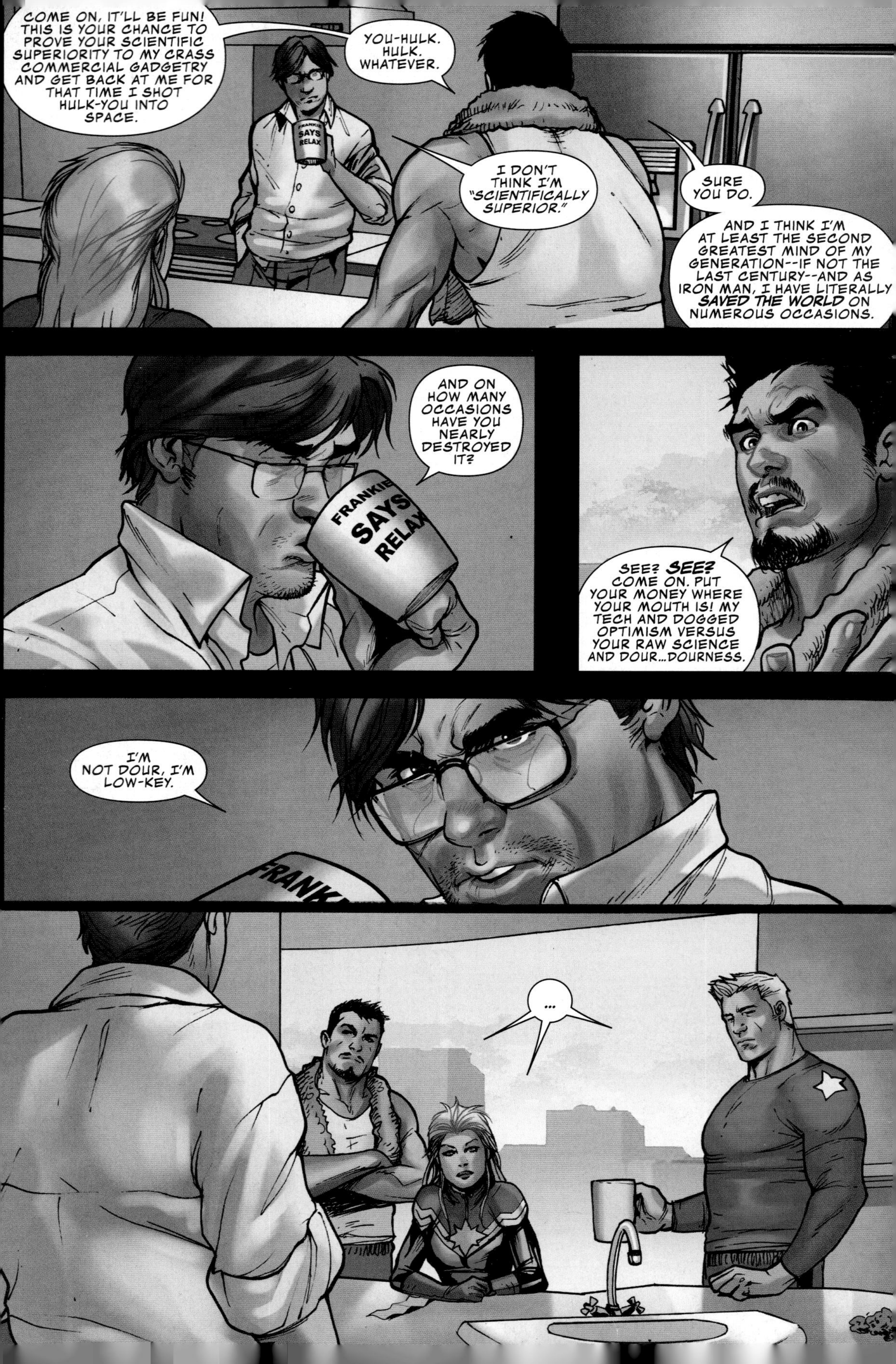
COME ON, IT'LL BE FUN! THIS IS YOUR CHANCE TO PROVE YOUR SCIENTIFIC SUPERIORITY TO MY CRASS COMMERCIAL GADGETRY AND GET BACK AT ME FOR THAT TIME I SHOT HULK-YOU INTO SPACE.
YOU-HULK. HULK. WHATEVER.
FRANKIE SAYS RELAX
I DON'T THINK I'M "SCIENTIFICALLY SUPERIOR."
SURE YOU DO.
AND I THINK I'M AT LEAST THE SECOND GREATEST MIND OF MY GENERATION--IF NOT THE LAST CENTURY--AND AS IRON MAN, I HAVE LITERALLY SAVED THE WORLD ON NUMEROUS OCCASIONS.
AND ON HOW MANY OCCASIONS HAVE YOU NEARLY DESTROYED IT?
FRANKIE SAYS RELAX
SEE? SEE? COME ON. PUT YOUR MONEY WHERE YOUR MOUTH IS! MY TECH AND DOGGED OPTIMISM VERSUS YOUR RAW SCIENCE AND DOUR...DOURNESS.
I'M NOT DOUR, I'M LOW-KEY.
...

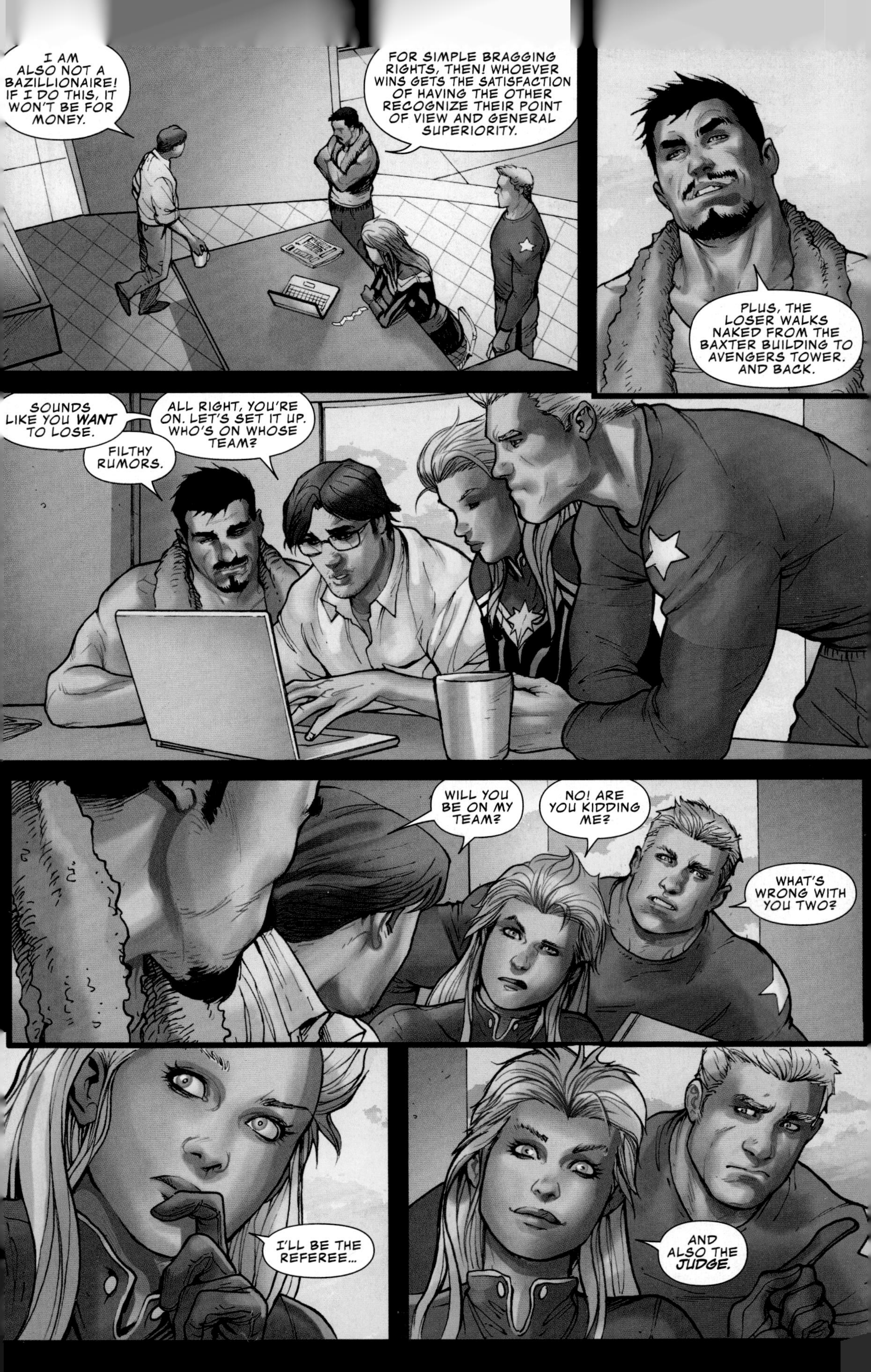
I AM ALSO NOT A BAZILLIONAIRE! IF I DO THIS, IT WON'T BE FOR MONEY.
FOR SIMPLE BRAGGING RIGHTS, THEN! WHOEVER WINS GETS THE SATISFACTION OF HAVING THE OTHER RECOGNIZE THEIR POINT OF VIEW AND GENERAL SUPERIORITY.
PLUS, THE LOSER WALKS NAKED FROM THE BAXTER BUILDING TO AVENGERS TOWER. AND BACK.
SOUNDS LIKE YOU *WANT* TO LOSE.
FILTHY RUMORS.
ALL RIGHT, YOU'RE ON. LET'S SET IT UP. WHO'S ON WHOSE TEAM?
WILL YOU BE ON MY TEAM?
NO! ARE YOU KIDDING ME?
WHAT'S WRONG WITH YOU TWO?
I'LL BE THE REFEREE...
AND ALSO THE *JUDGE.*

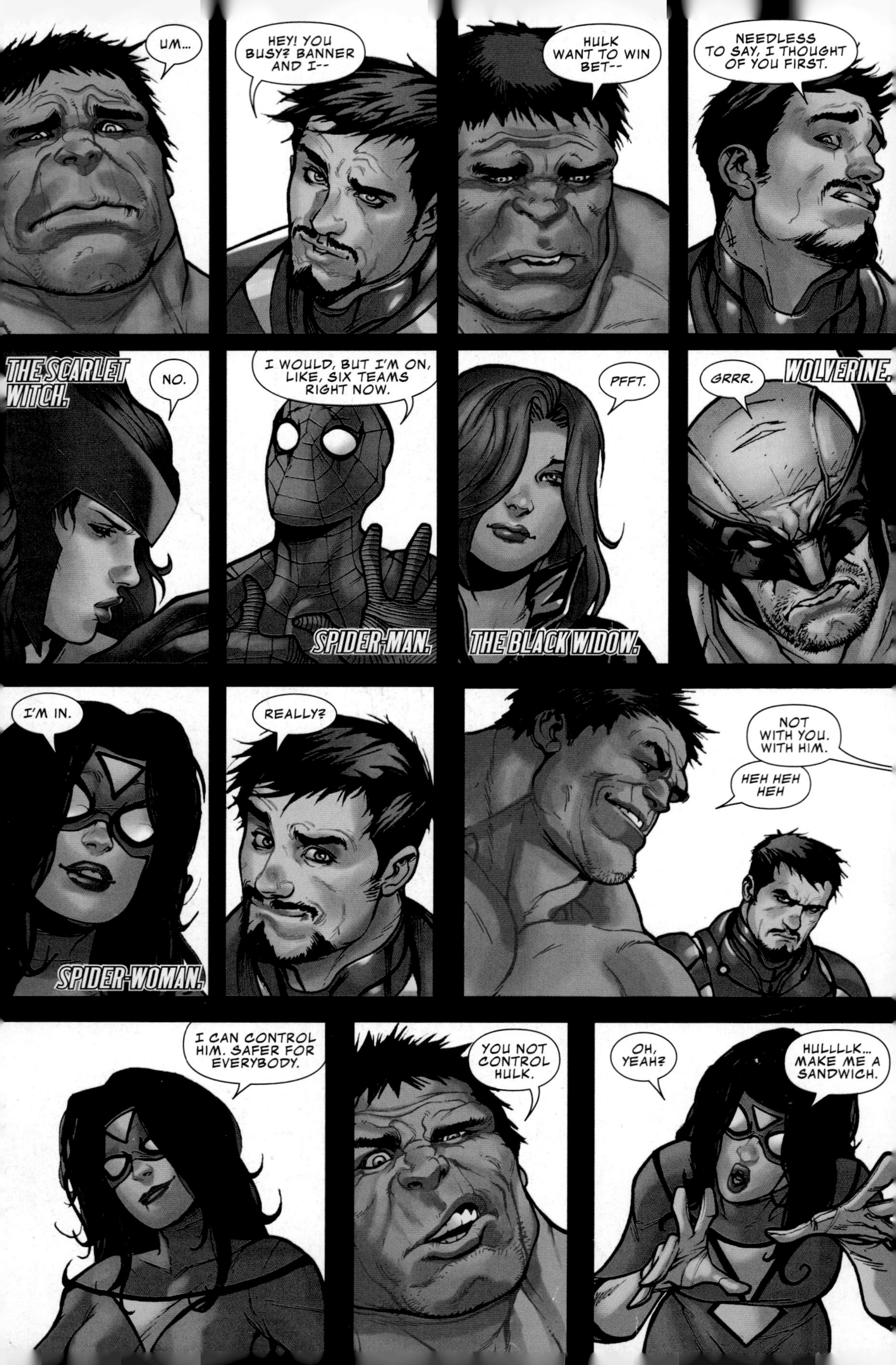
UM...
HEY! YOU BUSY? BANNER AND I--
HULK WANT TO WIN BET--
NEEDLESS TO SAY, I THOUGHT OF YOU FIRST.
THE SCARLET WITCH.
NO.
I WOULD, BUT I'M ON, LIKE, SIX TEAMS RIGHT NOW.
SPIDER-MAN.
PFFT.
THE BLACK WIDOW.
GRRR.
WOLVERINE.
I'M IN.
SPIDER-WOMAN.
REALLY?
NOT WITH YOU. WITH HIM.
HEH HEH HEH
I CAN CONTROL HIM. SAFER FOR EVERYBODY.
YOU NOT CONTROL HULK.
OH, YEAH?
HULLLLK... MAKE ME A SANDWICH.

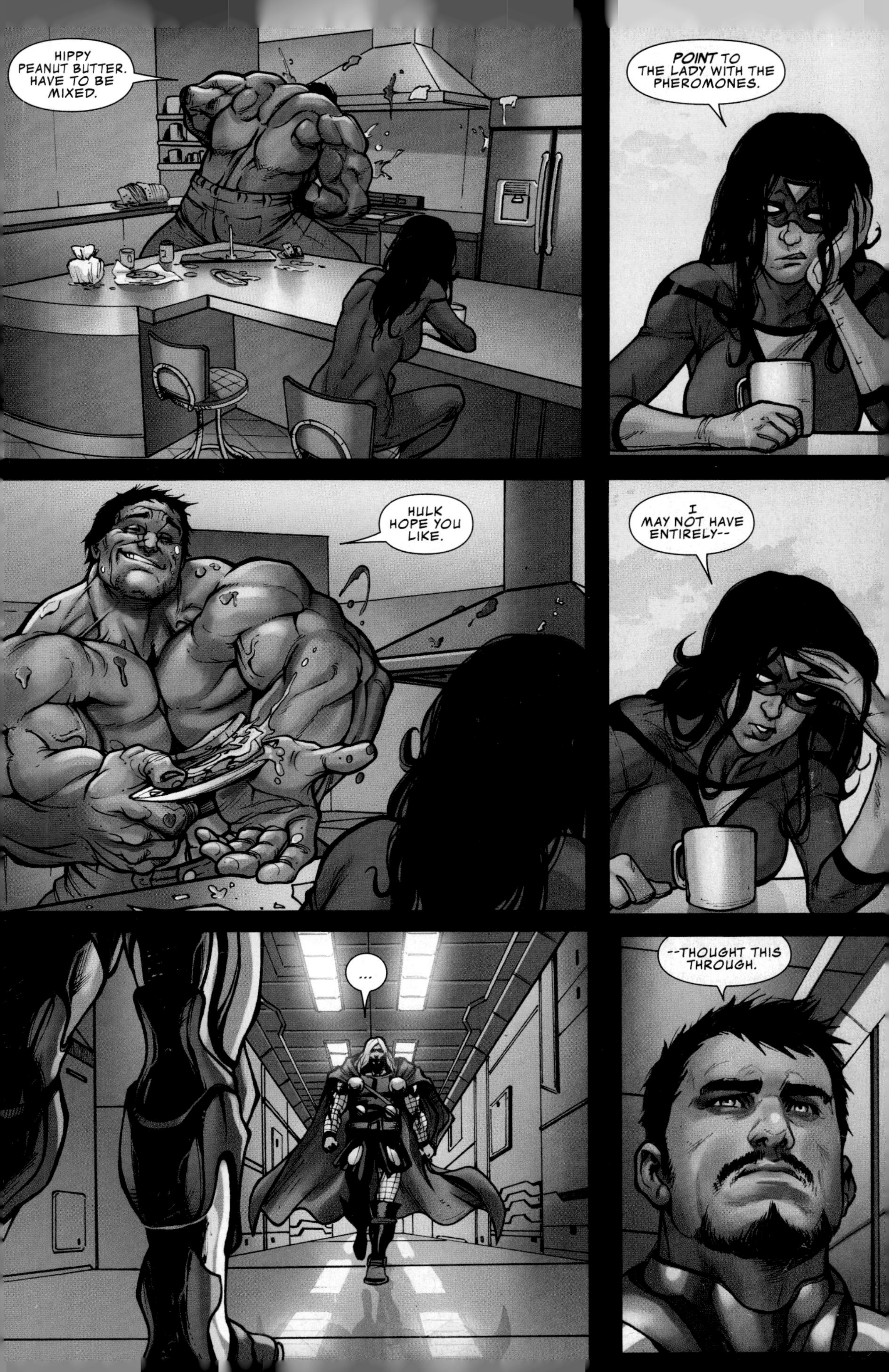
HIPPY PEANUT BUTTER. HAVE TO BE MIXED.
POINT TO THE LADY WITH THE PHEROMONES.
HULK HOPE YOU LIKE.
I MAY NOT HAVE ENTIRELY--
...
--THOUGHT THIS THROUGH.

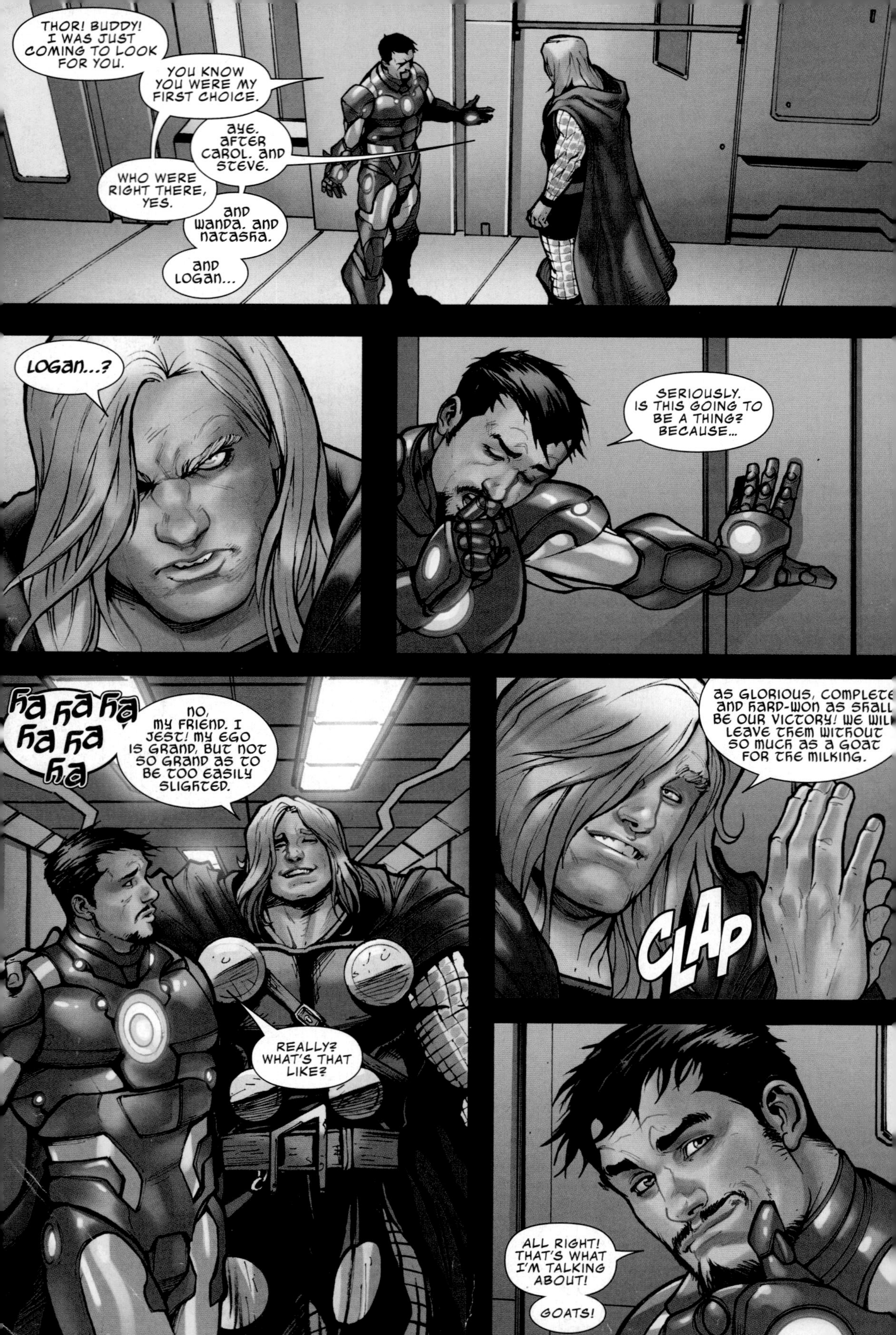
THOR! BUDDY! I WAS JUST COMING TO LOOK FOR YOU.
YOU KNOW YOU WERE MY FIRST CHOICE.
AYE. AFTER CAROL. AND STEVE.
WHO WERE RIGHT THERE, YES.
AND WANDA. AND NATASHA.
AND LOGAN...
LOGAN...?
SERIOUSLY. IS THIS GOING TO BE A THING? BECAUSE...
HA HA HA HA HA HA HA
NO, MY FRIEND. I JEST! MY EGO IS GRAND, BUT NOT SO GRAND AS TO BE TOO EASILY SLIGHTED.
REALLY? WHAT'S THAT LIKE?
AS GLORIOUS, COMPLETE AND HARD-WON AS SHALL BE OUR VICTORY! WE WILL LEAVE THEM WITHOUT SO MUCH AS A GOAT FOR THE MILKING.
CLAP
ALL RIGHT! THAT'S WHAT I'M TALKING ABOUT!
GOATS!

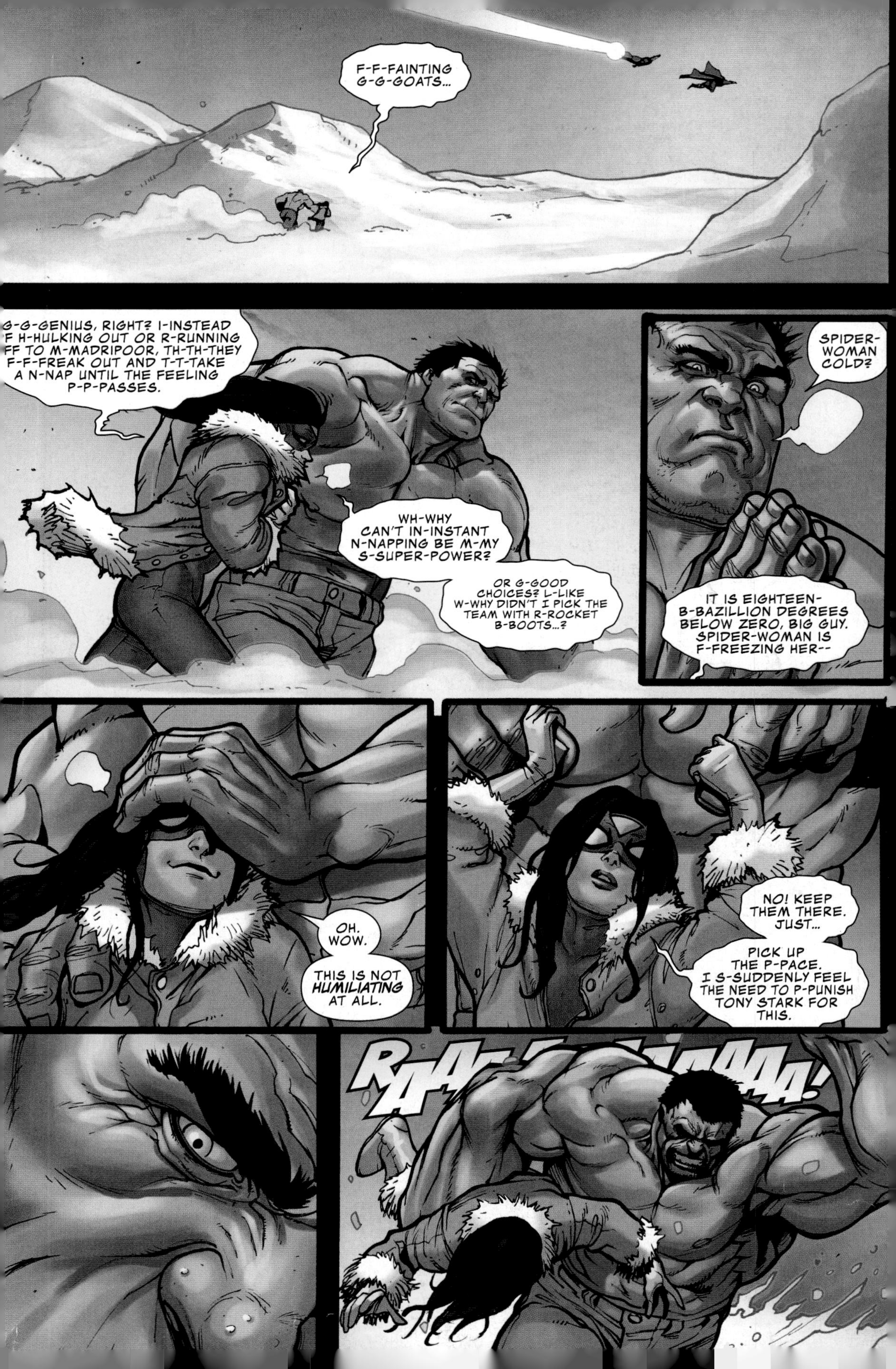
F-F-FAINTING G-G-GOATS...
G-G-GENIUS, RIGHT? I-INSTEAD F H-HULKING OUT OR R-RUNNING FF TO M-MADRIPOOR, TH-TH-THEY F-F-FREAK OUT AND T-T-TAKE A N-NAP UNTIL THE FEELING P-P-PASSES.
WH-WHY CAN'T IN-INSTANT N-NAPPING BE M-MY S-SUPER-POWER?
OR G-GOOD CHOICES? L-LIKE W-WHY DIDN'T I PICK THE TEAM WITH R-ROCKET B-BOOTS...?
SPIDER-WOMAN COLD?
IT IS EIGHTEEN-B-BAZILLION DEGREES BELOW ZERO, BIG GUY. SPIDER-WOMAN IS F-FREEZING HER--
OH. WOW.
THIS IS NOT *HUMILIATING* AT ALL.
NO! KEEP THEM THERE. JUST...
PICK UP THE P-PACE. I S-SUDDENLY FEEL THE NEED TO P-PUNISH TONY STARK FOR THIS.

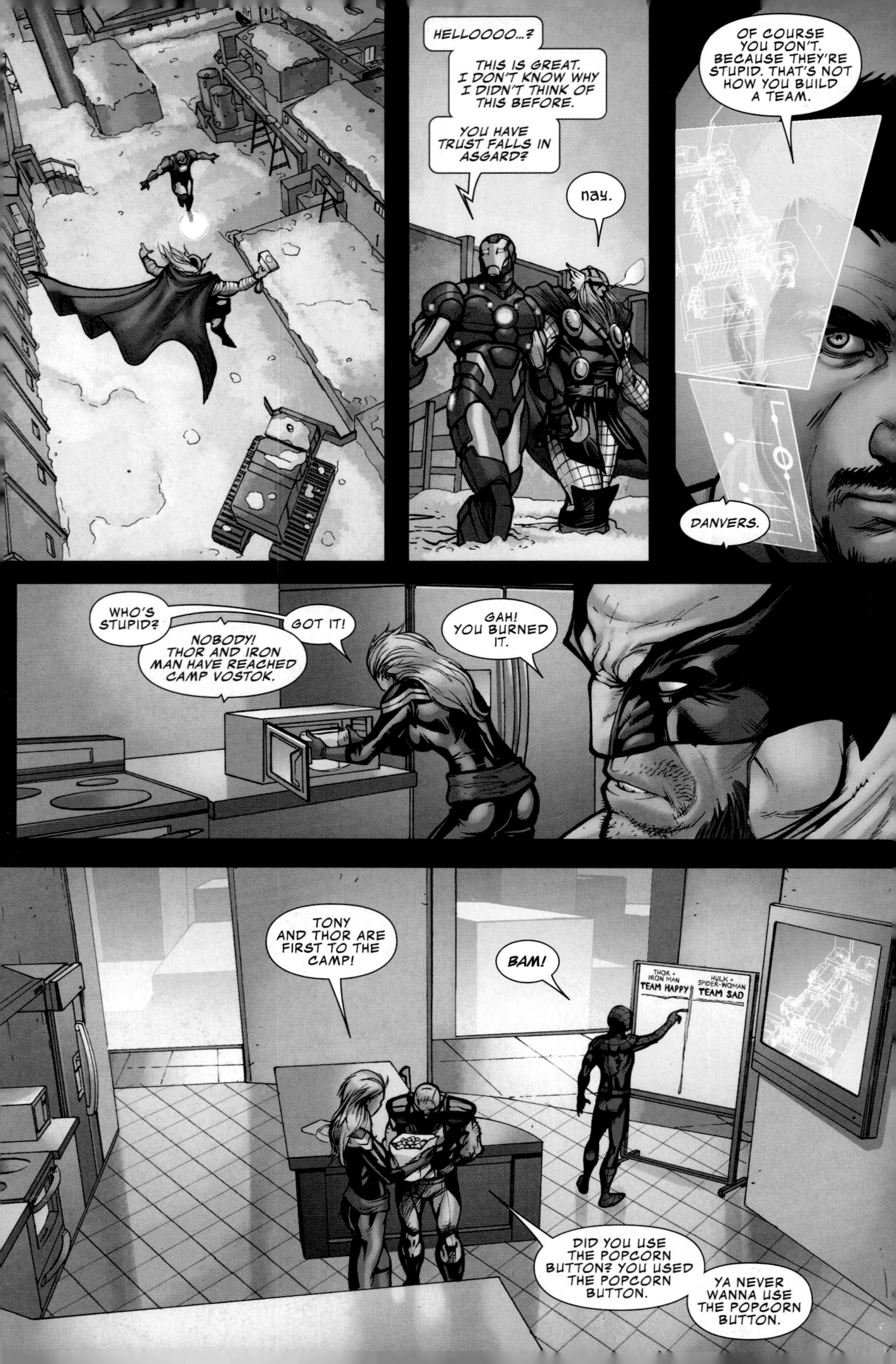
HELLOOOO...?
THIS IS GREAT. I DON'T KNOW WHY I DIDN'T THINK OF THIS BEFORE.
YOU HAVE TRUST FALLS IN ASGARD?
nay.
OF COURSE YOU DON'T. BECAUSE THEY'RE STUPID. THAT'S NOT HOW YOU BUILD A TEAM.
DANVERS.
WHO'S STUPID?
NOBODY! THOR AND IRON MAN HAVE REACHED CAMP VOSTOK.
GOT IT!
GAH! YOU BURNED IT.
TONY AND THOR ARE FIRST TO THE CAMP!
BAM!
THOR + IRON MAN TEAM HAPPY
HULK + SPIDER-WOMAN TEAM SAD
DID YOU USE THE POPCORN BUTTON? YOU USED THE POPCORN BUTTON.
YA NEVER WANNA USE THE POPCORN BUTTON.

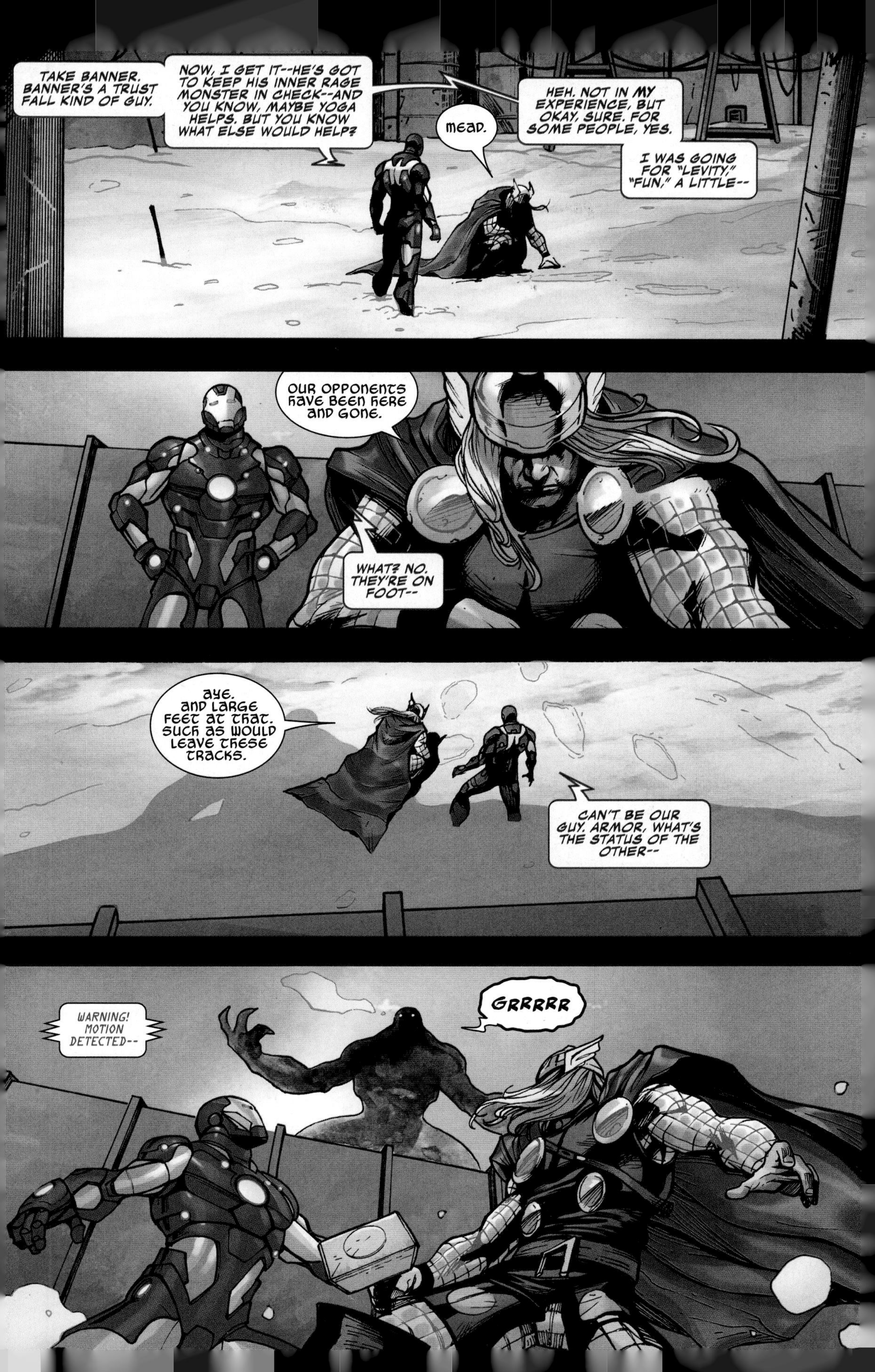
TAKE BANNER. BANNER'S A TRUST FALL KIND OF GUY.
NOW, I GET IT--HE'S GOT TO KEEP HIS INNER RAGE MONSTER IN CHECK--AND YOU KNOW, MAYBE YOGA HELPS. BUT YOU KNOW WHAT ELSE WOULD HELP?
MEAD.
HEH. NOT IN MY EXPERIENCE, BUT OKAY, SURE. FOR SOME PEOPLE, YES.
I WAS GOING FOR "LEVITY," "FUN," A LITTLE--
OUR OPPONENTS HAVE BEEN HERE AND GONE.
WHAT? NO. THEY'RE ON FOOT--
AYE. AND LARGE FEET AT THAT. SUCH AS WOULD LEAVE THESE TRACKS.
CAN'T BE OUR GUY. ARMOR, WHAT'S THE STATUS OF THE OTHER--
WARNING! MOTION DETECTED--
GRRRRR

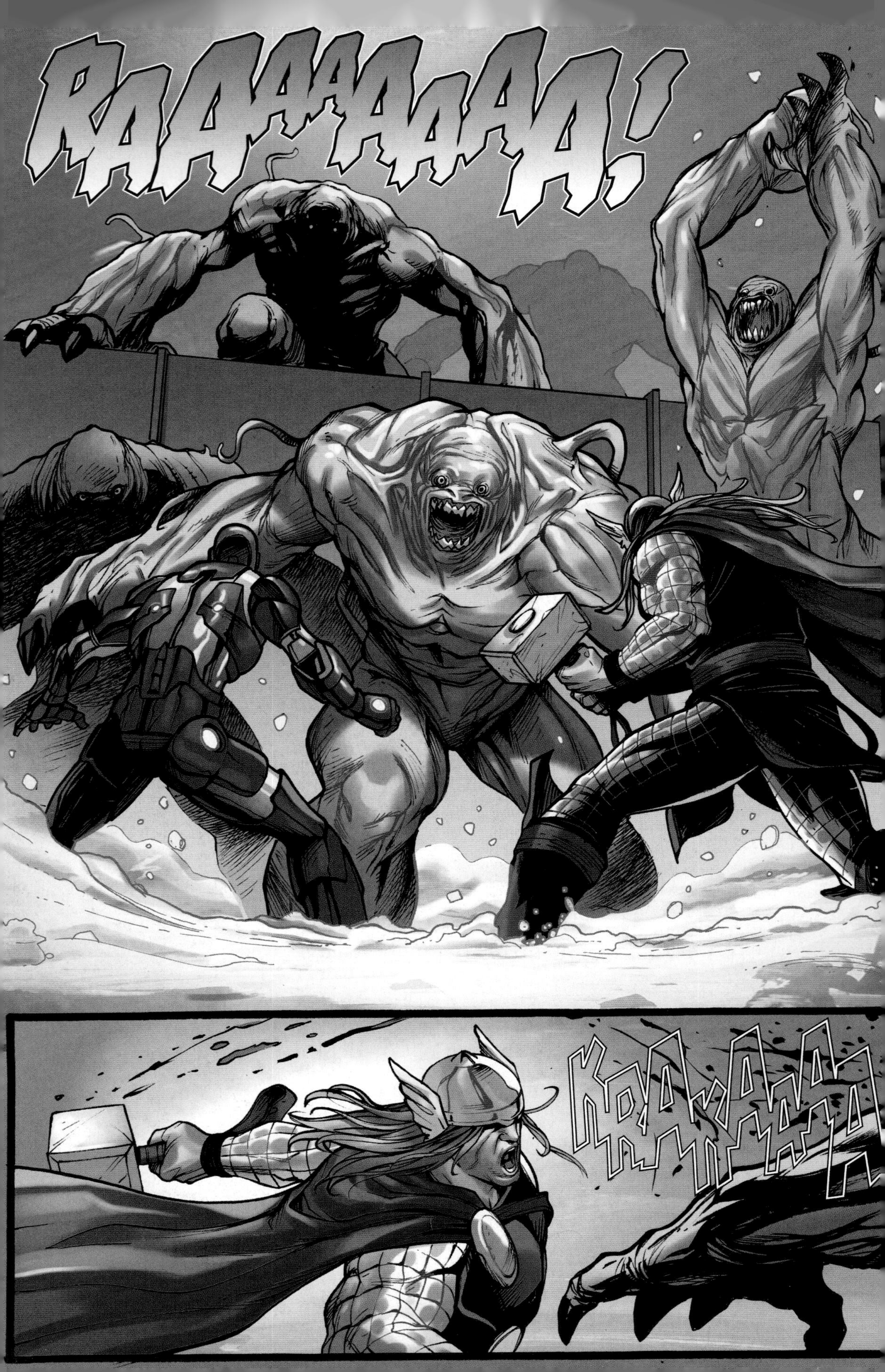
RAAAAAAAAA!
KRAKAAAAA

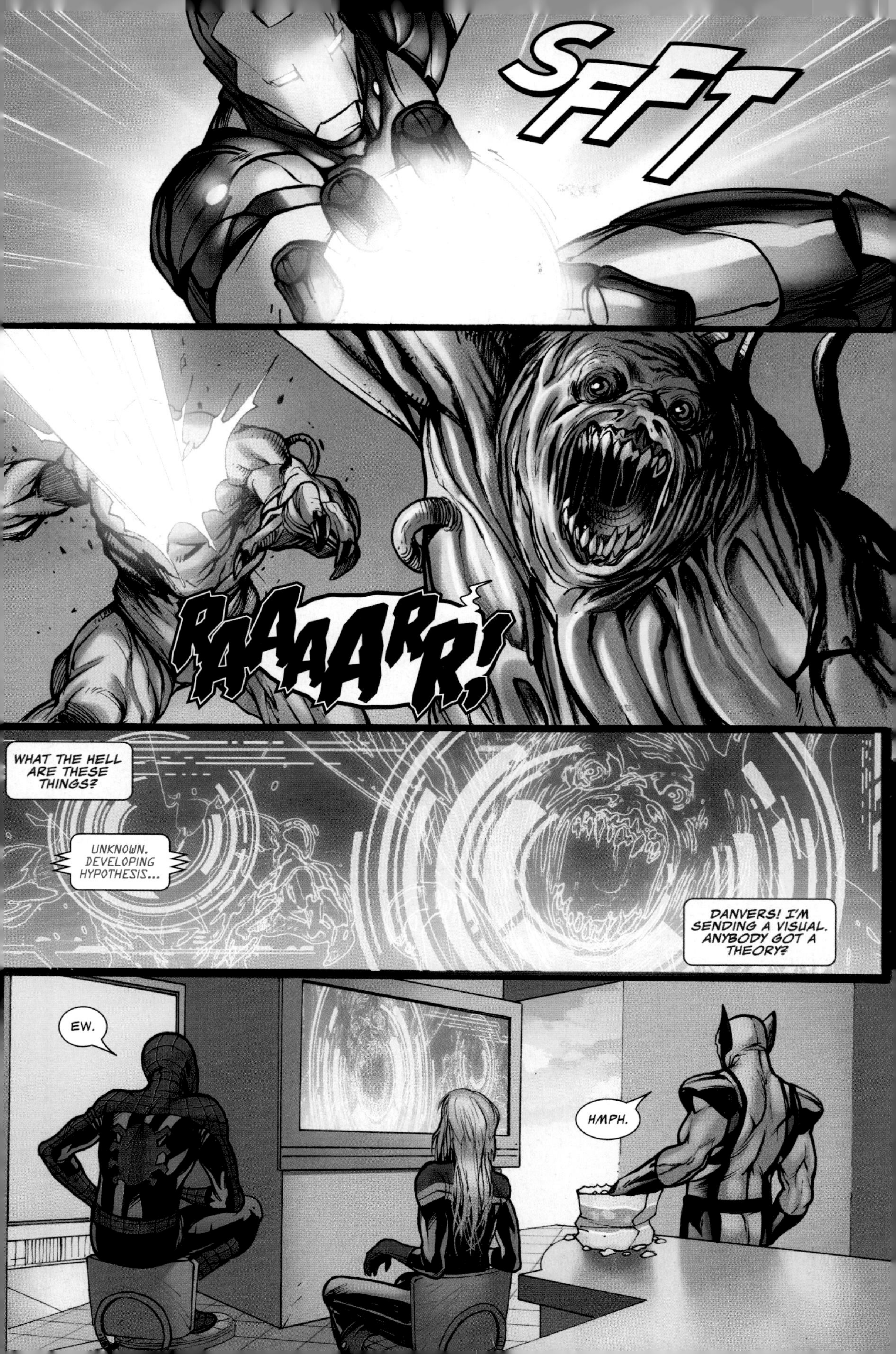
SFFT
RAAAARRR!
WHAT THE HELL ARE THESE THINGS?
UNKNOWN. DEVELOPING HYPOTHESIS...
DANVERS! I'M SENDING A VISUAL. ANYBODY GOT A THEORY?
EW.
HMPH.

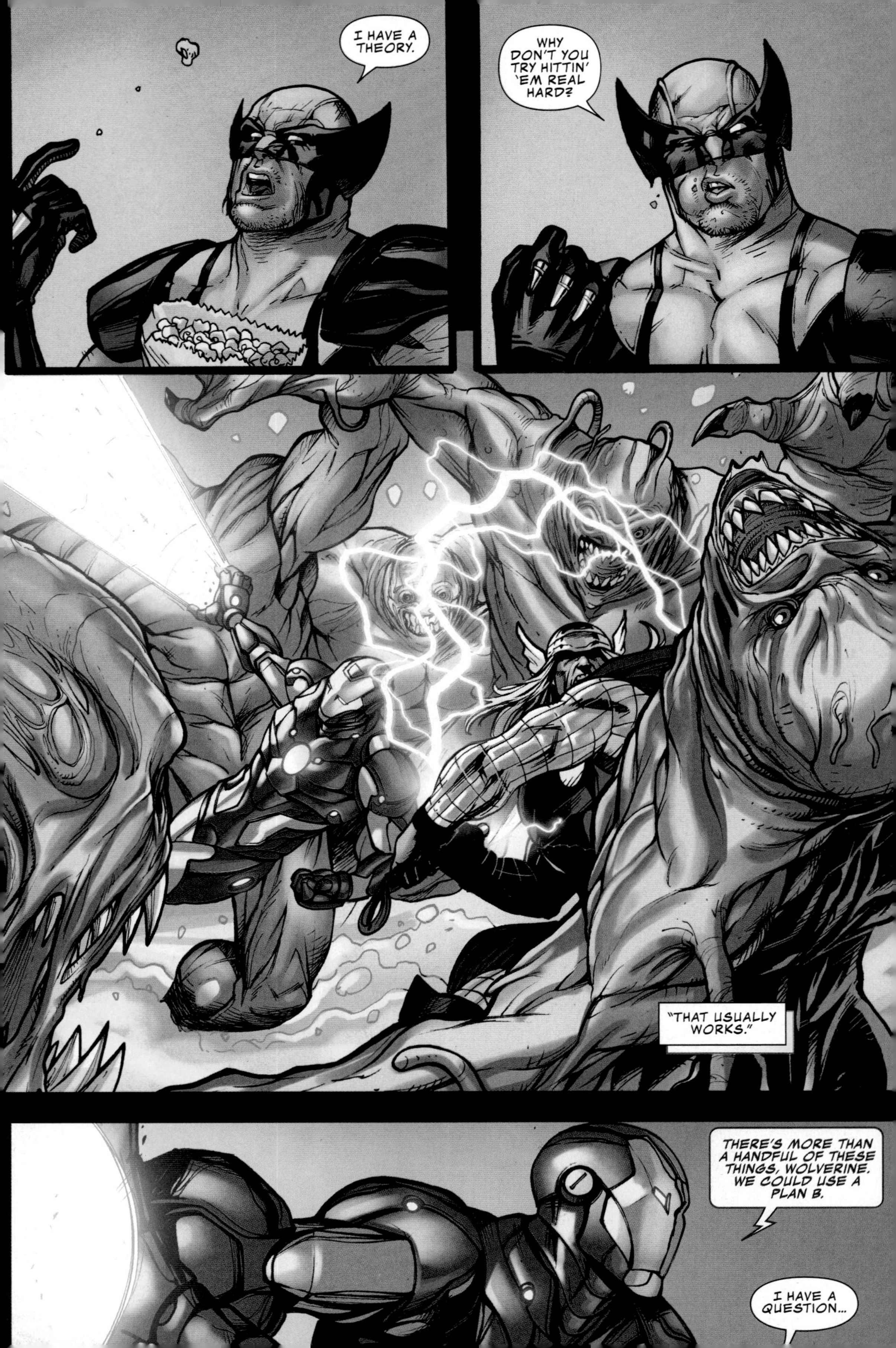
I HAVE A THEORY.
WHY DON'T YOU TRY HITTIN' 'EM REAL HARD?
"THAT USUALLY WORKS."
THERE'S MORE THAN A HANDFUL OF THESE THINGS, WOLVERINE. WE COULD USE A PLAN B.
I HAVE A QUESTION...

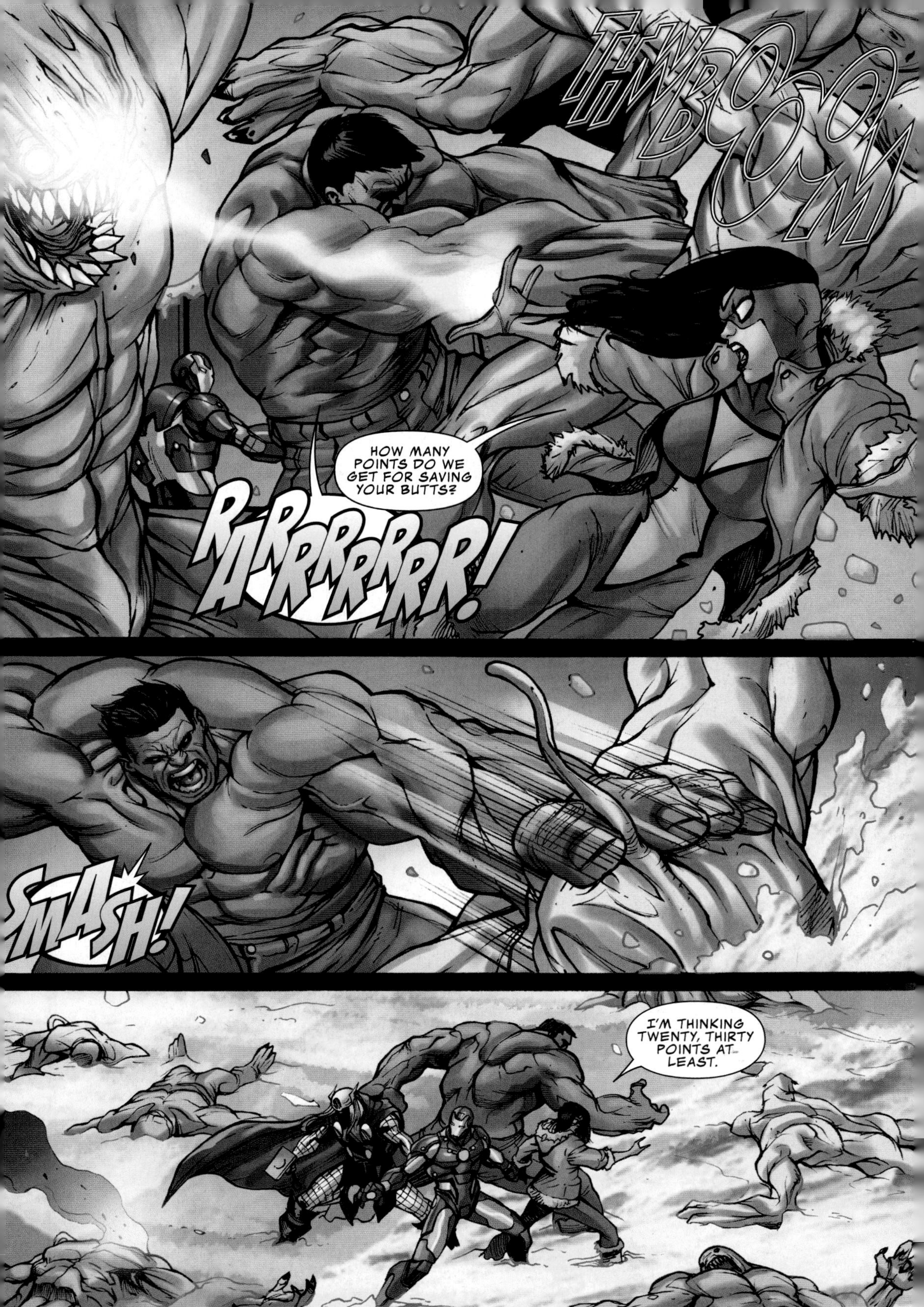
THWOOOOM
HOW MANY POINTS DO WE GET FOR SAVING YOUR BUTTS?
RARRRRRRR!
SMASH!
I'M THINKING TWENTY, THIRTY POINTS AT LEAST.

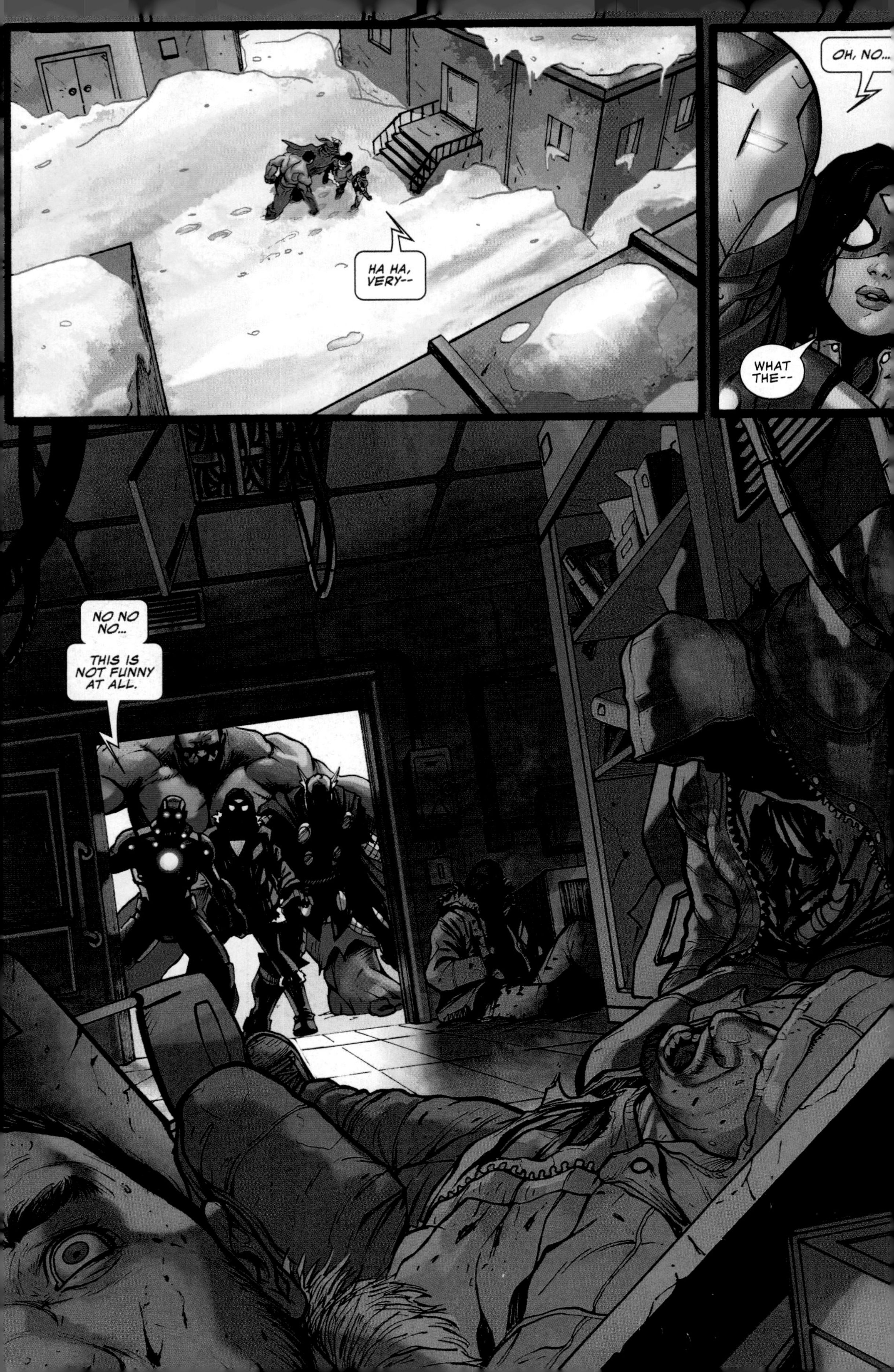
HA HA, VERY--
OH, NO...
WHAT THE--
NO NO NO...
THIS IS NOT FUNNY AT ALL.

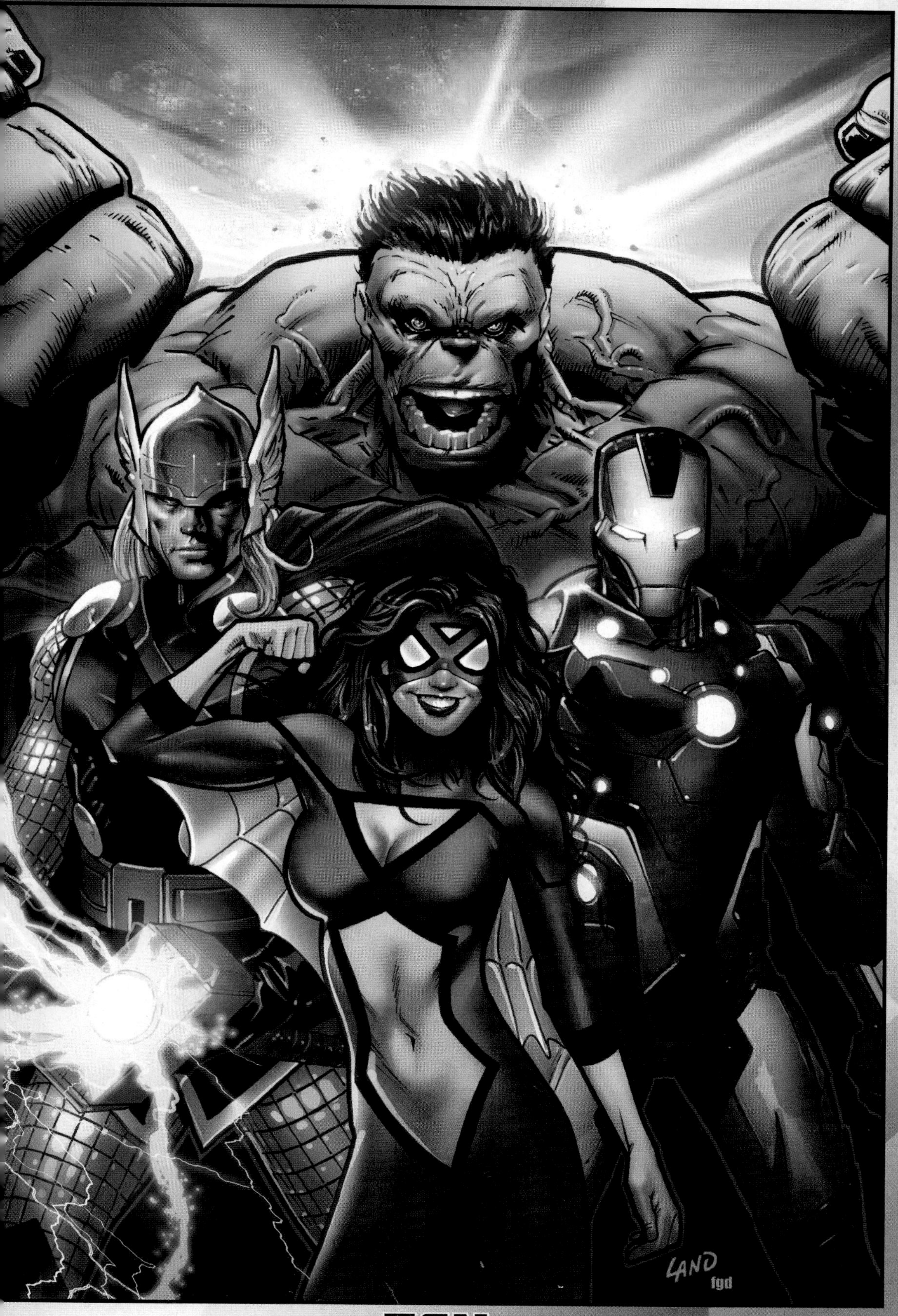
LAND
fgd

TEN

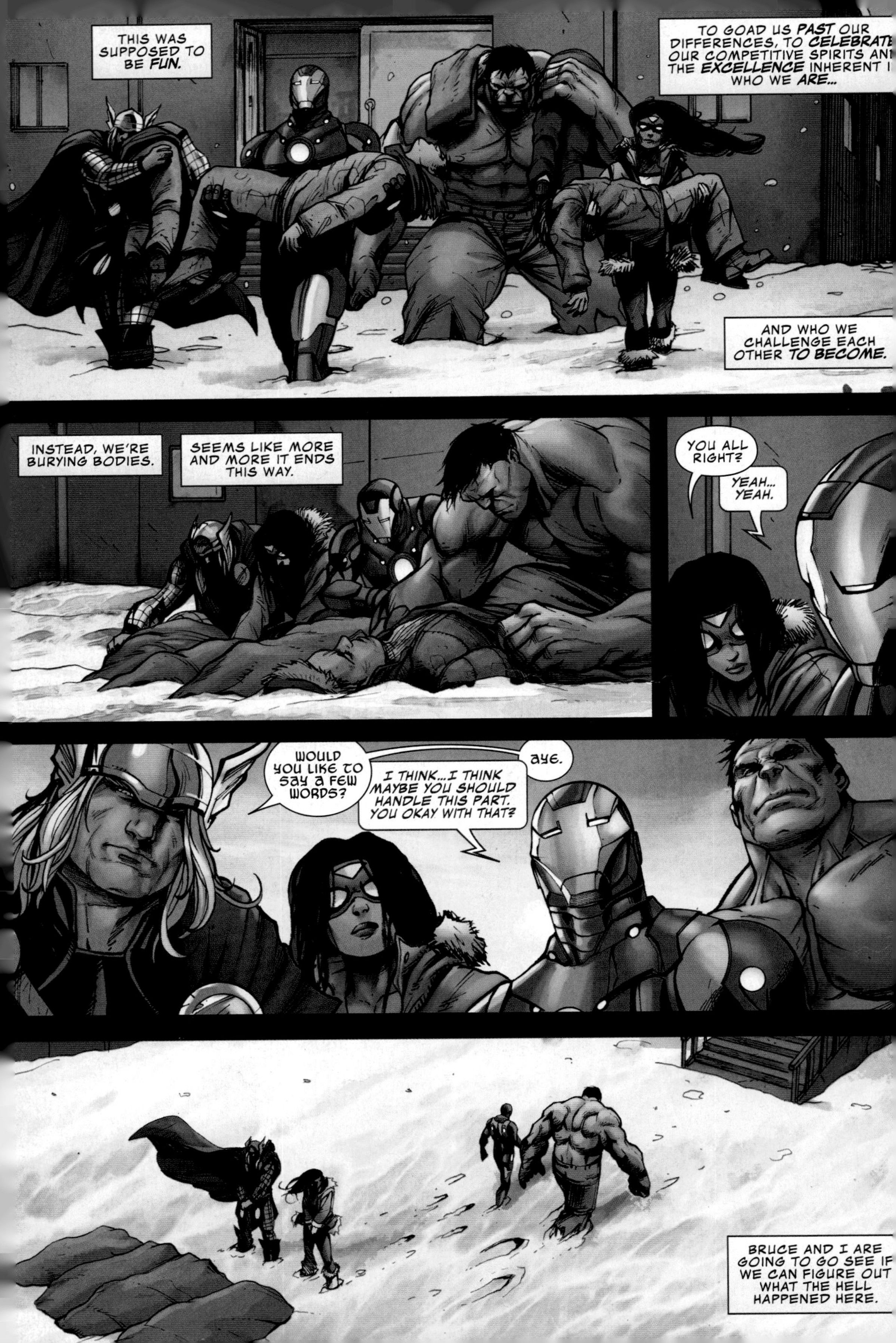

THIS WAS SUPPOSED TO BE FUN.
TO GOAD US PAST OUR DIFFERENCES, TO CELEBRATE OUR COMPETITIVE SPIRITS AND THE EXCELLENCE INHERENT IN WHO WE ARE...
AND WHO WE CHALLENGE EACH OTHER TO BECOME.
INSTEAD, WE'RE BURYING BODIES.
SEEMS LIKE MORE AND MORE IT ENDS THIS WAY.
YOU ALL RIGHT?
YEAH... YEAH.
WOULD YOU LIKE TO SAY A FEW WORDS?
I THINK...I THINK MAYBE YOU SHOULD HANDLE THIS PART. YOU OKAY WITH THAT?
AYE.
BRUCE AND I ARE GOING TO GO SEE IF WE CAN FIGURE OUT WHAT THE HELL HAPPENED HERE.

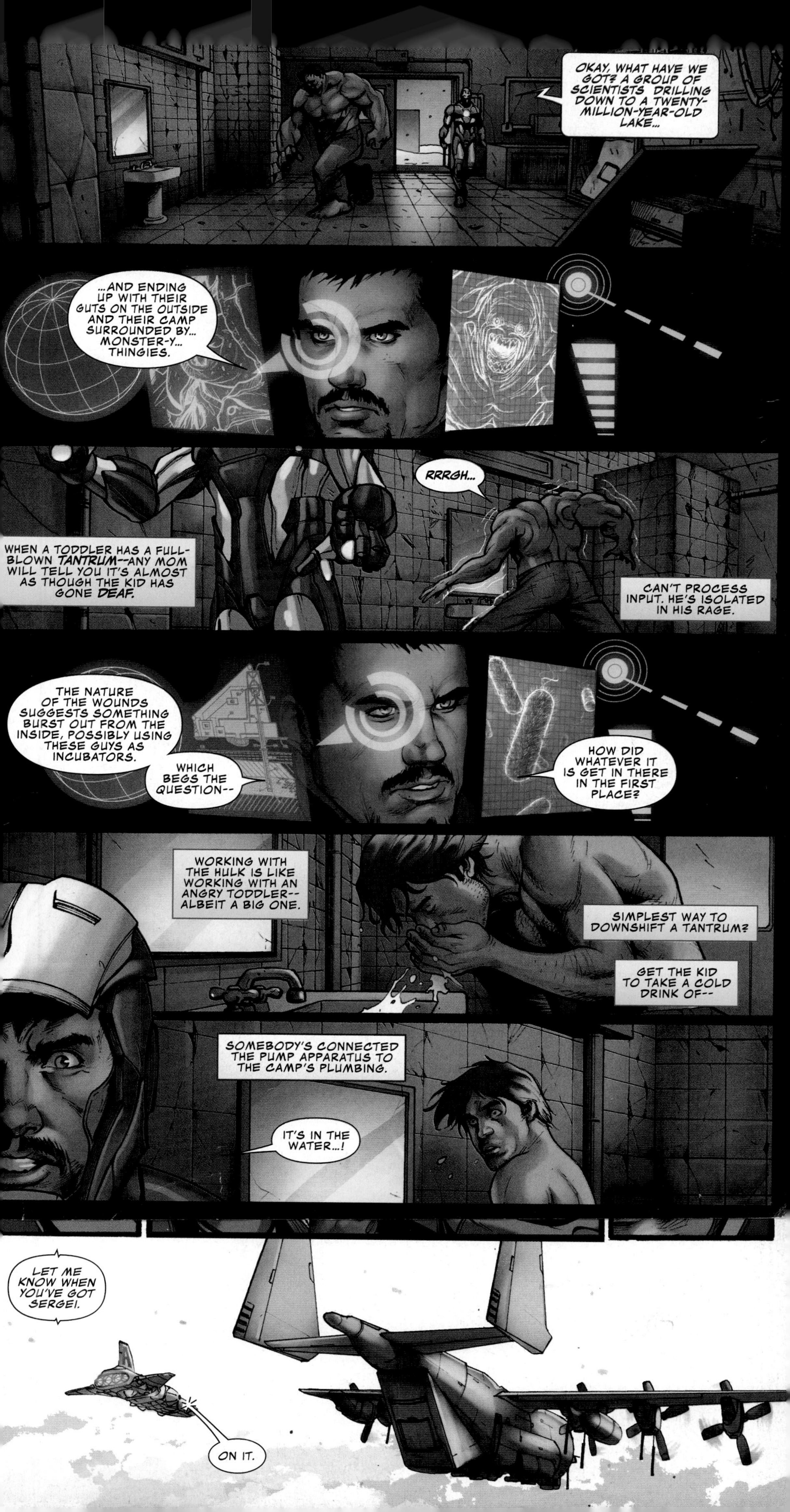

OKAY, WHAT HAVE WE GOT? A GROUP OF SCIENTISTS DRILLING DOWN TO A TWENTY-MILLION-YEAR-OLD LAKE...
...AND ENDING UP WITH THEIR GUTS ON THE OUTSIDE AND THEIR CAMP SURROUNDED BY... MONSTER-Y... THINGIES.
WHEN A TODDLER HAS A FULL-BLOWN TANTRUM--ANY MOM WILL TELL YOU IT'S ALMOST AS THOUGH THE KID HAS GONE DEAF.
RRRGH...
CAN'T PROCESS INPUT. HE'S ISOLATED IN HIS RAGE.
THE NATURE OF THE WOUNDS SUGGESTS SOMETHING BURST OUT FROM THE INSIDE, POSSIBLY USING THESE GUYS AS INCUBATORS.
WHICH BEGS THE QUESTION--
HOW DID WHATEVER IT IS GET IN THERE IN THE FIRST PLACE?
WORKING WITH THE HULK IS LIKE WORKING WITH AN ANGRY TODDLER--ALBEIT A BIG ONE.
SIMPLEST WAY TO DOWNSHIFT A TANTRUM?
GET THE KID TO TAKE A COLD DRINK OF--
SOMEBODY'S CONNECTED THE PUMP APPARATUS TO THE CAMP'S PLUMBING.
IT'S IN THE WATER...!
LET ME KNOW WHEN YOU'VE GOT SERGEI.
ON IT.

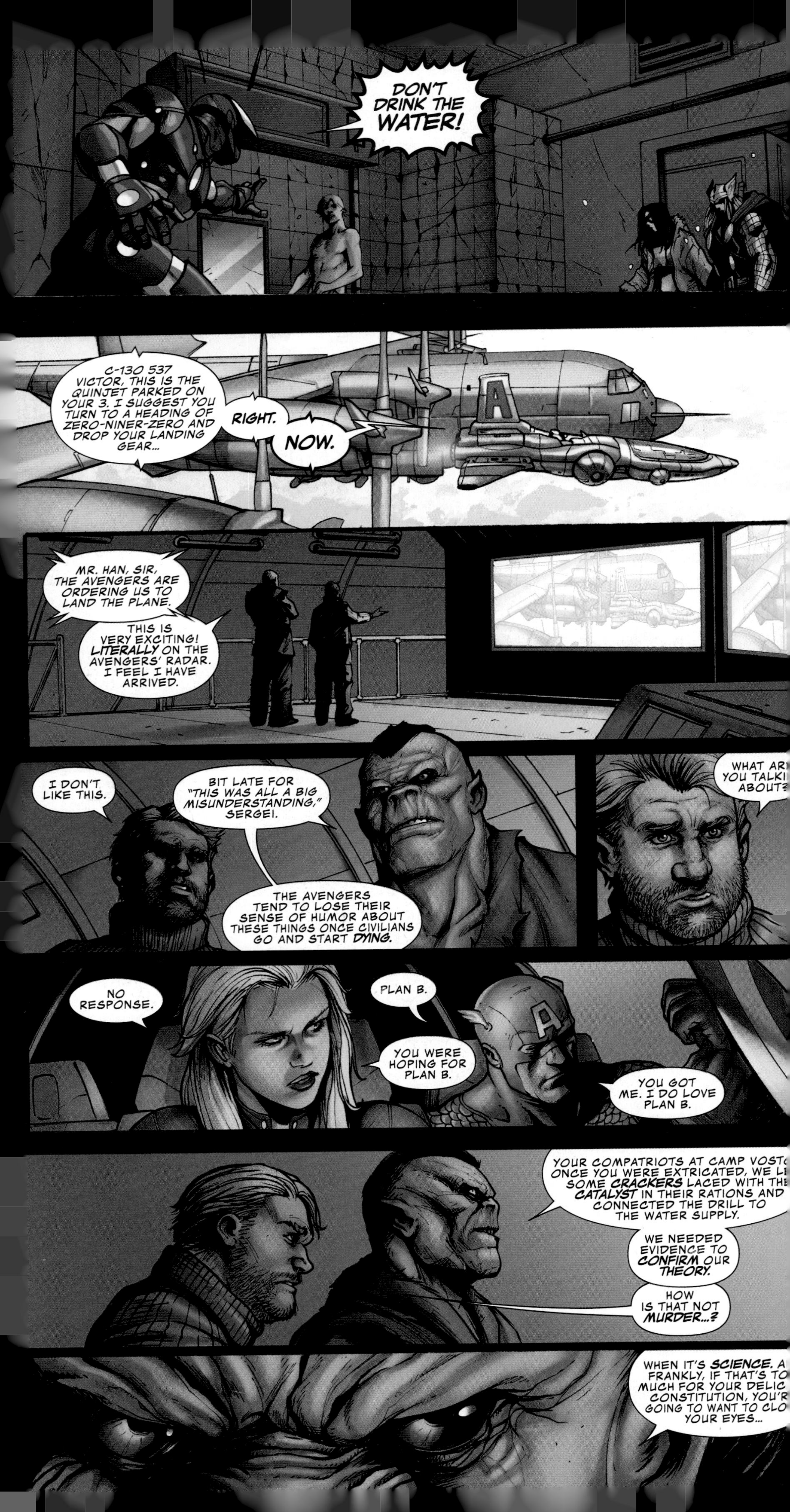
DON'T DRINK THE WATER!
C-130 537 VICTOR, THIS IS THE QUINJET PARKED ON YOUR 3. I SUGGEST YOU TURN TO A HEADING OF ZERO-NINER-ZERO AND DROP YOUR LANDING GEAR...
RIGHT.
NOW.
MR. HAN, SIR, THE AVENGERS ARE ORDERING US TO LAND THE PLANE.
THIS IS VERY EXCITING! LITERALLY ON THE AVENGERS' RADAR. I FEEL I HAVE ARRIVED.
I DON'T LIKE THIS.
BIT LATE FOR "THIS WAS ALL A BIG MISUNDERSTANDING," SERGEI.
THE AVENGERS TEND TO LOSE THEIR SENSE OF HUMOR ABOUT THESE THINGS ONCE CIVILIANS GO AND START DYING.
NO RESPONSE.
PLAN B.
YOU WERE HOPING FOR PLAN B.
YOU GOT ME. I DO LOVE PLAN B.
SOME CRACKERS LACED WITH THE CATALYST IN THEIR RATIONS AND CONNECTED THE DRILL TO THE WATER SUPPLY.
WE NEEDED EVIDENCE TO CONFIRM OUR THEORY.
HOW IS THAT NOT MURDER...?
YOUR EYES...

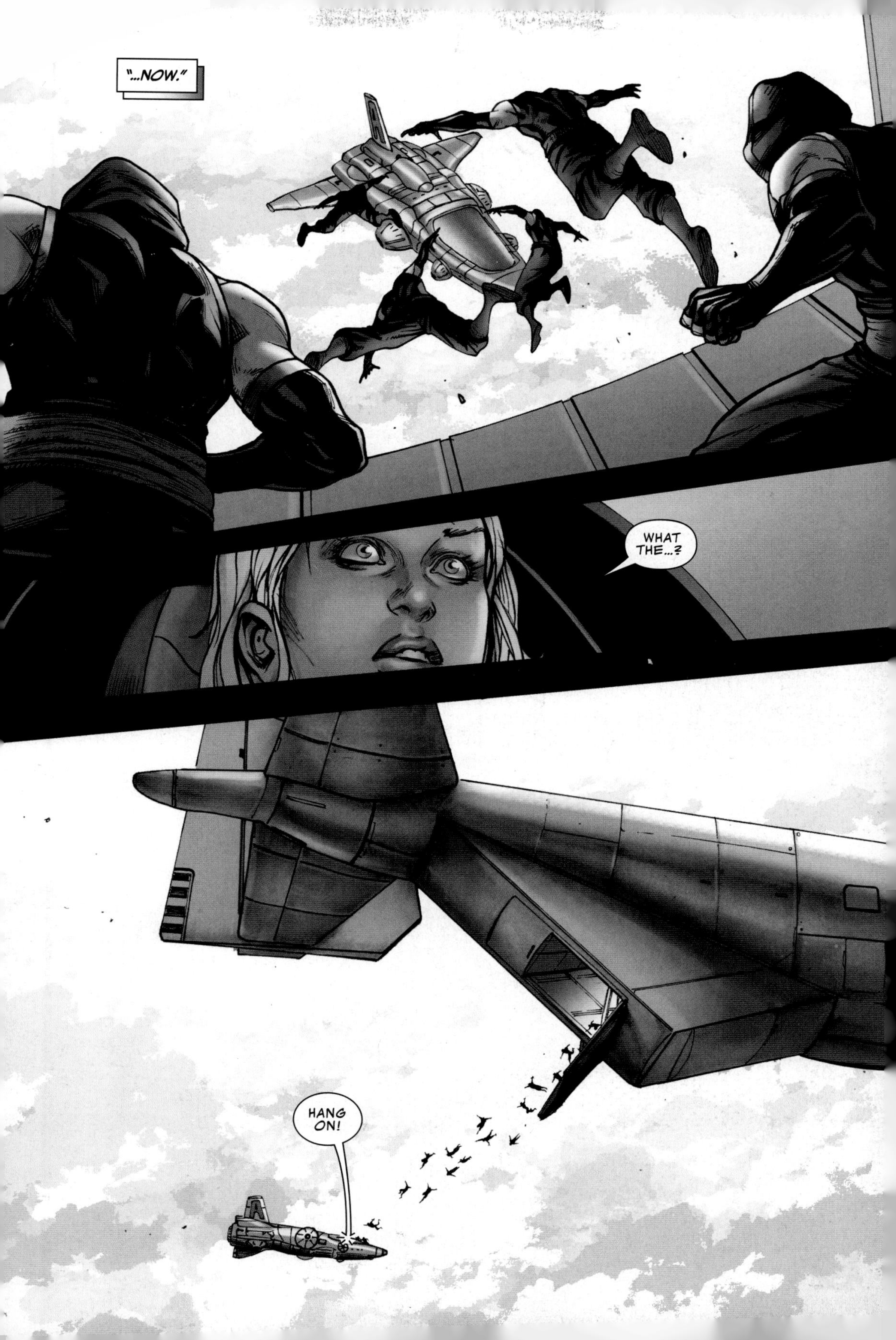
"...NOW."
WHAT THE...?
HANG ON!

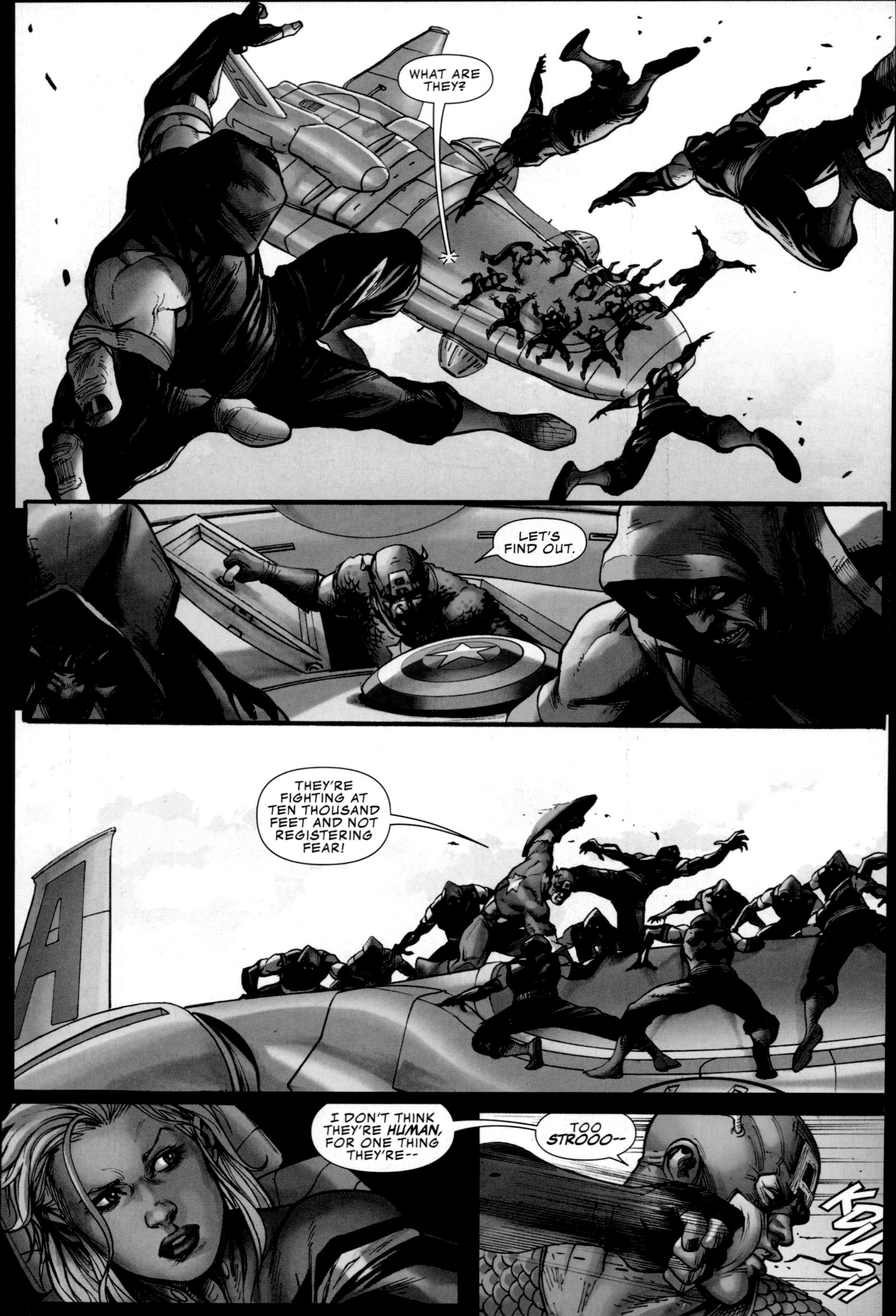
WHAT ARE THEY?
LET'S FIND OUT.
THEY'RE FIGHTING AT TEN THOUSAND FEET AND NOT REGISTERING FEAR!
I DON'T THINK THEY'RE HUMAN, FOR ONE THING THEY'RE--
TOO STROOO--
KOOSH

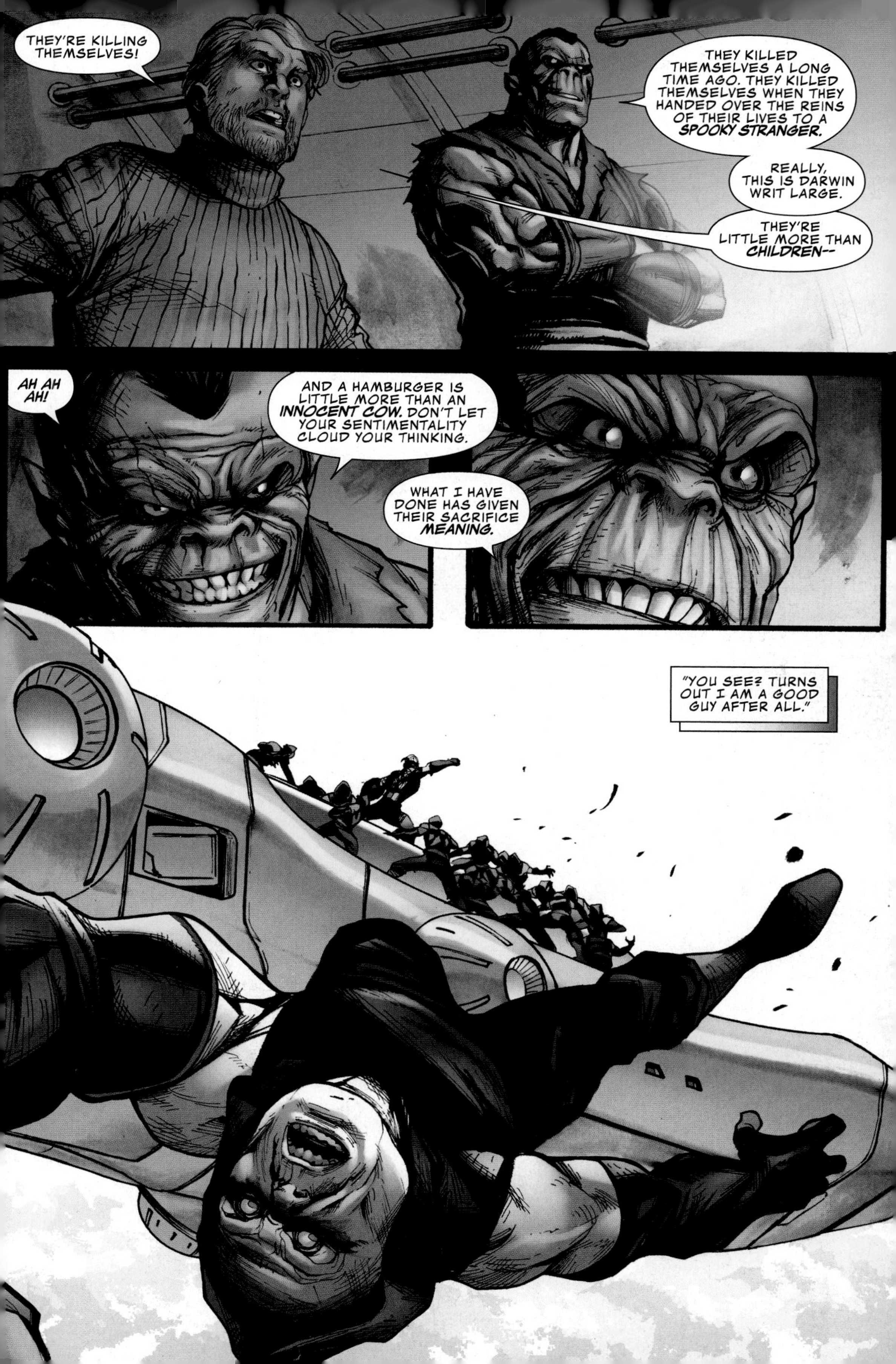
THEY'RE KILLING THEMSELVES!
THEY KILLED THEMSELVES A LONG TIME AGO. THEY KILLED THEMSELVES WHEN THEY HANDED OVER THE REINS OF THEIR LIVES TO A SPOOKY STRANGER.
REALLY, THIS IS DARWIN WRIT LARGE.
THEY'RE LITTLE MORE THAN CHILDREN--
AH AH AH!
AND A HAMBURGER IS LITTLE MORE THAN AN INNOCENT COW. DON'T LET YOUR SENTIMENTALITY CLOUD YOUR THINKING.
WHAT I HAVE DONE HAS GIVEN THEIR SACRIFICE MEANING.
"YOU SEE? TURNS OUT I AM A GOOD GUY AFTER ALL."

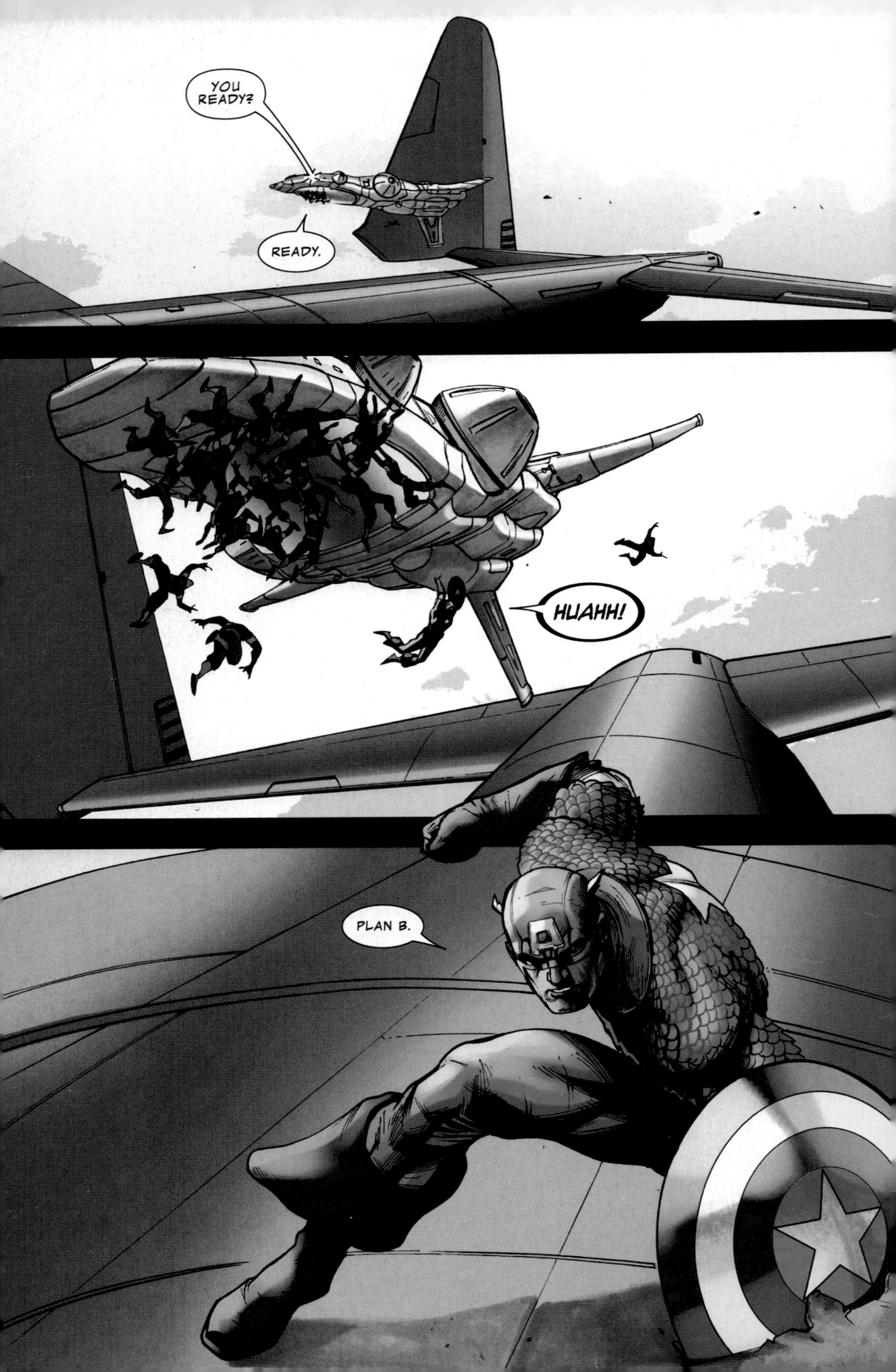
YOU READY?
READY.
HUAHH!
PLAN B.

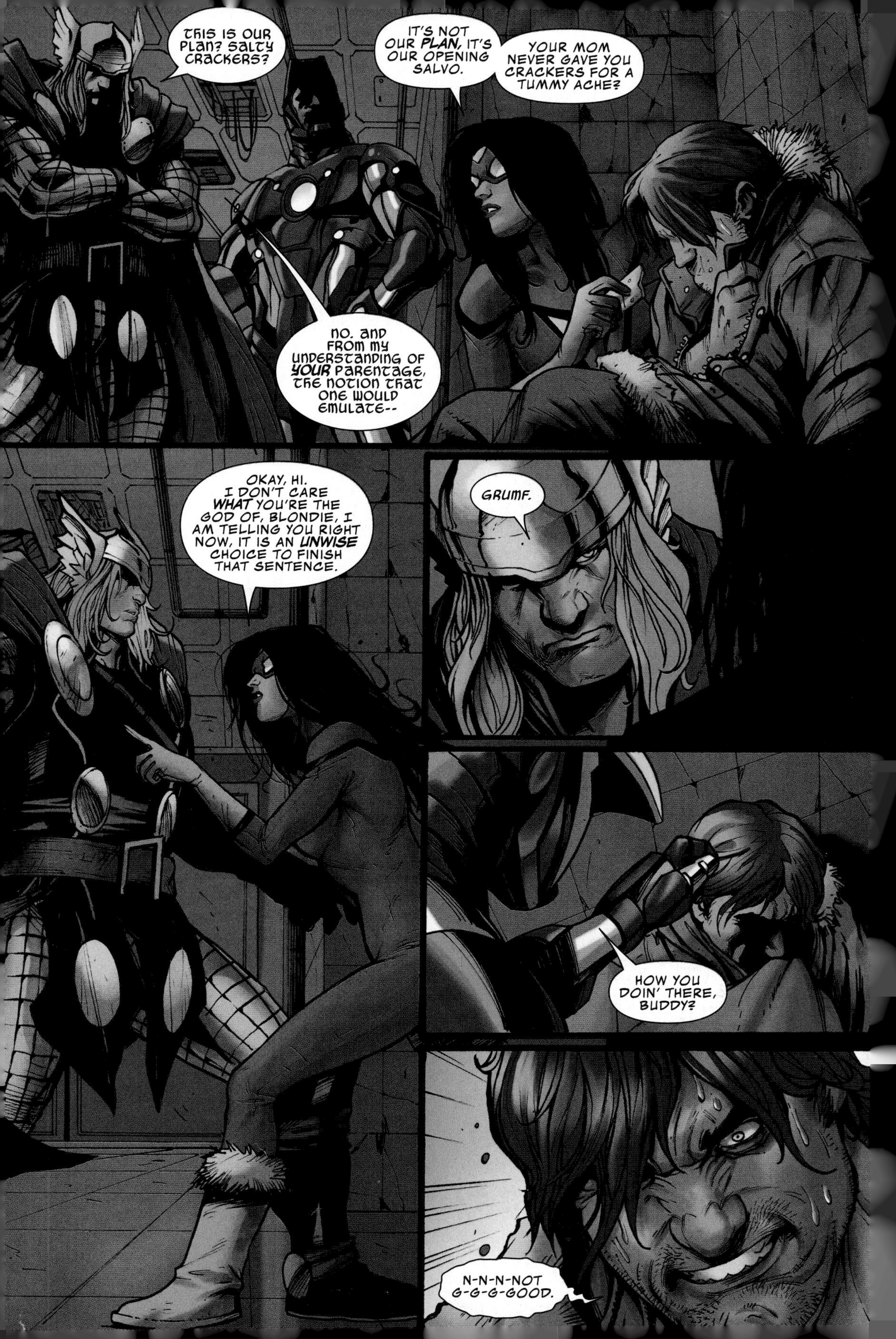
THIS IS OUR PLAN? SALTY CRACKERS?
IT'S NOT OUR PLAN, IT'S OUR OPENING SALVO.
YOUR MOM NEVER GAVE YOU CRACKERS FOR A TUMMY ACHE?
NO. AND FROM MY UNDERSTANDING OF YOUR PARENTAGE, THE NOTION THAT ONE WOULD EMULATE--
OKAY, HI. I DON'T CARE WHAT YOU'RE THE GOD OF, BLONDIE, I AM TELLING YOU RIGHT NOW, IT IS AN UNWISE CHOICE TO FINISH THAT SENTENCE.
GRUMF.
HOW YOU DOIN' THERE, BUDDY?
N-N-N-NOT G-G-G-GOOD.

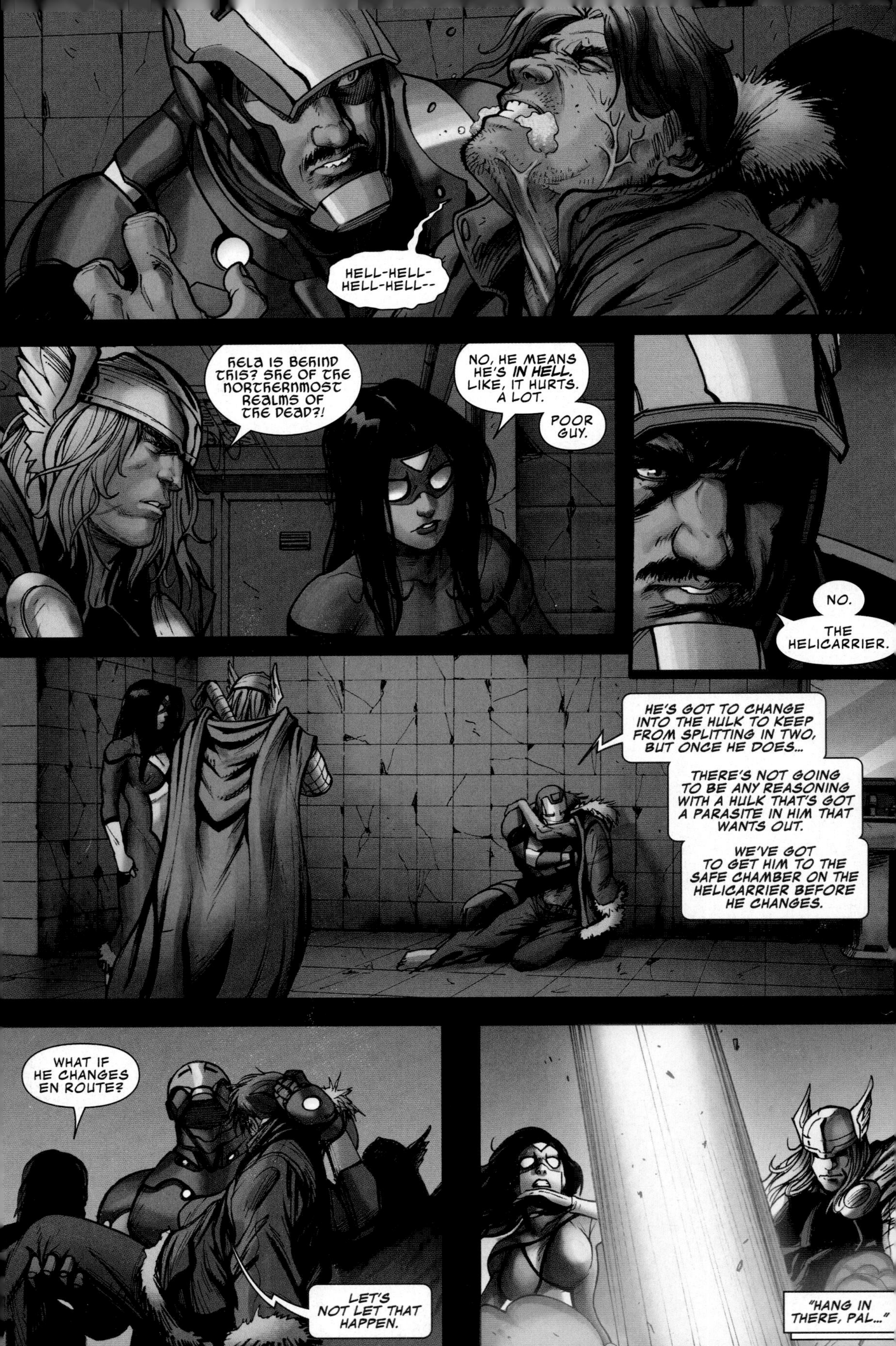
HELL-HELL-
HELL-HELL--
HELA IS BEHIND THIS? SHE OF THE NORTHERNMOST REALMS OF THE DEAD?!
NO, HE MEANS HE'S IN HELL. LIKE, IT HURTS. A LOT.
POOR GUY.
NO.
THE HELICARRIER.
HE'S GOT TO CHANGE INTO THE HULK TO KEEP FROM SPLITTING IN TWO, BUT ONCE HE DOES...
THERE'S NOT GOING TO BE ANY REASONING WITH A HULK THAT'S GOT A PARASITE IN HIM THAT WANTS OUT.
WE'VE GOT TO GET HIM TO THE SAFE CHAMBER ON THE HELICARRIER BEFORE HE CHANGES.
WHAT IF HE CHANGES EN ROUTE?
LET'S NOT LET THAT HAPPEN.
"HANG IN THERE, PAL..."

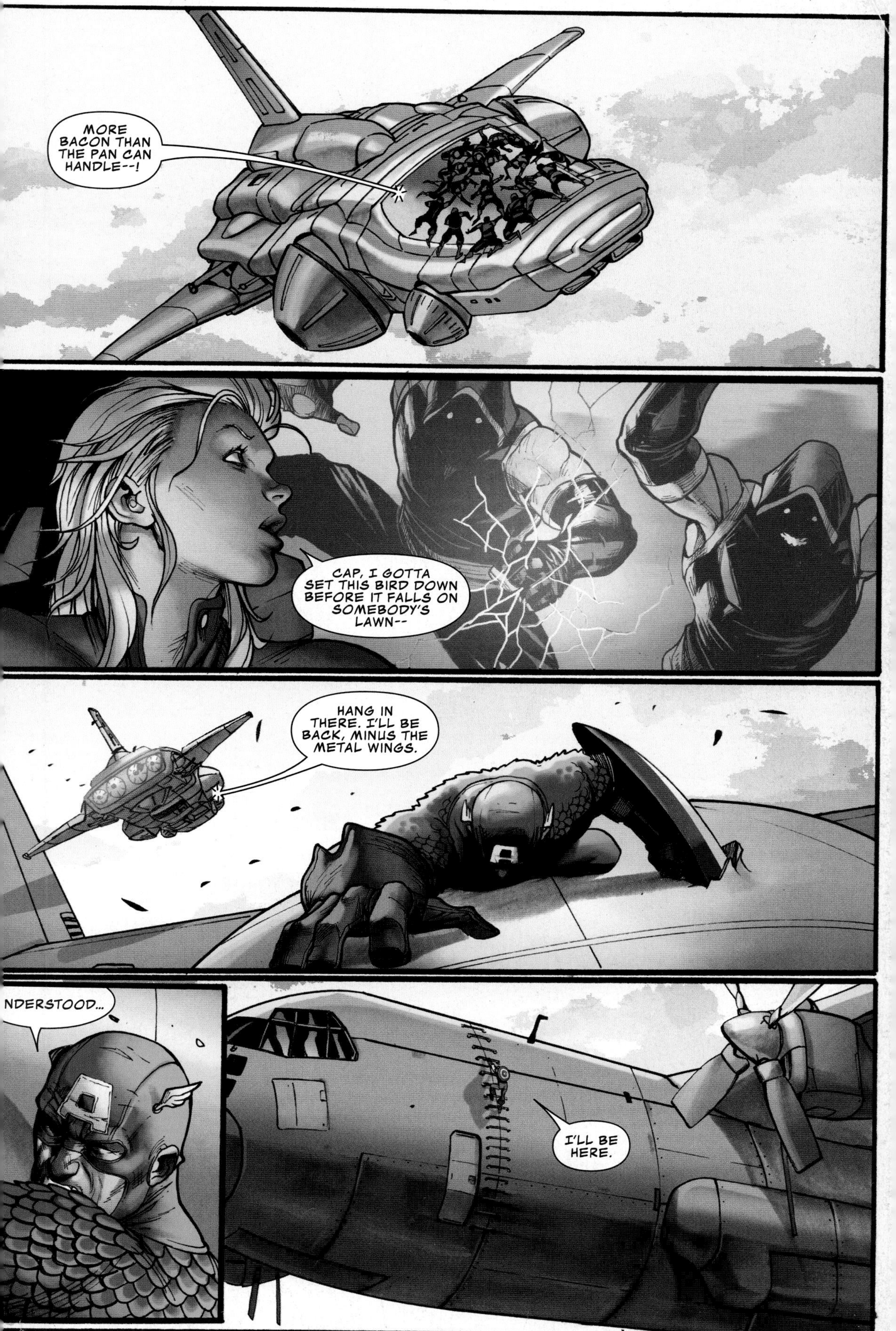
MORE BACON THAN THE PAN CAN HANDLE--!
CAP, I GOTTA SET THIS BIRD DOWN BEFORE IT FALLS ON SOMEBODY'S LAWN--
HANG IN THERE. I'LL BE BACK, MINUS THE METAL WINGS.
NDERSTOOD...
I'LL BE HERE.

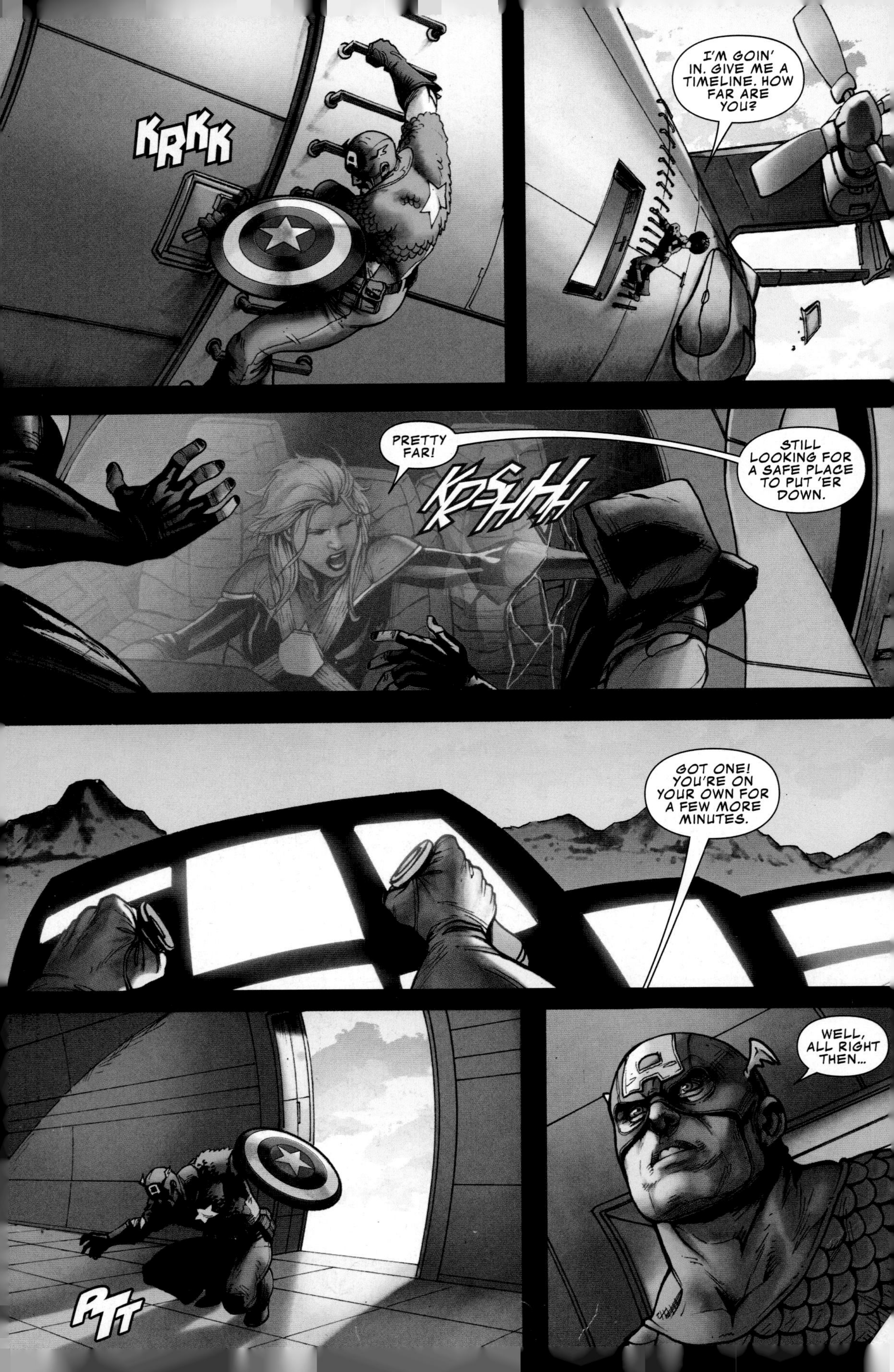
KRKK
I'M GOIN' IN. GIVE ME A TIMELINE. HOW FAR ARE YOU?
PRETTY FAR!
KRSHHH
STILL LOOKING FOR A SAFE PLACE TO PUT 'ER DOWN.
GOT ONE! YOU'RE ON YOUR OWN FOR A FEW MORE MINUTES.
PTT
WELL, ALL RIGHT THEN...

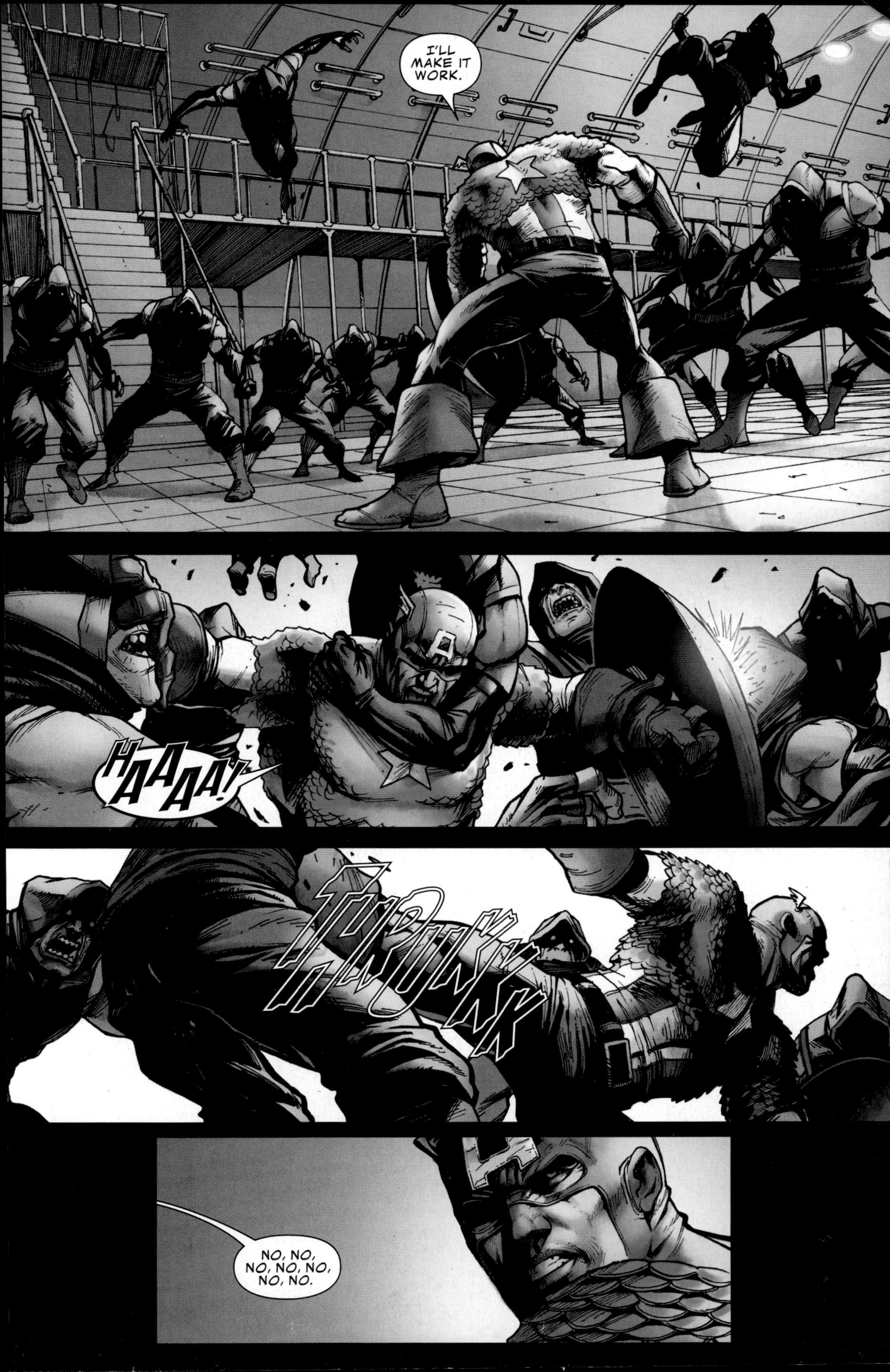
I'LL MAKE IT WORK.
HAAAA!
THUNK
NO, NO, NO, NO, NO, NO, NO.

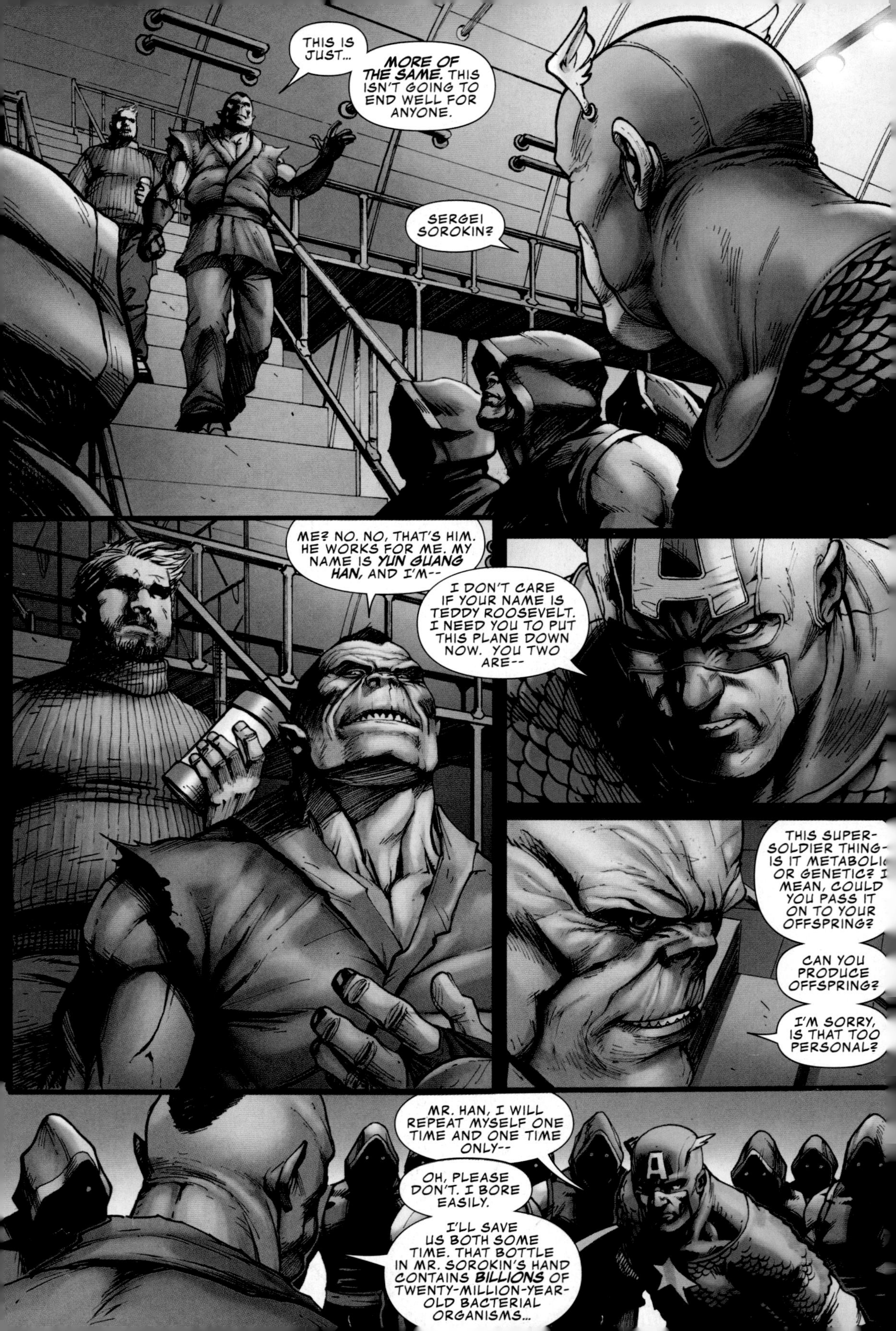
THIS IS JUST...
MORE OF THE SAME. THIS ISN'T GOING TO END WELL FOR ANYONE.
SERGEI SOROKIN?
ME? NO. NO, THAT'S HIM. HE WORKS FOR ME. MY NAME IS YUN GUANG HAN, AND I'M--
I DON'T CARE IF YOUR NAME IS TEDDY ROOSEVELT. I NEED YOU TO PUT THIS PLANE DOWN NOW. YOU TWO ARE--
THIS SUPER-SOLDIER THING--IS IT METABOLIC OR GENETIC? I MEAN, COULD YOU PASS IT ON TO YOUR OFFSPRING?
CAN YOU PRODUCE OFFSPRING?
I'M SORRY, IS THAT TOO PERSONAL?
MR. HAN, I WILL REPEAT MYSELF ONE TIME AND ONE TIME ONLY--
OH, PLEASE DON'T. I BORE EASILY.
I'LL SAVE US BOTH SOME TIME. THAT BOTTLE IN MR. SOROKIN'S HAND CONTAINS BILLIONS OF TWENTY-MILLION-YEAR-OLD BACTERIAL ORGANISMS...

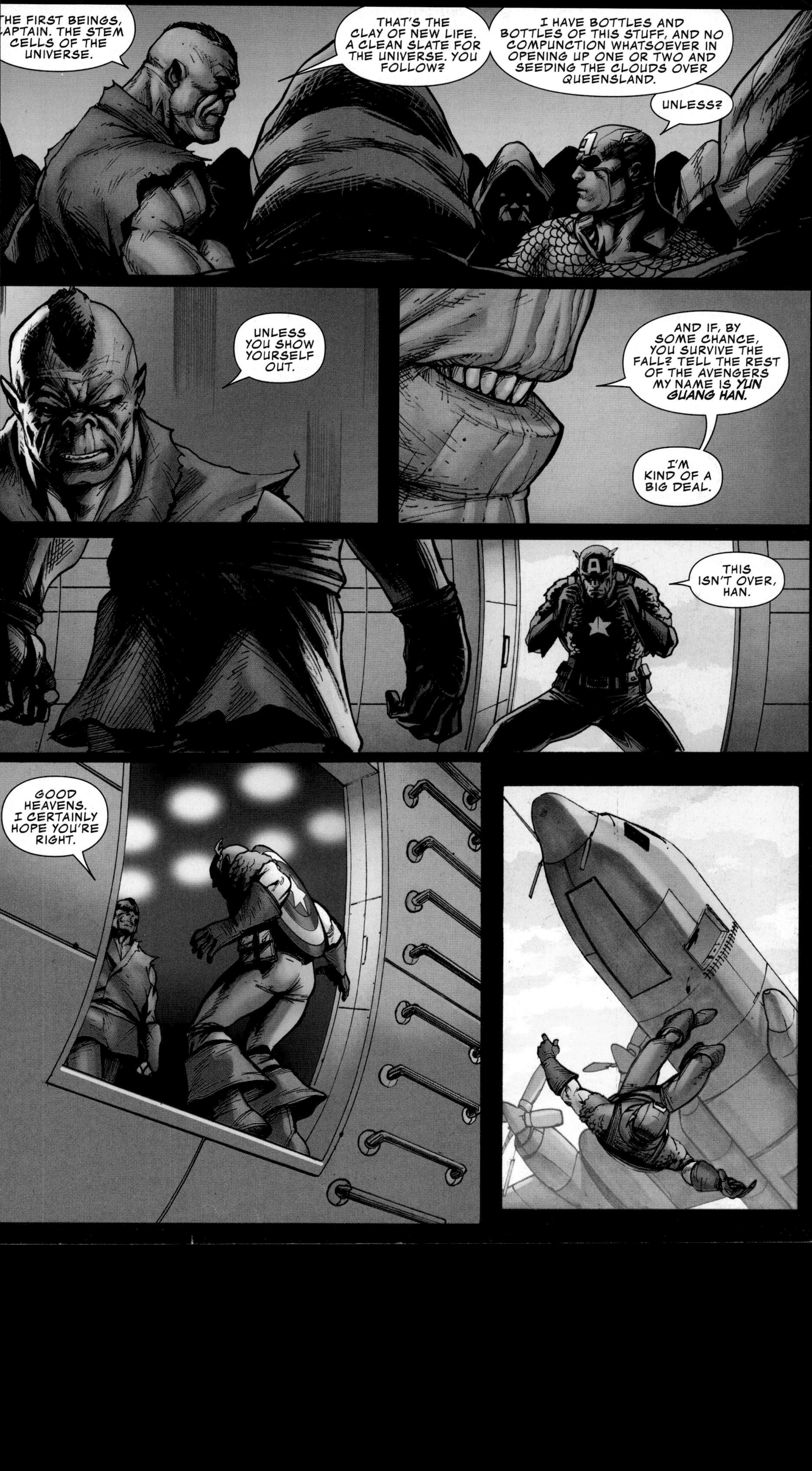

THE FIRST BEINGS, CAPTAIN. THE STEM CELLS OF THE UNIVERSE.
THAT'S THE CLAY OF NEW LIFE. A CLEAN SLATE FOR THE UNIVERSE. YOU FOLLOW?
I HAVE BOTTLES AND BOTTLES OF THIS STUFF, AND NO COMPUNCTION WHATSOEVER IN OPENING UP ONE OR TWO AND SEEDING THE CLOUDS OVER QUEENSLAND.
UNLESS?
UNLESS YOU SHOW YOURSELF OUT.
AND IF, BY SOME CHANCE, YOU SURVIVE THE FALL? TELL THE REST OF THE AVENGERS MY NAME IS *YUN GUANG HAN.*
I'M KIND OF A BIG DEAL.
THIS ISN'T OVER, HAN.
GOOD HEAVENS. I CERTAINLY HOPE YOU'RE RIGHT.

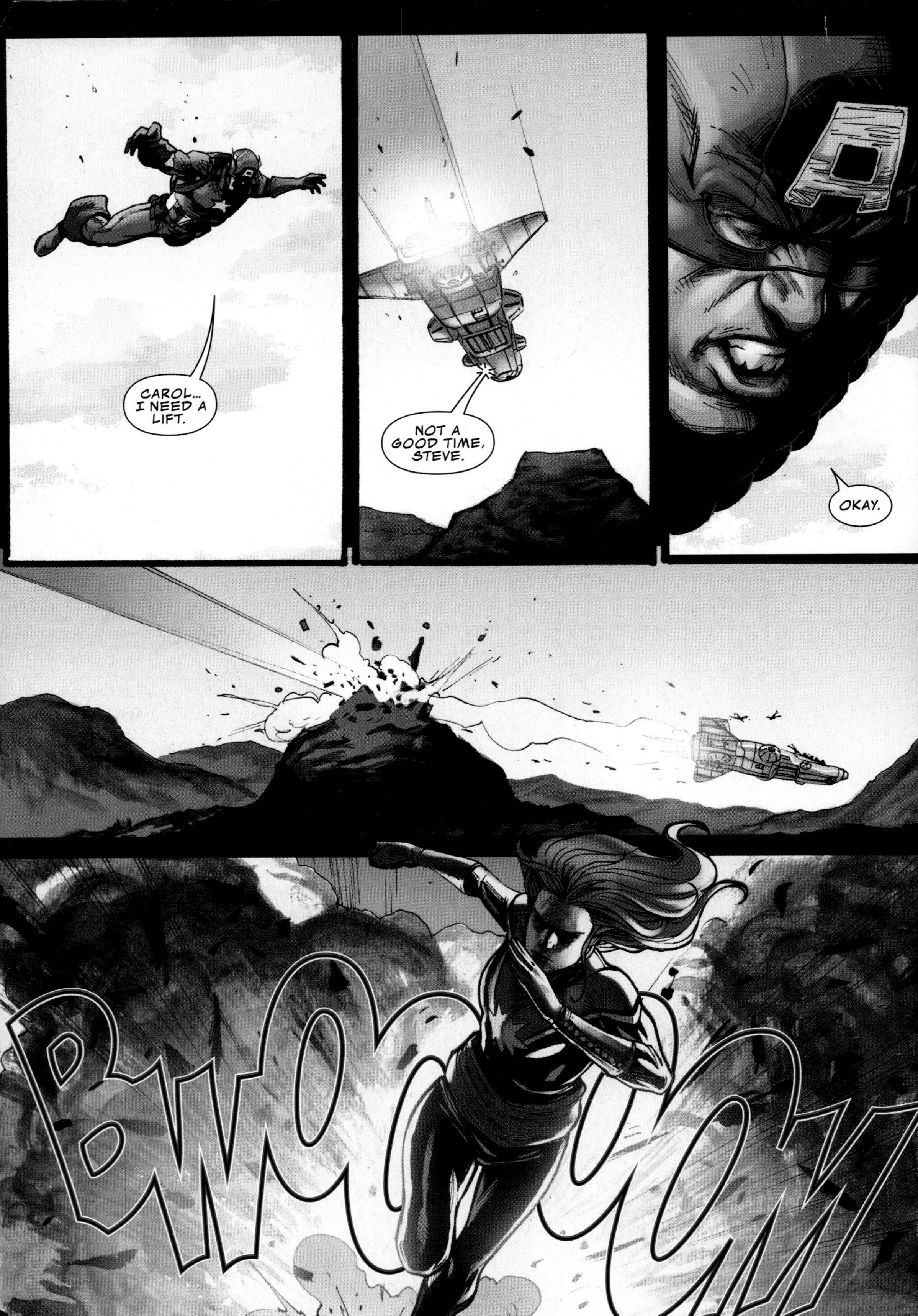
CAROL... I NEED A LIFT.
NOT A GOOD TIME, STEVE.
OKAY.
BWOOOOM

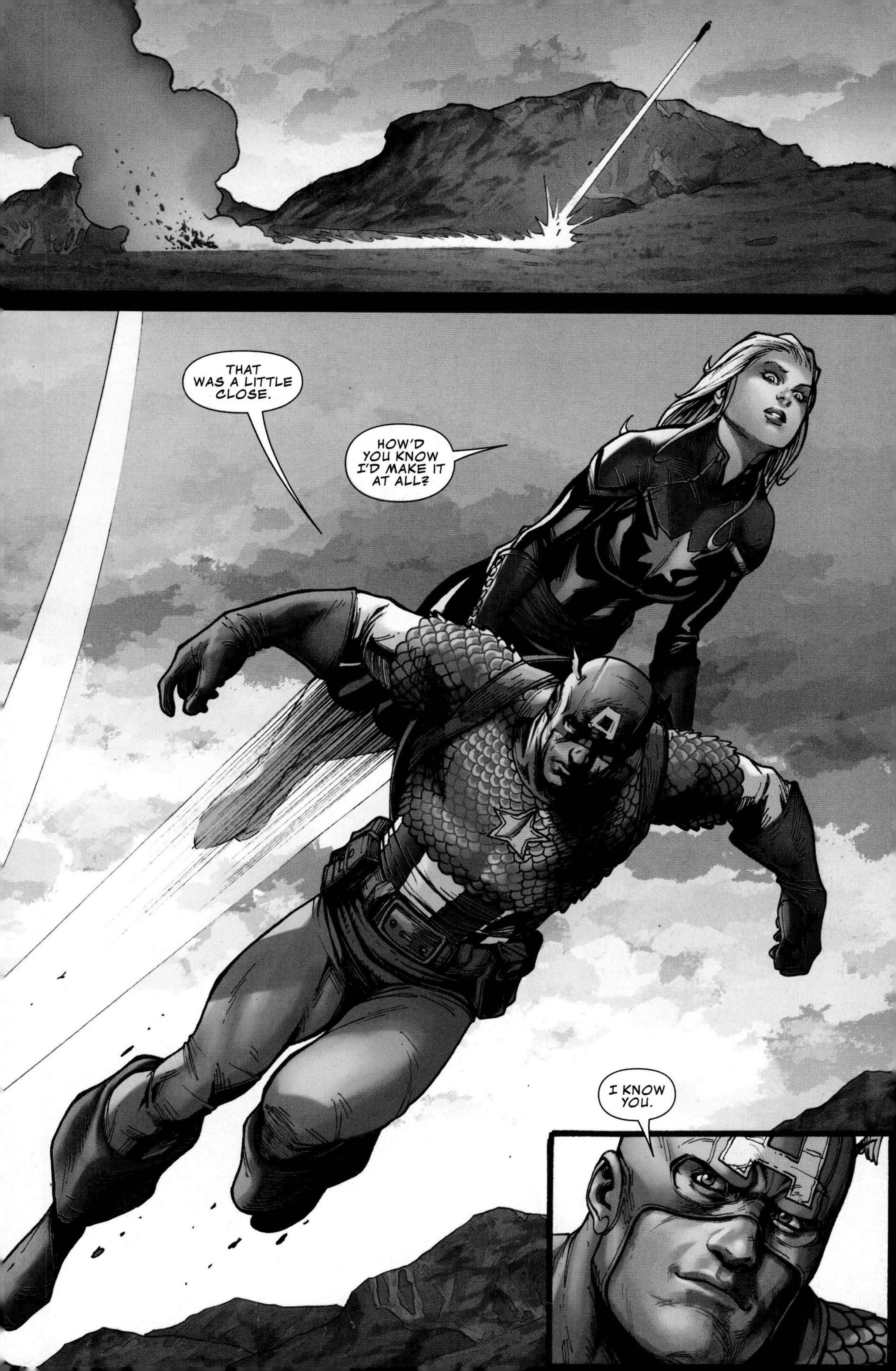
THAT WAS A LITTLE CLOSE.
HOW'D YOU KNOW I'D MAKE IT AT ALL?
I KNOW YOU.

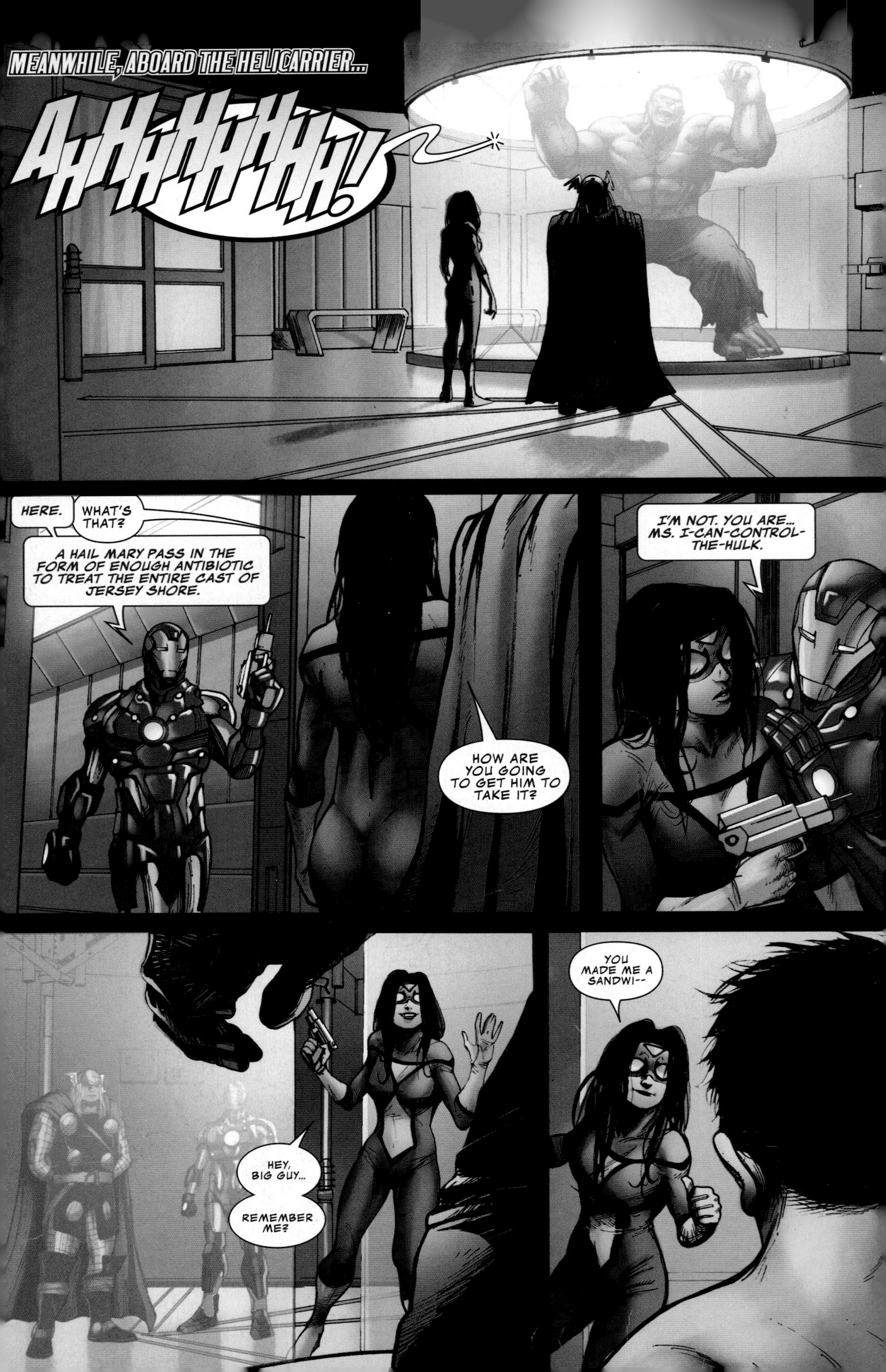

MEANWHILE, ABOARD THE HELICARRIER...
AHHHHHHH!
HERE.
WHAT'S THAT?
A HAIL MARY PASS IN THE FORM OF ENOUGH ANTIBIOTIC TO TREAT THE ENTIRE CAST OF JERSEY SHORE.
HOW ARE YOU GOING TO GET HIM TO TAKE IT?
I'M NOT. YOU ARE... MS. I-CAN-CONTROL-THE-HULK.
HEY, BIG GUY...
REMEMBER ME?
YOU MADE ME A SANDWI--

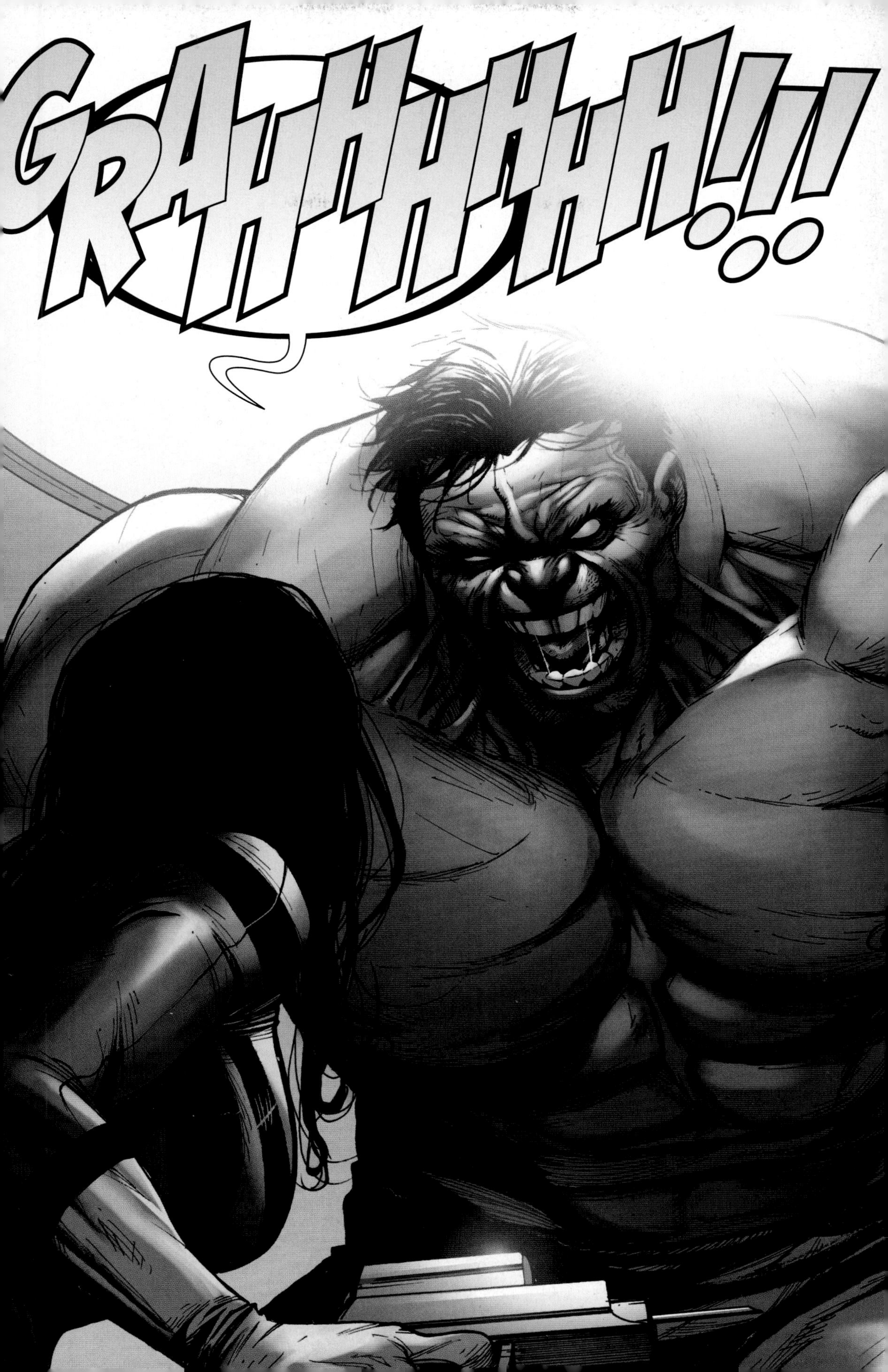
GRAHHHHHH!!!

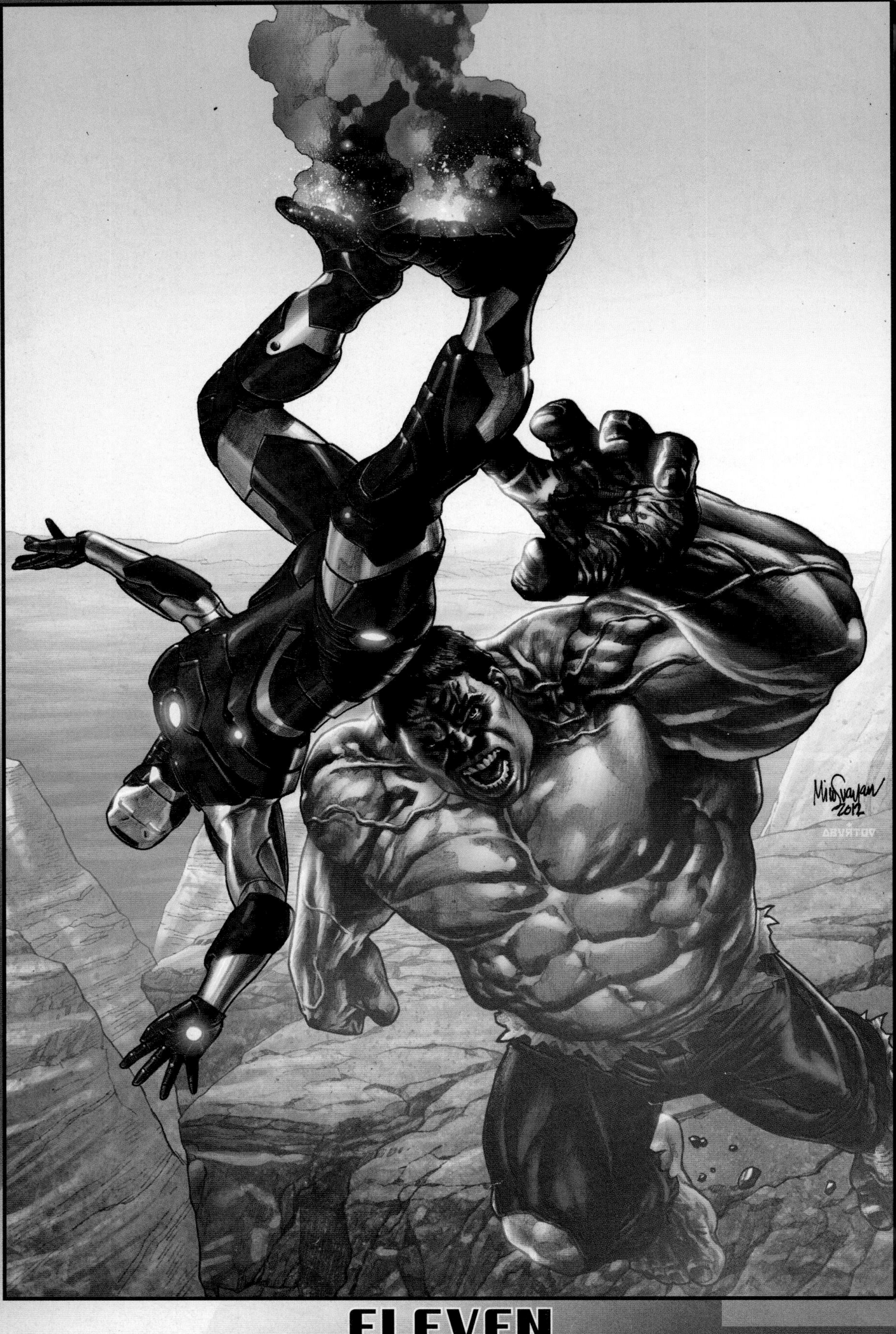

ELEVEN

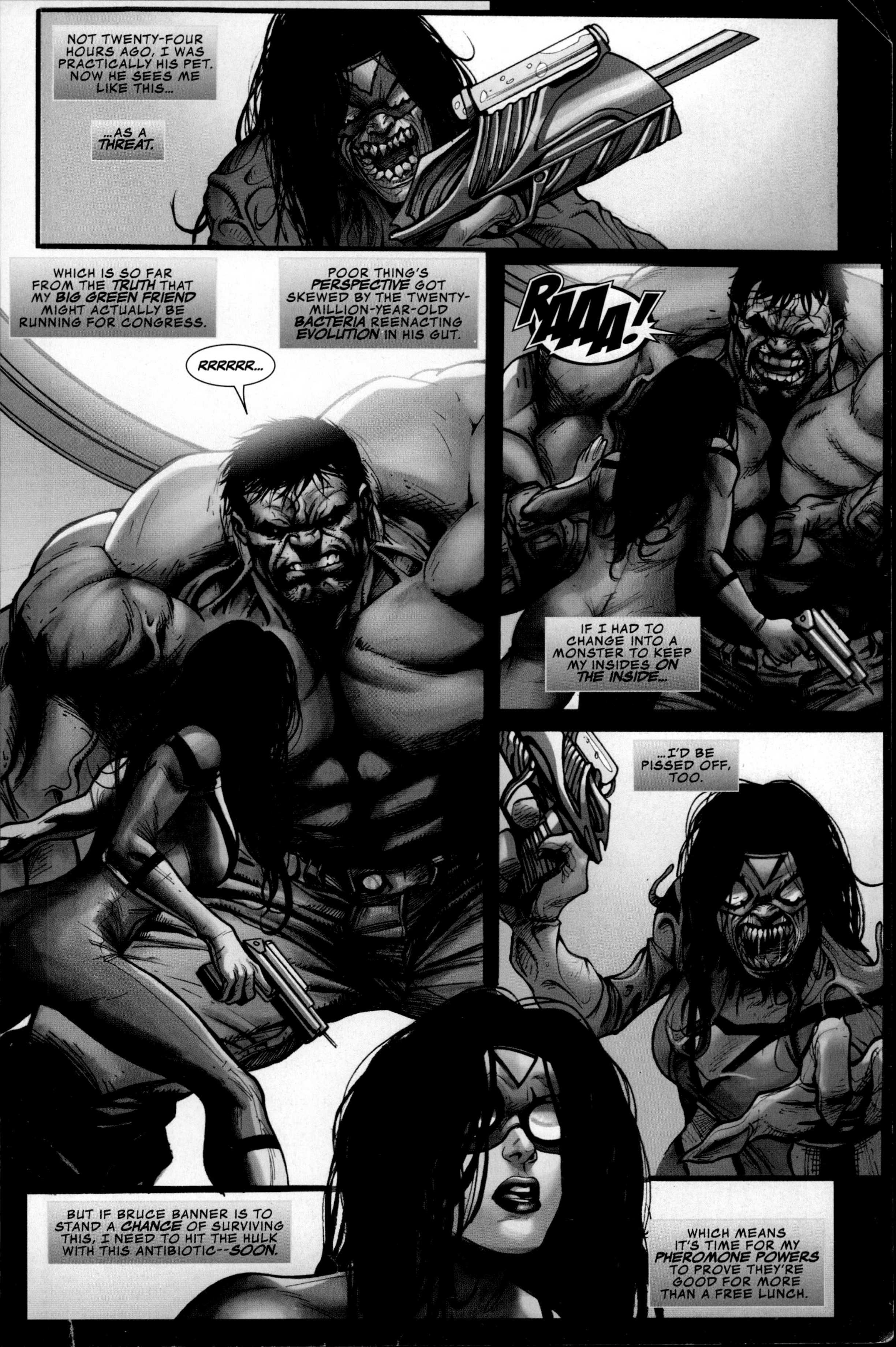
NOT TWENTY-FOUR HOURS AGO, I WAS PRACTICALLY HIS PET. NOW HE SEES ME LIKE THIS...
...AS A THREAT.
WHICH IS SO FAR FROM THE TRUTH THAT MY BIG GREEN FRIEND MIGHT ACTUALLY BE RUNNING FOR CONGRESS.
POOR THING'S PERSPECTIVE GOT SKEWED BY THE TWENTY-MILLION-YEAR-OLD BACTERIA REENACTING EVOLUTION IN HIS GUT.
RRRRRR...
RAAAA!
IF I HAD TO CHANGE INTO A MONSTER TO KEEP MY INSIDES ON THE INSIDE...
...I'D BE PISSED OFF, TOO.
BUT IF BRUCE BANNER IS TO STAND A CHANCE OF SURVIVING THIS, I NEED TO HIT THE HULK WITH THIS ANTIBIOTIC--SOON.
WHICH MEANS IT'S TIME FOR MY PHEROMONE POWERS TO PROVE THEY'RE GOOD FOR MORE THAN A FREE LUNCH.

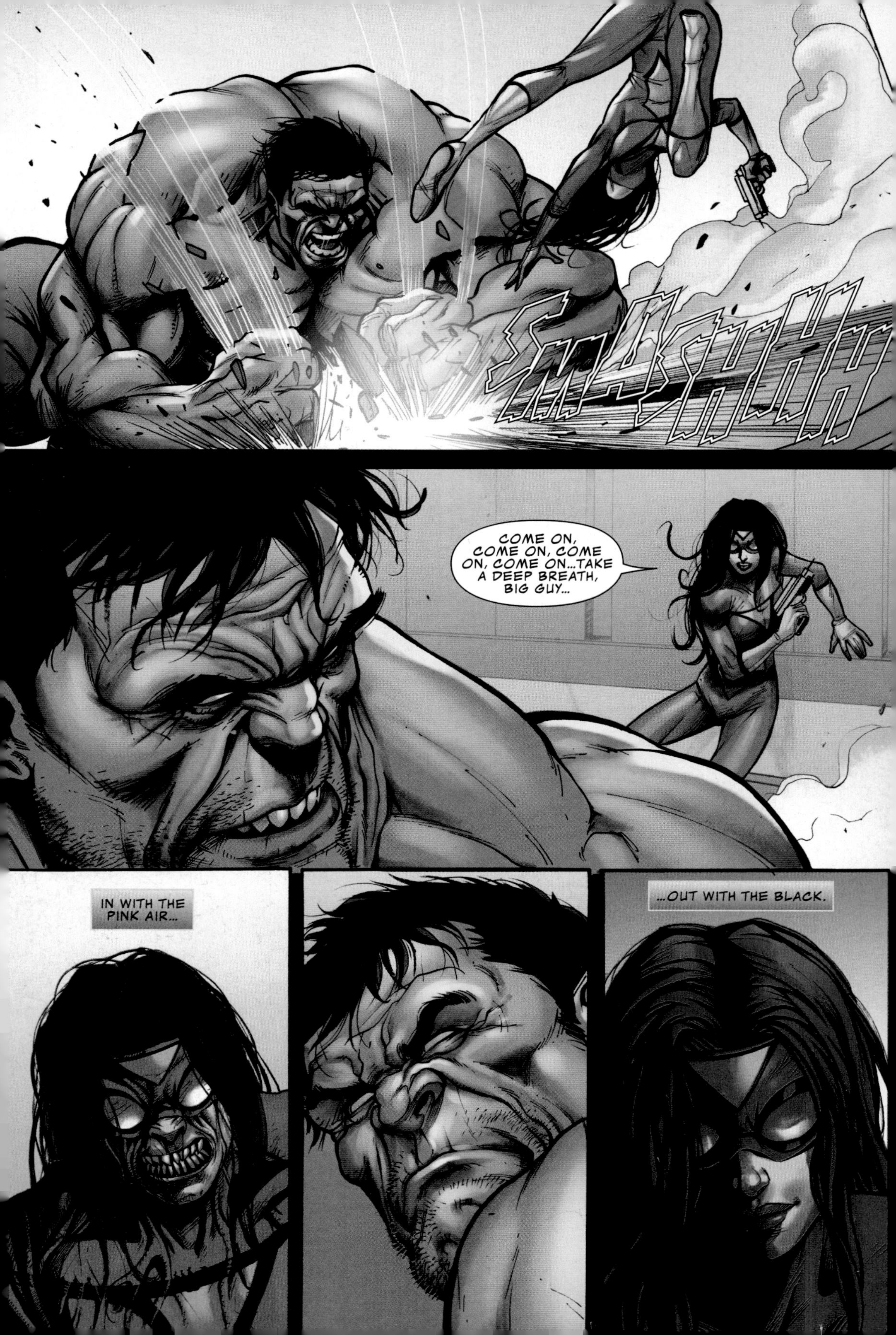
SMASHHH
COME ON, COME ON, COME ON, COME ON...TAKE A DEEP BREATH, BIG GUY...
IN WITH THE PINK AIR...
...OUT WITH THE BLACK.

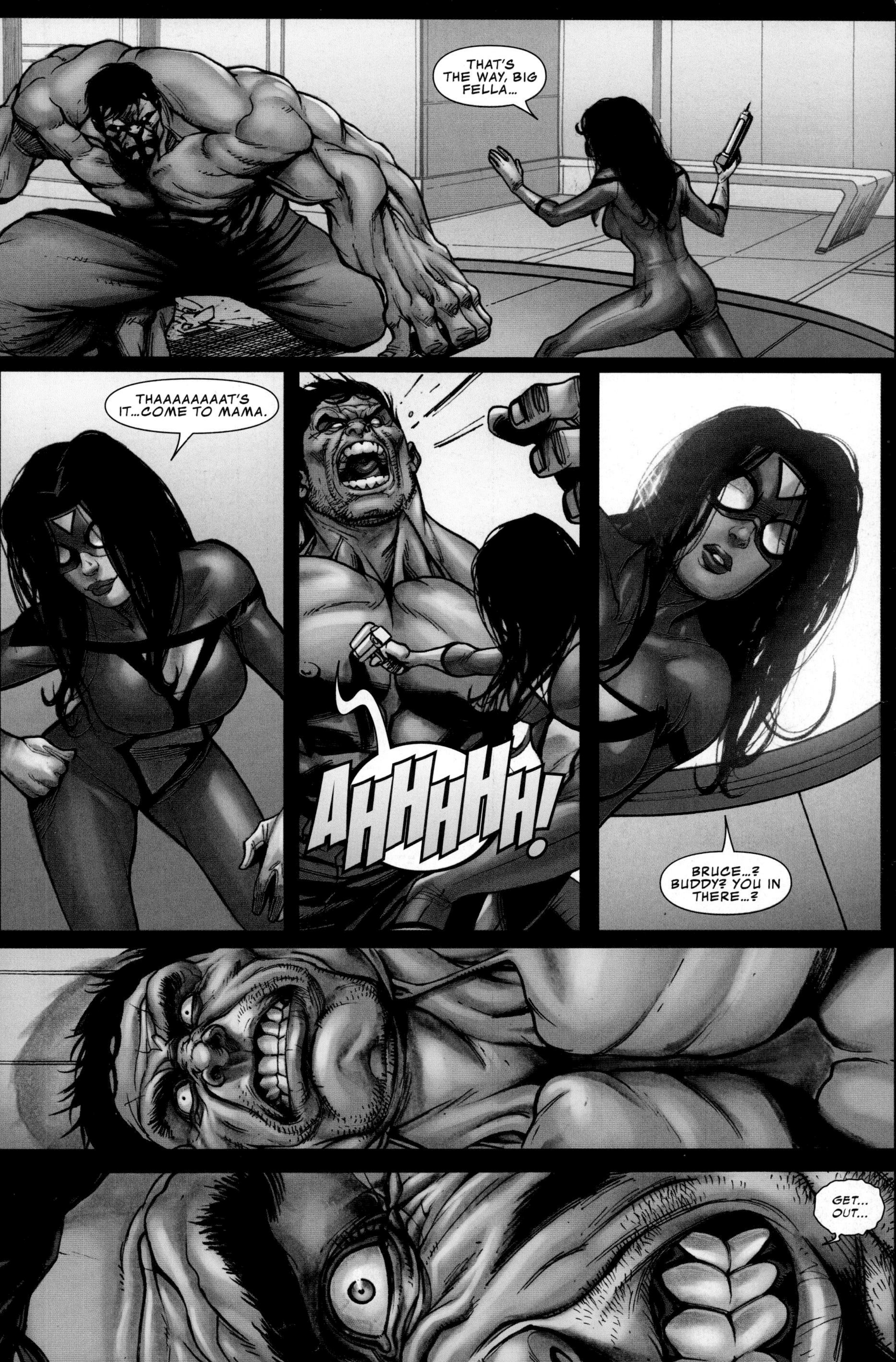
THAT'S THE WAY, BIG FELLA...
THAAAAAAAAT'S IT...COME TO MAMA.
AHHHHH!
BRUCE...? BUDDY? YOU IN THERE...?
GET... OUT...

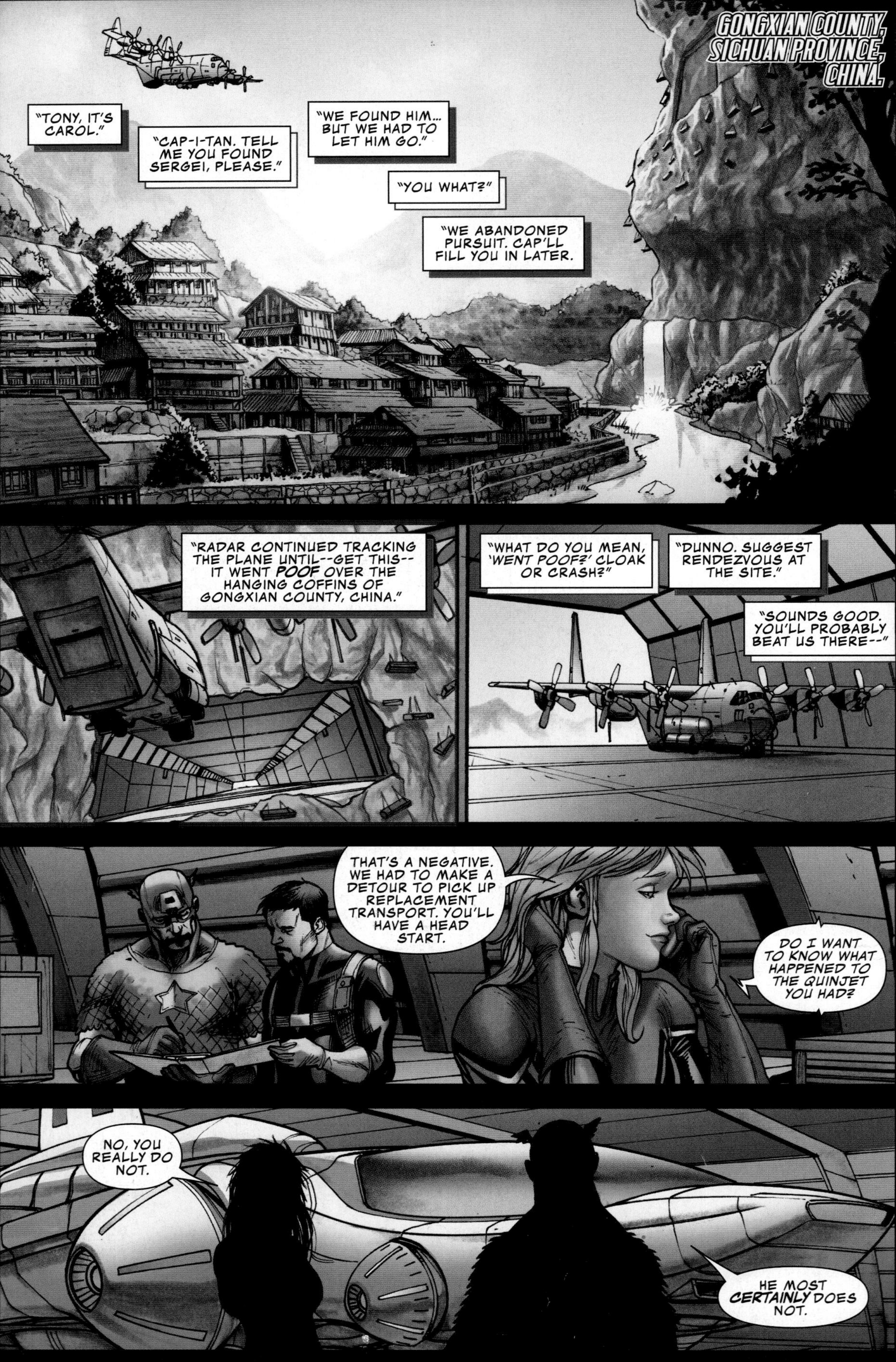
GONGXIAN COUNTY, SICHUAN PROVINCE, CHINA.
"TONY, IT'S CAROL."
"CAP-I-TAN. TELL ME YOU FOUND SERGEI, PLEASE."
"WE FOUND HIM... BUT WE HAD TO LET HIM GO."
"YOU WHAT?"
"WE ABANDONED PURSUIT. CAP'LL FILL YOU IN LATER.
"RADAR CONTINUED TRACKING THE PLANE UNTIL--GET THIS--IT WENT POOF OVER THE HANGING COFFINS OF GONGXIAN COUNTY, CHINA."
"WHAT DO YOU MEAN, 'WENT POOF?' CLOAK OR CRASH?"
"DUNNO. SUGGEST RENDEZVOUS AT THE SITE."
"SOUNDS GOOD. YOU'LL PROBABLY BEAT US THERE--"
THAT'S A NEGATIVE. WE HAD TO MAKE A DETOUR TO PICK UP REPLACEMENT TRANSPORT. YOU'LL HAVE A HEAD START.
DO I WANT TO KNOW WHAT HAPPENED TO THE QUINJET YOU HAD?
NO, YOU REALLY DO NOT.
HE MOST CERTAINLY DOES NOT.

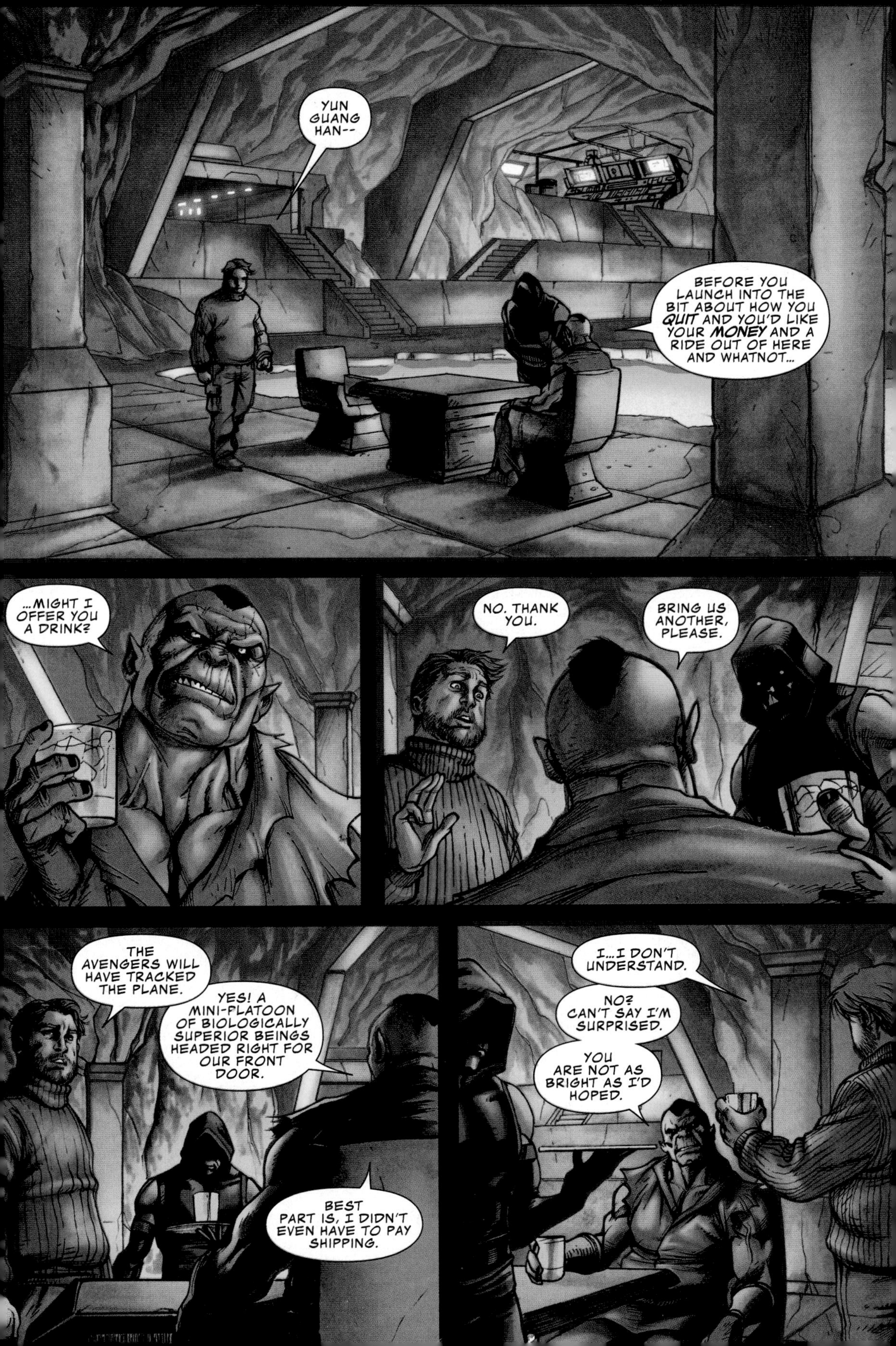
YUN GUANG HAN--
BEFORE YOU LAUNCH INTO THE BIT ABOUT HOW YOU QUIT AND YOU'D LIKE YOUR MONEY AND A RIDE OUT OF HERE AND WHATNOT...
...MIGHT I OFFER YOU A DRINK?
NO. THANK YOU.
BRING US ANOTHER, PLEASE.
THE AVENGERS WILL HAVE TRACKED THE PLANE.
YES! A MINI-PLATOON OF BIOLOGICALLY SUPERIOR BEINGS HEADED RIGHT FOR OUR FRONT DOOR.
BEST PART IS, I DIDN'T EVEN HAVE TO PAY SHIPPING.
I...I DON'T UNDERSTAND.
NO? CAN'T SAY I'M SURPRISED.
YOU ARE NOT AS BRIGHT AS I'D HOPED.

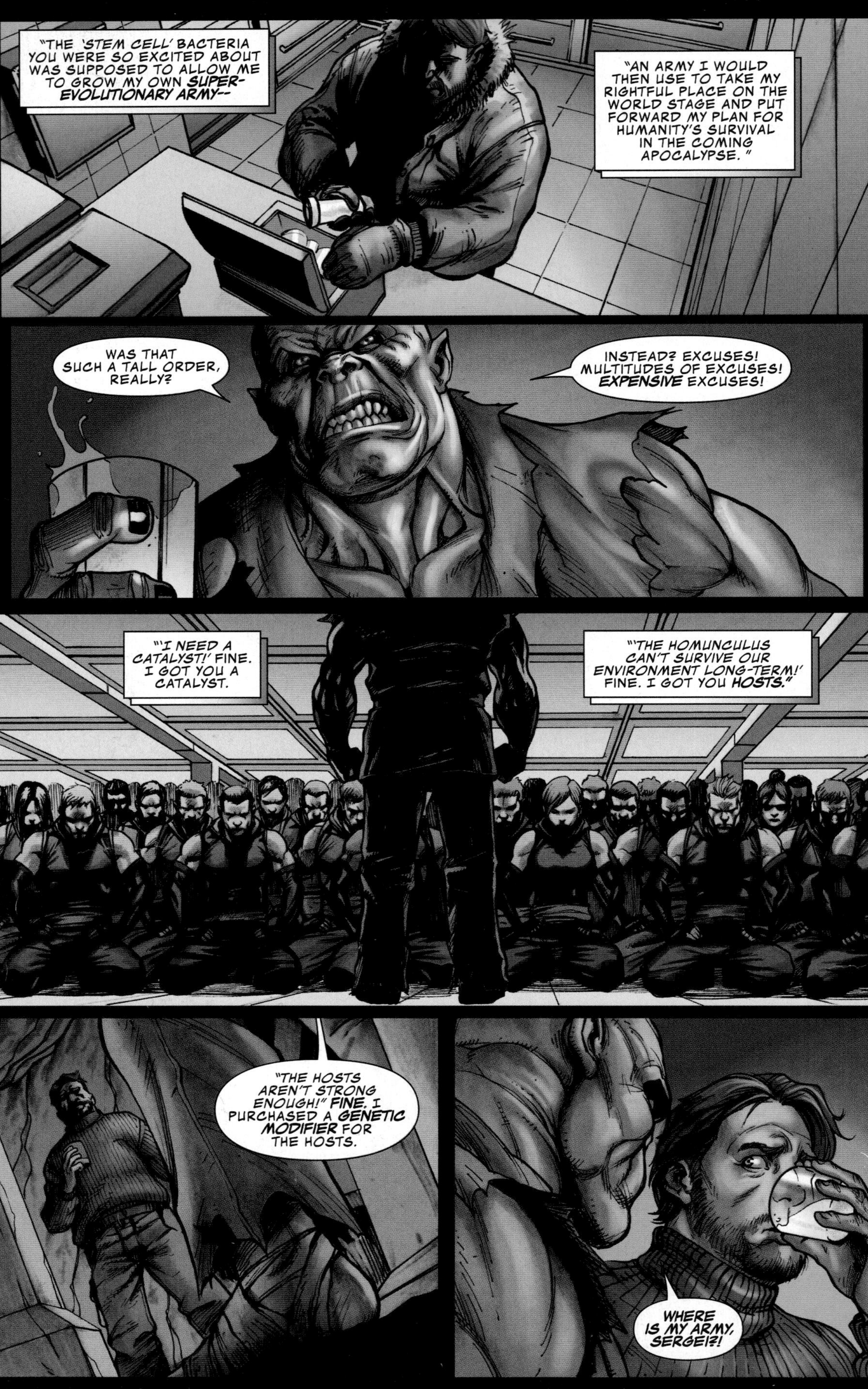
"THE 'STEM CELL' BACTERIA YOU WERE SO EXCITED ABOUT WAS SUPPOSED TO ALLOW ME TO GROW MY OWN SUPER-EVOLUTIONARY ARMY--
"AN ARMY I WOULD THEN USE TO TAKE MY RIGHTFUL PLACE ON THE WORLD STAGE AND PUT FORWARD MY PLAN FOR HUMANITY'S SURVIVAL IN THE COMING APOCALYPSE."
WAS THAT SUCH A TALL ORDER, REALLY?
INSTEAD? EXCUSES! MULTITUDES OF EXCUSES! EXPENSIVE EXCUSES!
"'I NEED A CATALYST!' FINE. I GOT YOU A CATALYST.
"'THE HOMUNCULUS CAN'T SURVIVE OUR ENVIRONMENT LONG-TERM!' FINE. I GOT YOU HOSTS."
"THE HOSTS AREN'T STRONG ENOUGH!" FINE. I PURCHASED A GENETIC MODIFIER FOR THE HOSTS.
WHERE IS MY ARMY, SERGEI?!

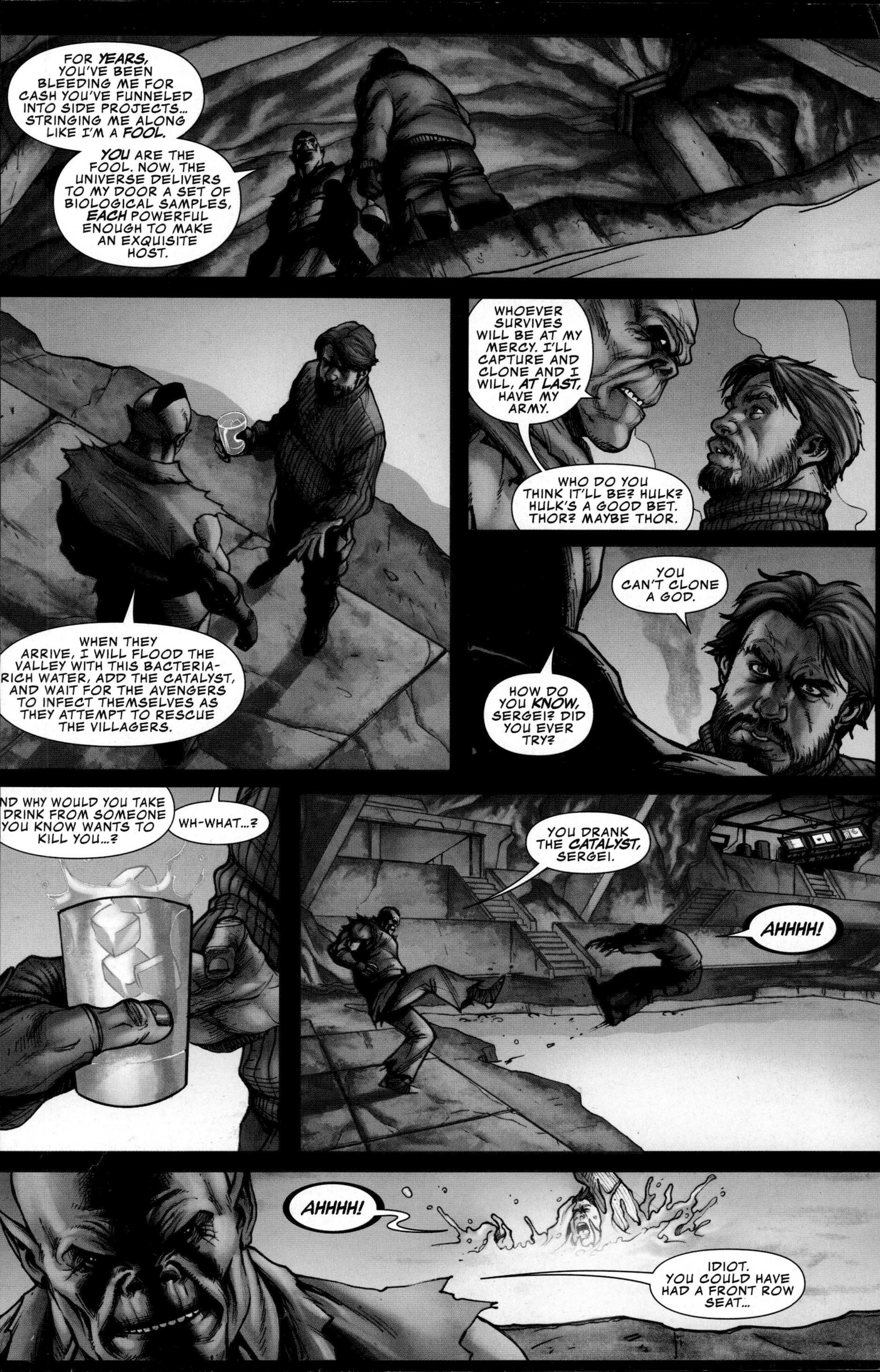
FOR YEARS, YOU'VE BEEN BLEEDING ME FOR CASH YOU'VE FUNNELED INTO SIDE PROJECTS... STRINGING ME ALONG LIKE I'M A FOOL.
YOU ARE THE FOOL. NOW, THE UNIVERSE DELIVERS TO MY DOOR A SET OF BIOLOGICAL SAMPLES, EACH POWERFUL ENOUGH TO MAKE AN EXQUISITE HOST.
WHEN THEY ARRIVE, I WILL FLOOD THE VALLEY WITH THIS BACTERIA-RICH WATER, ADD THE CATALYST, AND WAIT FOR THE AVENGERS TO INFECT THEMSELVES AS THEY ATTEMPT TO RESCUE THE VILLAGERS.
WHOEVER SURVIVES WILL BE AT MY MERCY. I'LL CAPTURE AND CLONE AND I WILL, AT LAST, HAVE MY ARMY.
WHO DO YOU THINK IT'LL BE? HULK? HULK'S A GOOD BET. THOR? MAYBE THOR.
YOU CAN'T CLONE A GOD.
HOW DO YOU KNOW, SERGEI? DID YOU EVER TRY?
ND WHY WOULD YOU TAKE DRINK FROM SOMEONE YOU KNOW WANTS TO KILL YOU...?
WH-WHAT...?
YOU DRANK THE CATALYST, SERGEI.
AHHHH!
AHHHH!
IDIOT. YOU COULD HAVE HAD A FRONT ROW SEAT...

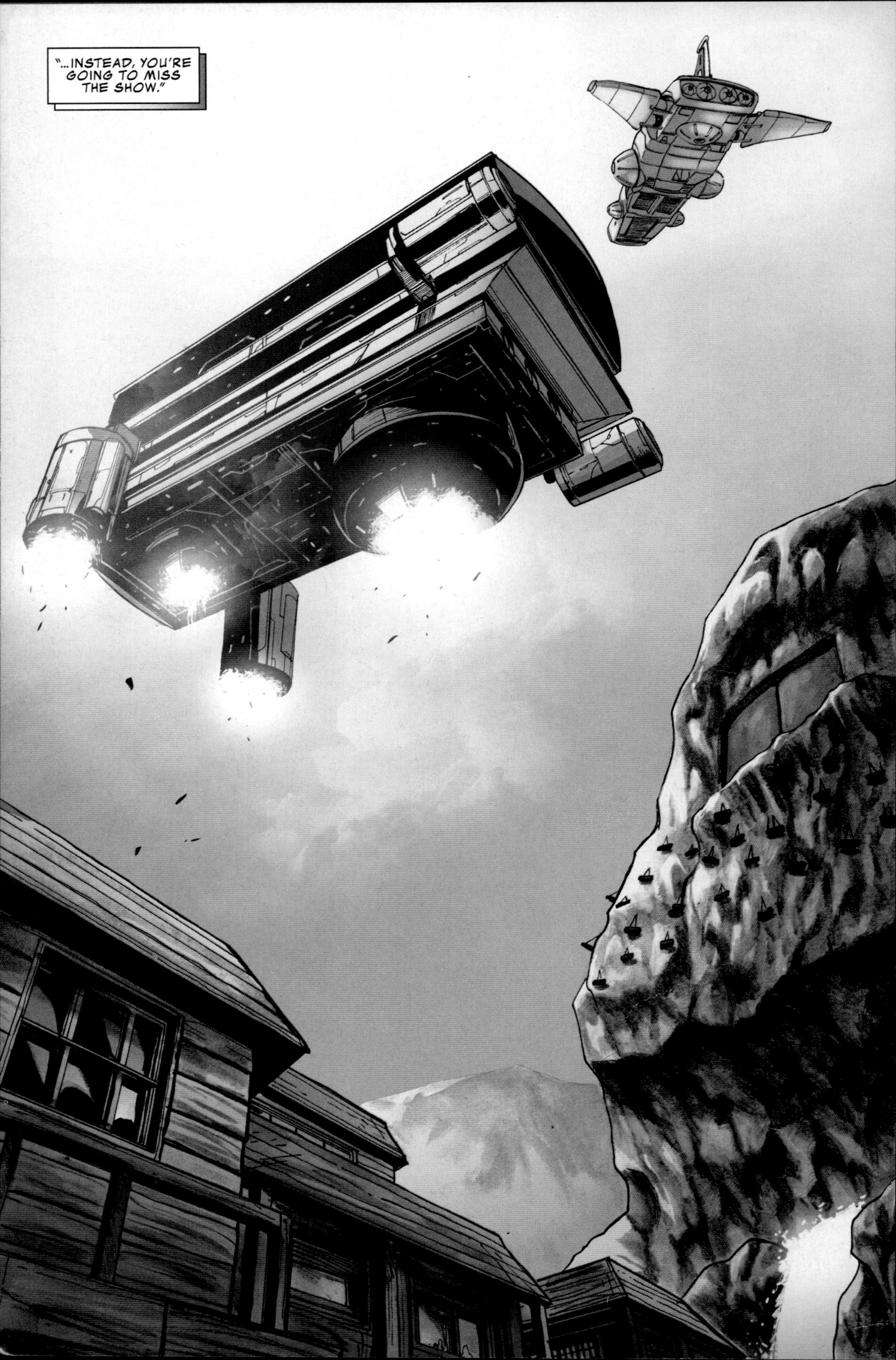
"...INSTEAD, YOU'RE GOING TO MISS THE SHOW."

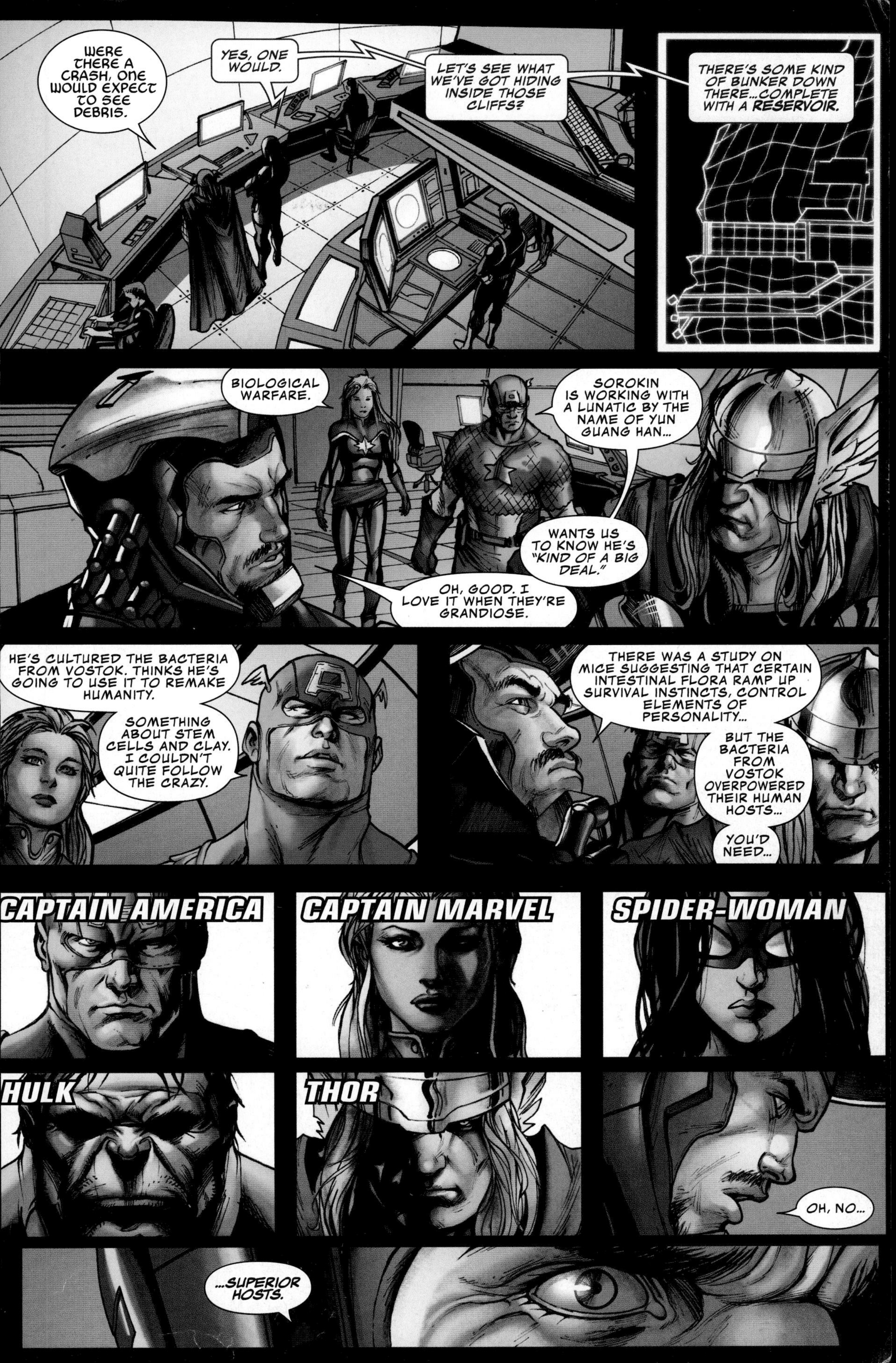
WERE THERE A CRASH, ONE WOULD EXPECT TO SEE DEBRIS.
YES, ONE WOULD.
LET'S SEE WHAT WE'VE GOT HIDING INSIDE THOSE CLIFFS?
THERE'S SOME KIND OF BUNKER DOWN THERE...COMPLETE WITH A RESERVOIR.
BIOLOGICAL WARFARE.
SOROKIN IS WORKING WITH A LUNATIC BY THE NAME OF YUN GUANG HAN...
WANTS US TO KNOW HE'S "KIND OF A BIG DEAL."
OH, GOOD. I LOVE IT WHEN THEY'RE GRANDIOSE.
HE'S CULTURED THE BACTERIA FROM VOSTOK. THINKS HE'S GOING TO USE IT TO REMAKE HUMANITY.
SOMETHING ABOUT STEM CELLS AND CLAY. I COULDN'T QUITE FOLLOW THE CRAZY.
THERE WAS A STUDY ON MICE SUGGESTING THAT CERTAIN INTESTINAL FLORA RAMP UP SURVIVAL INSTINCTS, CONTROL ELEMENTS OF PERSONALITY...
BUT THE BACTERIA FROM VOSTOK OVERPOWERED THEIR HUMAN HOSTS...
YOU'D NEED...
CAPTAIN AMERICA
CAPTAIN MARVEL
SPIDER-WOMAN
HULK
THOR
OH, NO...
...SUPERIOR HOSTS.

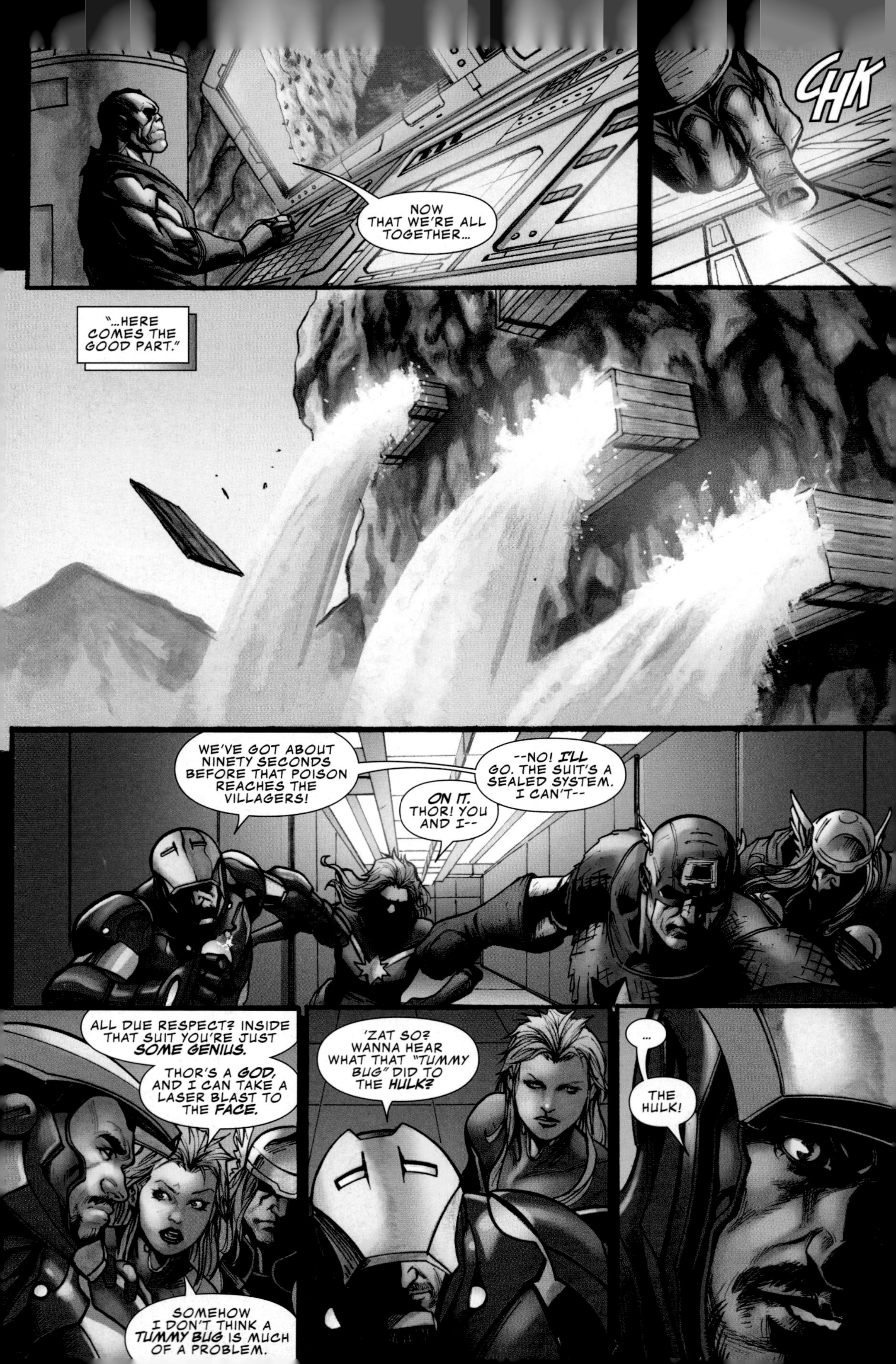
NOW THAT WE'RE ALL TOGETHER...
CHK
"...HERE COMES THE GOOD PART."
WE'VE GOT ABOUT NINETY SECONDS BEFORE THAT POISON REACHES THE VILLAGERS!
ON IT. THOR! YOU AND I--
--NO! I'LL GO. THE SUIT'S A SEALED SYSTEM. I CAN'T--
ALL DUE RESPECT? INSIDE THAT SUIT YOU'RE JUST SOME GENIUS.
THOR'S A GOD, AND I CAN TAKE A LASER BLAST TO THE FACE.
SOMEHOW I DON'T THINK A TUMMY BUG IS MUCH OF A PROBLEM.
'ZAT SO? WANNA HEAR WHAT THAT "TUMMY BUG" DID TO THE HULK?
...
THE HULK!

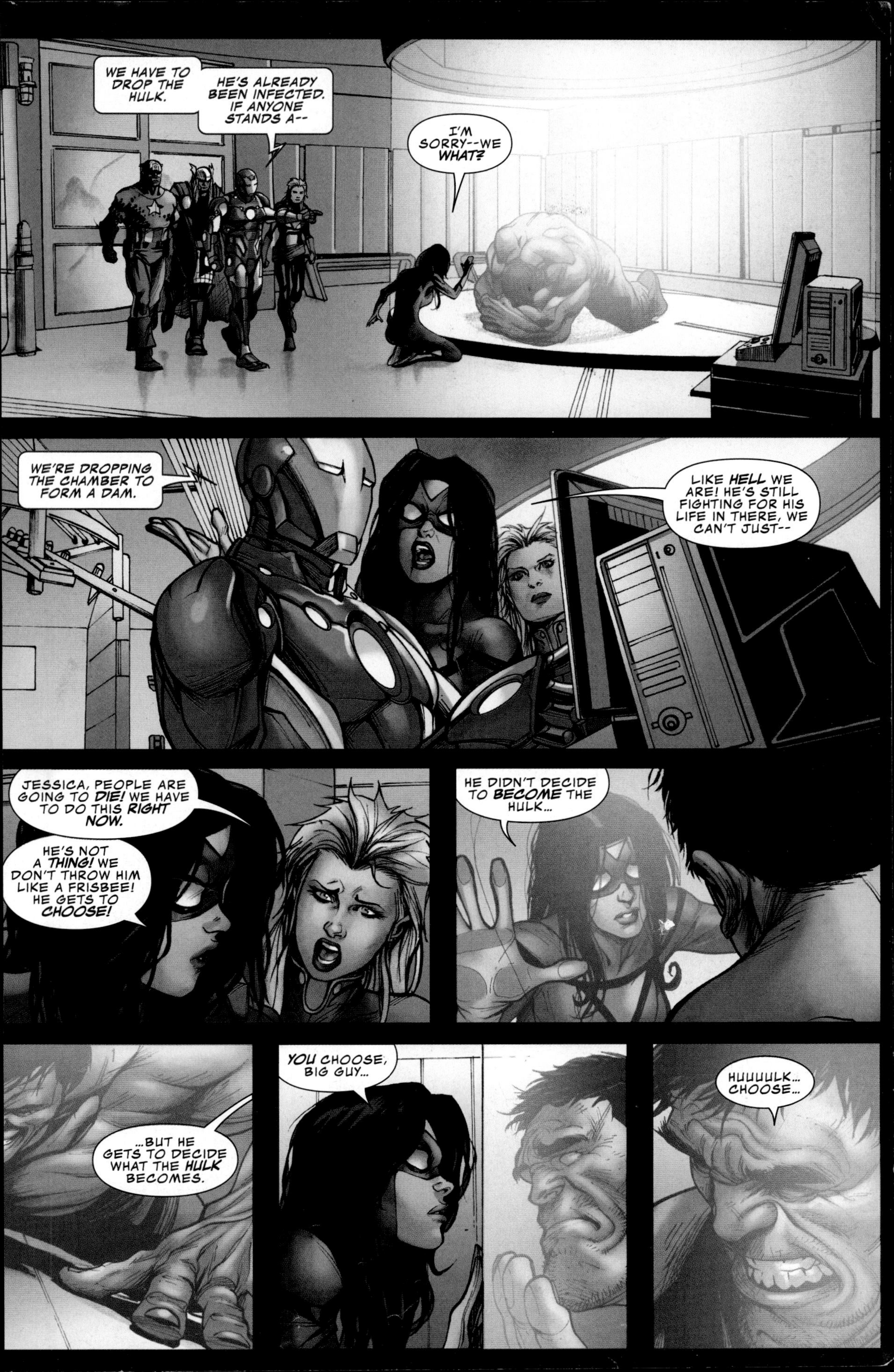
WE HAVE TO DROP THE HULK.
HE'S ALREADY BEEN INFECTED. IF ANYONE STANDS A--
I'M SORRY--WE WHAT?
WE'RE DROPPING THE CHAMBER TO FORM A DAM.
LIKE HELL WE ARE! HE'S STILL FIGHTING FOR HIS LIFE IN THERE, WE CAN'T JUST--
JESSICA, PEOPLE ARE GOING TO DIE! WE HAVE TO DO THIS RIGHT NOW.
HE'S NOT A THING! WE DON'T THROW HIM LIKE A FRISBEE! HE GETS TO CHOOSE!
HE DIDN'T DECIDE TO BECOME THE HULK...
...BUT HE GETS TO DECIDE WHAT THE HULK BECOMES.
YOU CHOOSE, BIG GUY...
HUUUULK... CHOOSE...

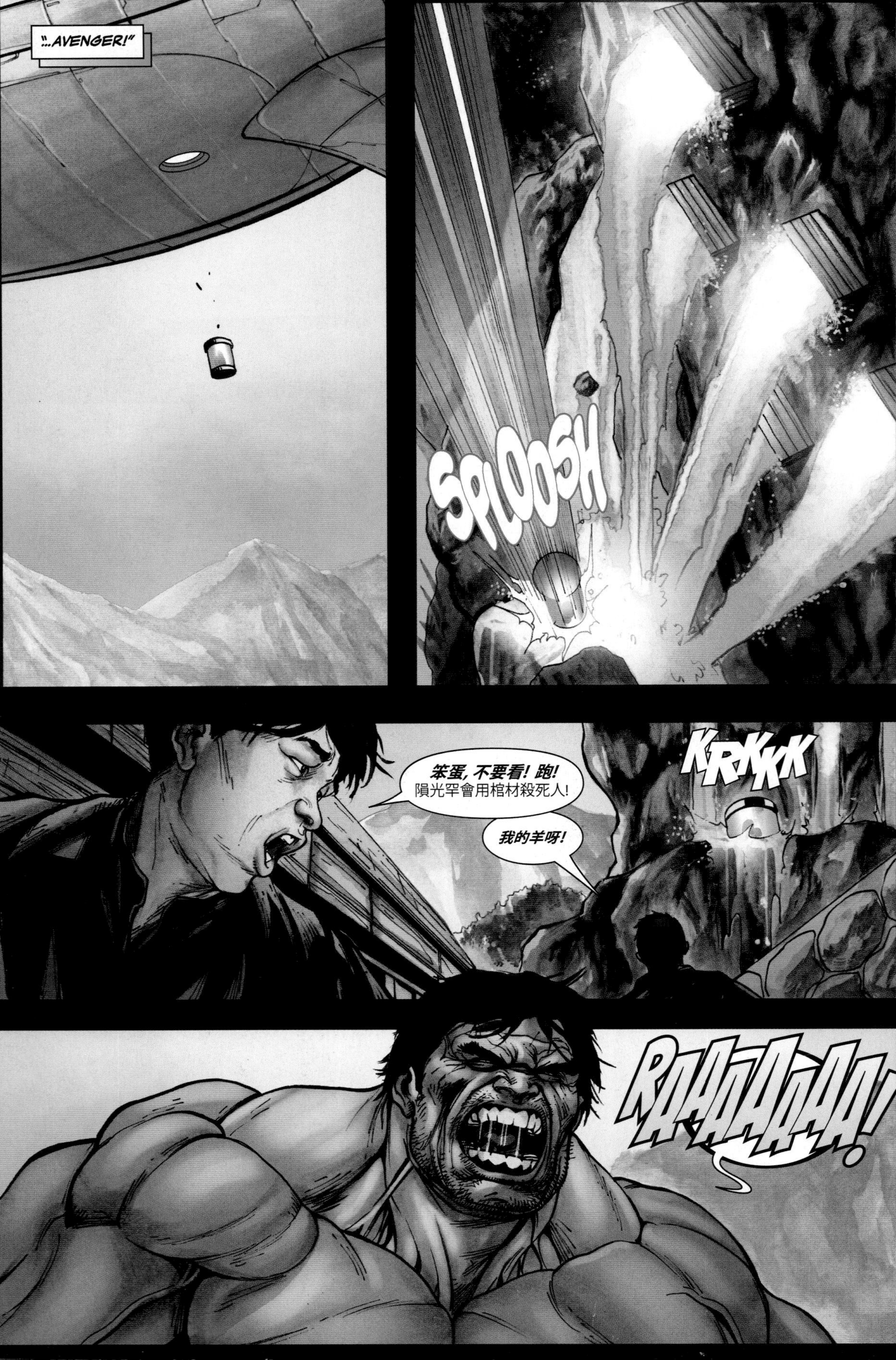
"...AVENGER!"
SPLOOSH
KRKKK
笨蛋, 不要看! 跑! 隕光罕會用棺材殺死人!
我的羊呀!
RAAAAAAA!

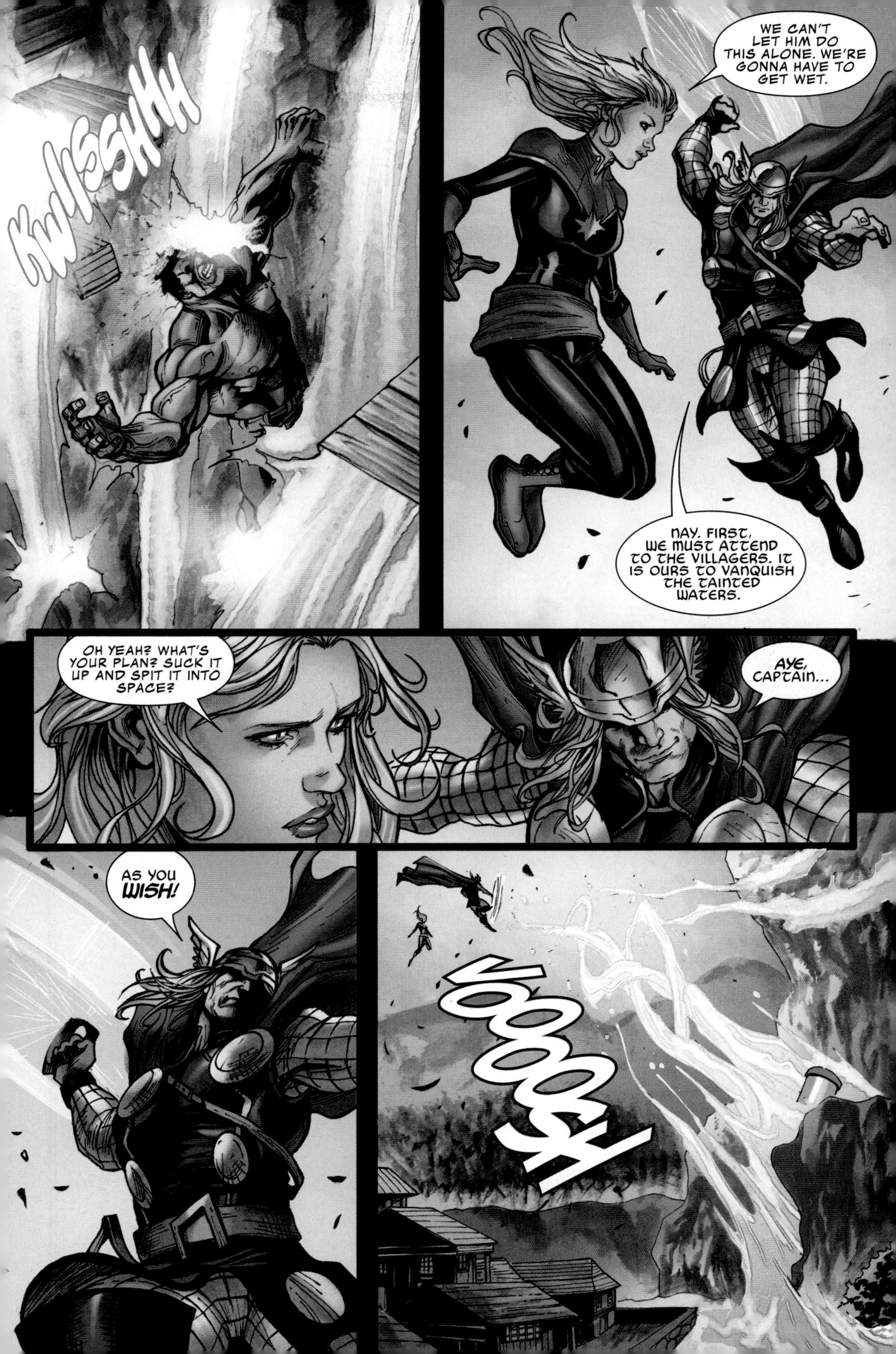
KWUSSHHH
WE CAN'T LET HIM DO THIS ALONE. WE'RE GONNA HAVE TO GET WET.
NAY. FIRST, WE MUST ATTEND TO THE VILLAGERS. IT IS OURS TO VANQUISH THE TAINTED WATERS.
OH YEAH? WHAT'S YOUR PLAN? SUCK IT UP AND SPIT IT INTO SPACE?
AYE, CAPTAIN...
AS YOU WISH!
VOOOOSH

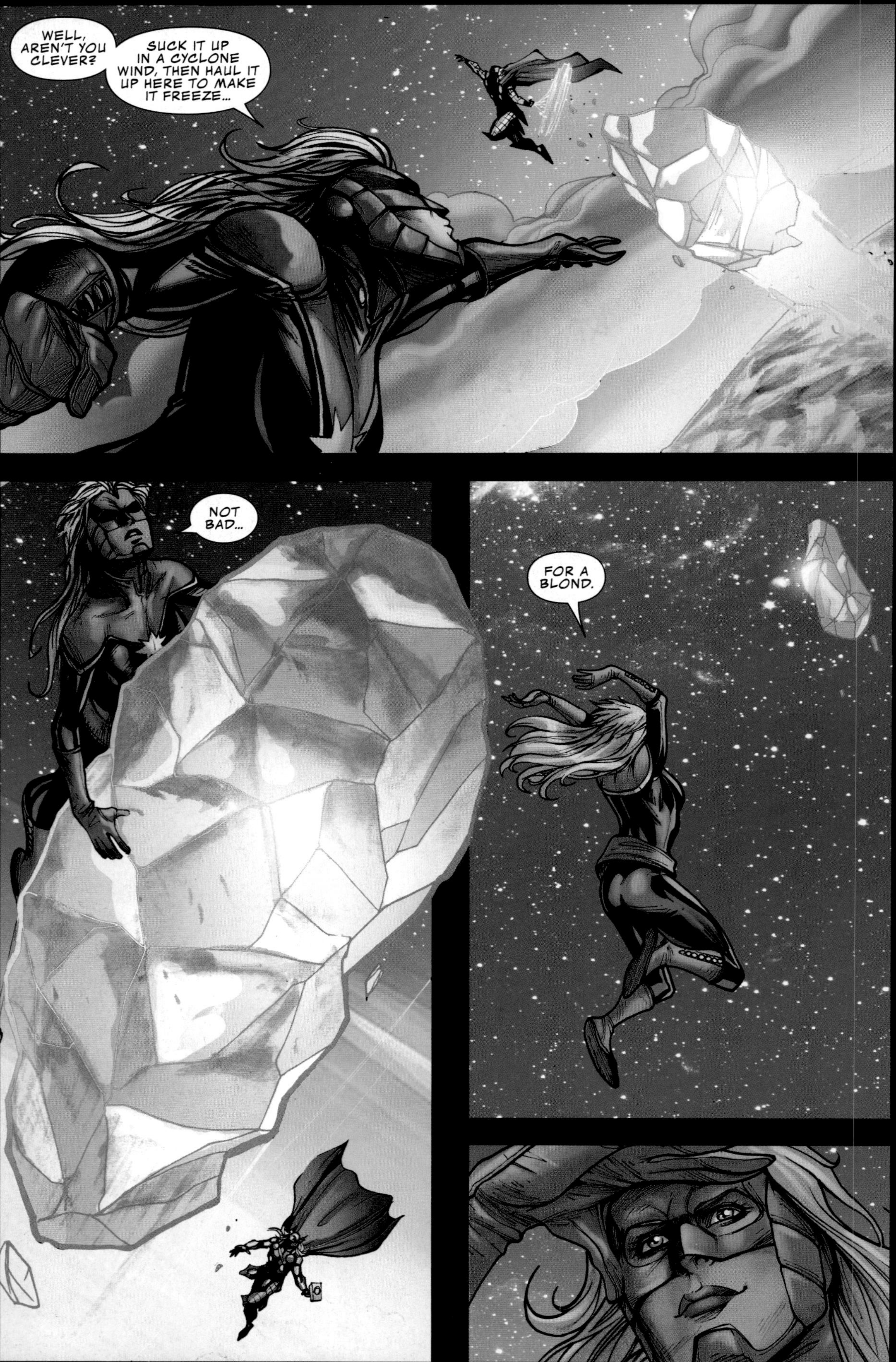
WELL, AREN'T YOU CLEVER?
SUCK IT UP IN A CYCLONE WIND, THEN HAUL IT UP HERE TO MAKE IT FREEZE...
NOT BAD...
FOR A BLOND.

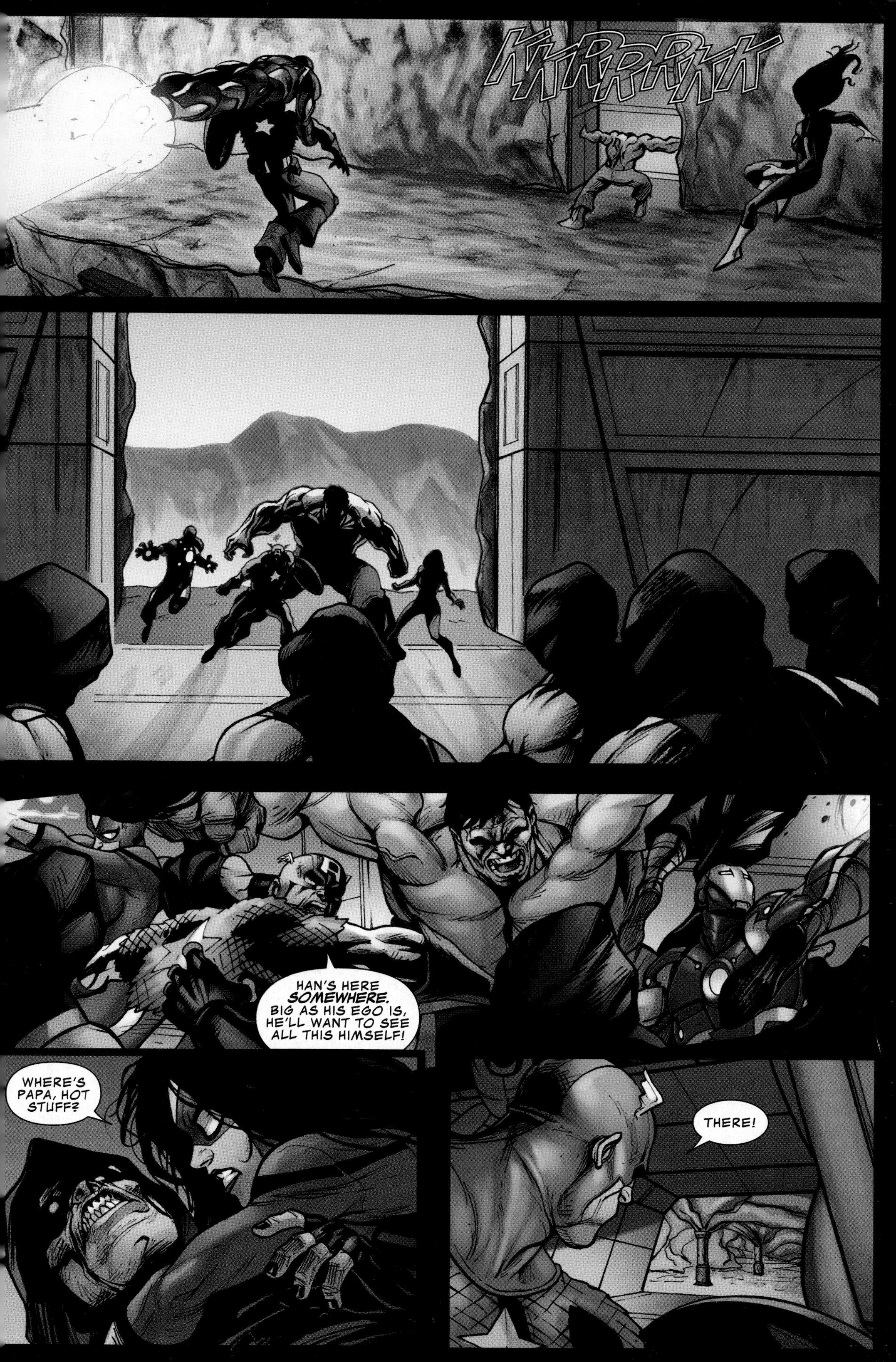
KKRRRRKK
HAN'S HERE *SOMEWHERE.* BIG AS HIS EGO IS, HE'LL WANT TO SEE ALL THIS HIMSELF!
WHERE'S PAPA, HOT STUFF?
THERE!

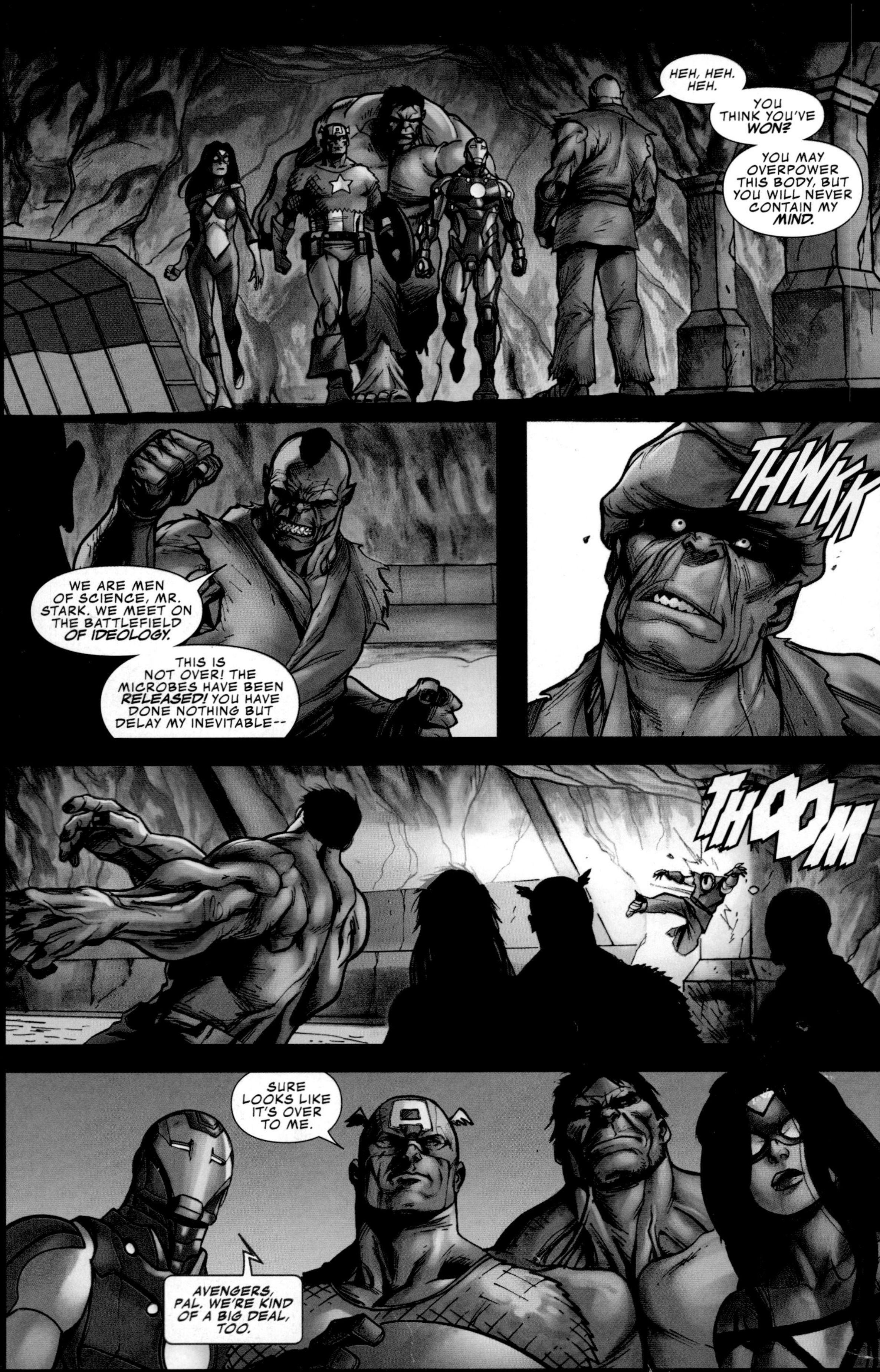
HEH, HEH. HEH.
YOU THINK YOU'VE WON?
YOU MAY OVERPOWER THIS BODY, BUT YOU WILL NEVER CONTAIN MY MIND.
WE ARE MEN OF SCIENCE, MR. STARK. WE MEET ON THE BATTLEFIELD OF IDEOLOGY.
THIS IS NOT OVER! THE MICROBES HAVE BEEN RELEASED! YOU HAVE DONE NOTHING BUT DELAY MY INEVITABLE--
THWKK
THOOM
SURE LOOKS LIKE IT'S OVER TO ME.
AVENGERS, PAL. WE'RE KIND OF A BIG DEAL, TOO.

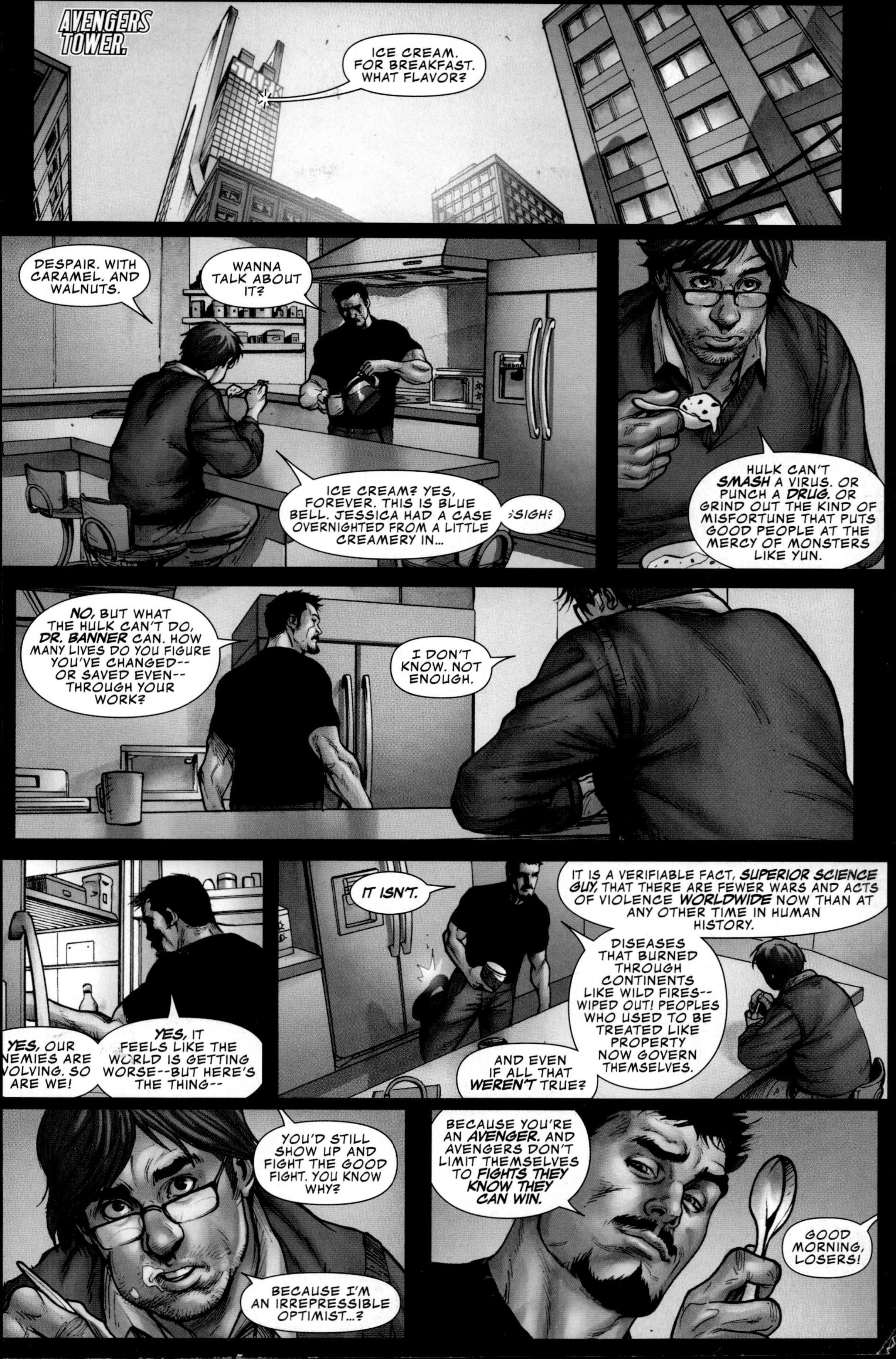
AVENGERS TOWER.
ICE CREAM. FOR BREAKFAST. WHAT FLAVOR?
DESPAIR. WITH CARAMEL. AND WALNUTS.
WANNA TALK ABOUT IT?
ICE CREAM? YES, FOREVER. THIS IS BLUE BELL. JESSICA HAD A CASE OVERNIGHTED FROM A LITTLE CREAMERY IN...
SIGH
HULK CAN'T SMASH A VIRUS. OR PUNCH A DRUG. OR GRIND OUT THE KIND OF MISFORTUNE THAT PUTS GOOD PEOPLE AT THE MERCY OF MONSTERS LIKE YUN.
NO, BUT WHAT THE HULK CAN'T DO, DR. BANNER CAN. HOW MANY LIVES DO YOU FIGURE YOU'VE CHANGED-- OR SAVED EVEN-- THROUGH YOUR WORK?
I DON'T KNOW. NOT ENOUGH.
YES, IT FEELS LIKE THE WORLD IS GETTING WORSE--BUT HERE'S THE THING--
YES, OUR NEMIES ARE VOLVING. SO ARE WE!
IT ISN'T.
IT IS A VERIFIABLE FACT, SUPERIOR SCIENCE GUY, THAT THERE ARE FEWER WARS AND ACTS OF VIOLENCE WORLDWIDE NOW THAN AT ANY OTHER TIME IN HUMAN HISTORY.
DISEASES THAT BURNED THROUGH CONTINENTS LIKE WILD FIRES-- WIPED OUT! PEOPLES WHO USED TO BE TREATED LIKE PROPERTY NOW GOVERN THEMSELVES.
AND EVEN IF ALL THAT WEREN'T TRUE?
YOU'D STILL SHOW UP AND FIGHT THE GOOD FIGHT. YOU KNOW WHY?
BECAUSE I'M AN IRREPRESSIBLE OPTIMIST...?
BECAUSE YOU'RE AN AVENGER. AND AVENGERS DON'T LIMIT THEMSELVES TO FIGHTS THEY KNOW THEY CAN WIN.
GOOD MORNING, LOSERS!

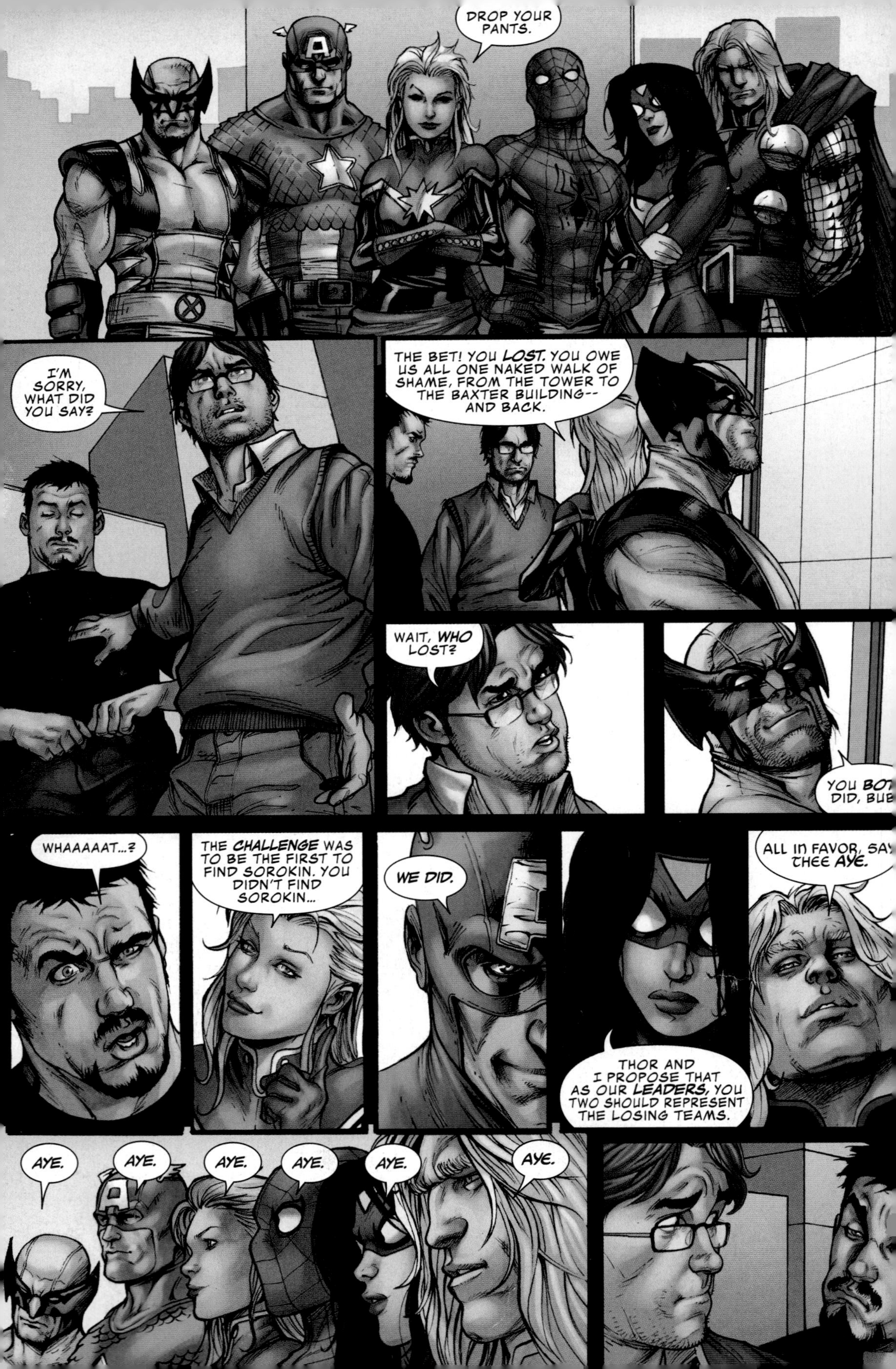
DROP YOUR PANTS.
I'M SORRY, WHAT DID YOU SAY?
THE BET! YOU LOST. YOU OWE US ALL ONE NAKED WALK OF SHAME, FROM THE TOWER TO THE BAXTER BUILDING-- AND BACK.
WAIT, WHO LOST?
YOU BOT DID, BUB
WHAAAAAT...?
THE CHALLENGE WAS TO BE THE FIRST TO FIND SOROKIN. YOU DIDN'T FIND SOROKIN...
WE DID.
THOR AND I PROPOSE THAT AS OUR LEADERS, YOU TWO SHOULD REPRESENT THE LOSING TEAMS.
ALL IN FAVOR, SAY THEE AYE.
AYE.
AYE.
AYE.
AYE.
AYE.
AYE.

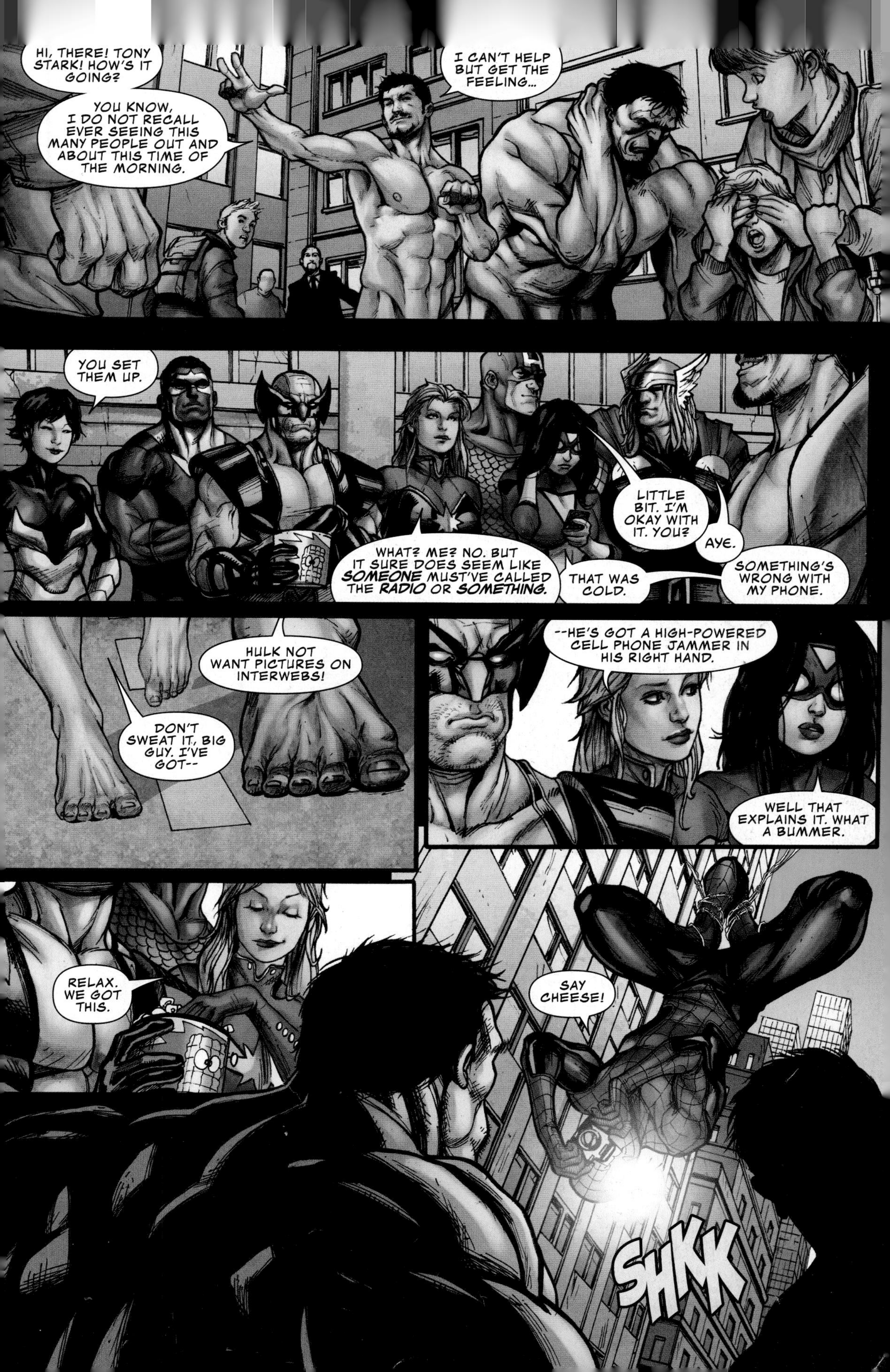

HI, THERE! TONY STARK! HOW'S IT GOING?
YOU KNOW, I DO NOT RECALL EVER SEEING THIS MANY PEOPLE OUT AND ABOUT THIS TIME OF THE MORNING.
I CAN'T HELP BUT GET THE FEELING...
YOU SET THEM UP.
WHAT? ME? NO. BUT IT SURE DOES SEEM LIKE SOMEONE MUST'VE CALLED THE RADIO OR SOMETHING.
LITTLE BIT. I'M OKAY WITH IT. YOU?
AYE.
THAT WAS COLD.
SOMETHING'S WRONG WITH MY PHONE.
HULK NOT WANT PICTURES ON INTERWEBS!
DON'T SWEAT IT, BIG GUY. I'VE GOT--
--HE'S GOT A HIGH-POWERED CELL PHONE JAMMER IN HIS RIGHT HAND.
WELL THAT EXPLAINS IT. WHAT A BUMMER.
RELAX. WE GOT THIS.
SAY CHEESE!
SHKK

| FINAL | # DAILY ☙ BUGLE® | SINCE 1897 ☆☆☆☆ $1.00 (in NYC $1.50 (outside cit' |

NEW YORK'S FINEST DAILY NEWSPAPER

NAKED JUSTICE

Celebrity Avengers bare souls and MORE. Fined for public indecency over wager gone awry, Stark make. donation matching fine to CDC.

By NE'ER CASCIO
Staff Writer

NEW YORK — 1/16/13 — (Reuters) — Commuters and shoppers along Broadway certainly got more than they bargained for in the early hours of Tuesday morning. According to witnesses interviewed by the Bugle, Avengers "the

Hulk" and Tony Stark (a/k/a "Iron Man" oft lauded for putting themselves at ris) were instead putting themselves display.

The act of public indecency (bo men were cited) was apparently the resu of a wager gone wrong. A spokesperse for the Avengers organization issued apology on behalf of… (CONT'D)

Opinion - A4: What can't super-powered stars buy their way out of

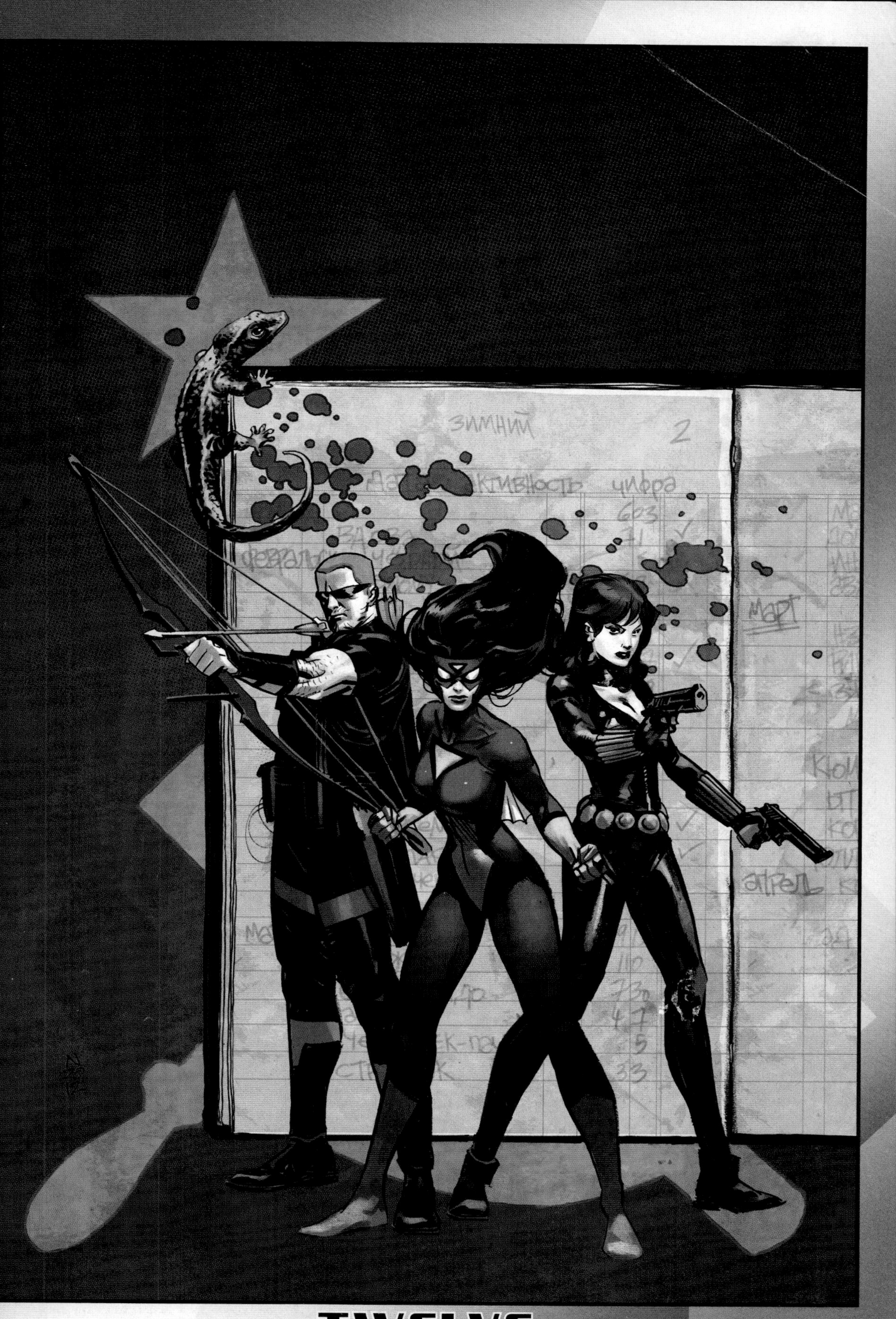
ЗИМНИЙ
2
цифра
МАРТ

TWELVE

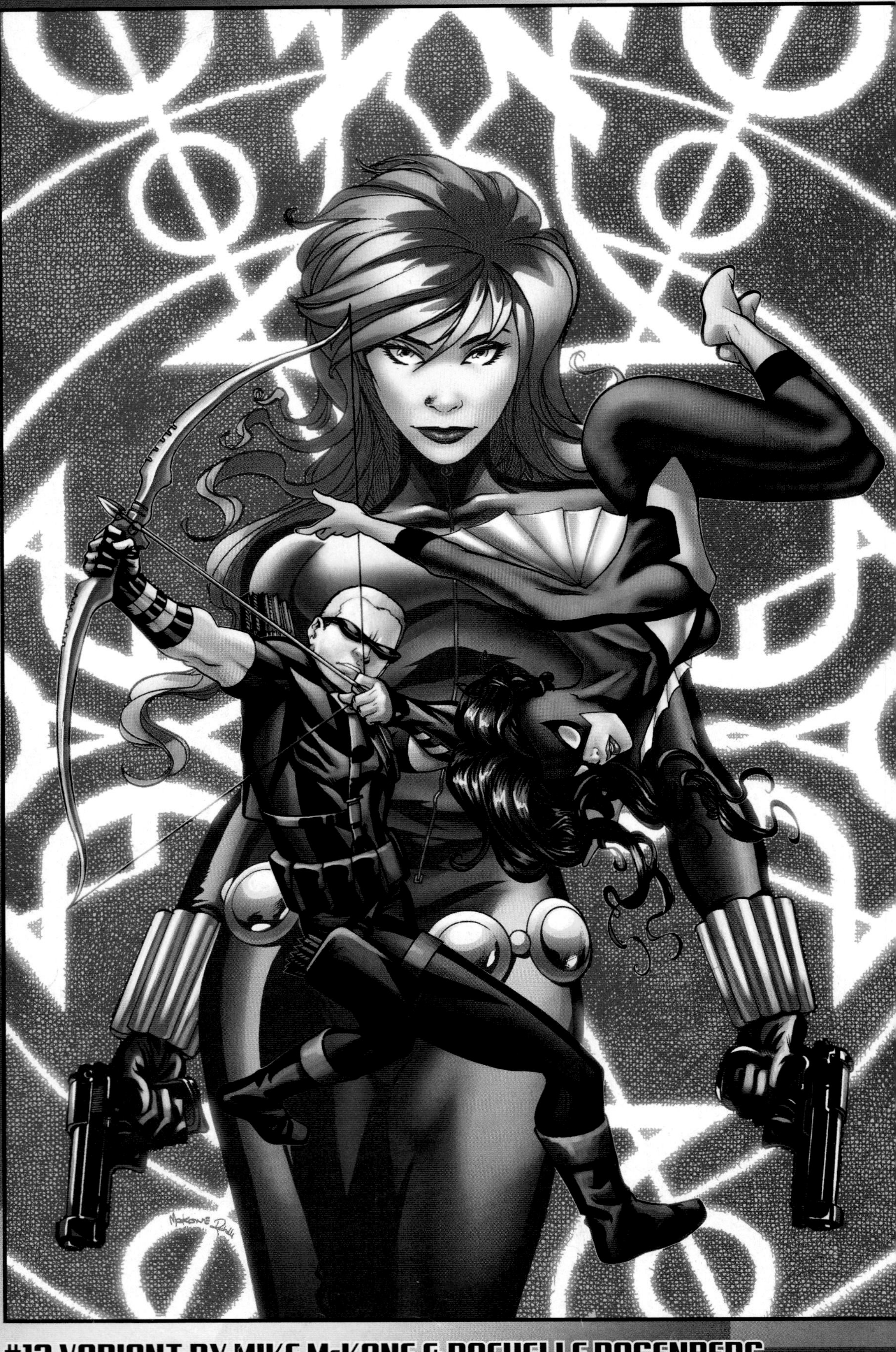

#12 VARIANT BY MIKE McKONE & RACHELLE ROSENBERG

AND THERE CAME A DAY, A DAY UNLIKE ANY OTHER, WHEN EARTH'S MIGHTIEST HEROES FOUND THEMSELVES UNITED AGAINST A COMMON THREAT! ON THAT DAY, THE AVENGERS WERE BORN, TO FIGHT THE FOES NO SINGLE SUPER HERO COULD WITHSTAND!

AVENGERS ASSEMBLE

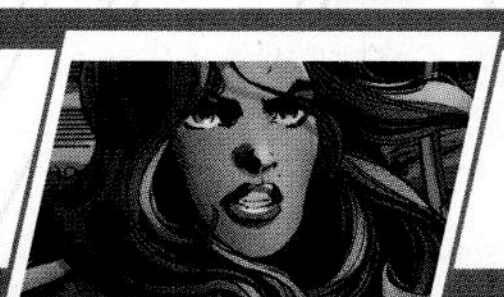

BLACK WIDOW
NATASHA ROMANOFF
EX-KGB SPY, COVERT SPECIALIST

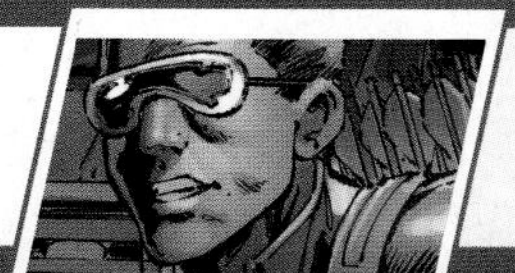

HAWKEYE
CLINT BARTON,
EXPERT MARKSMAN

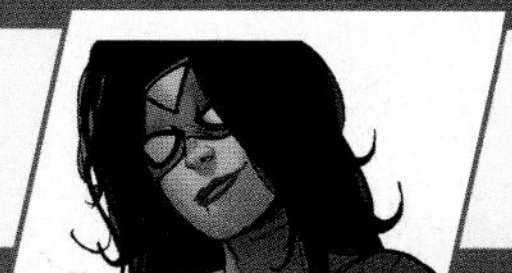

SPIDER-WOMAN
JESSICA DREW
SPIDER-POWERED SECRET AGENT

FILE: N_ROMANOFF

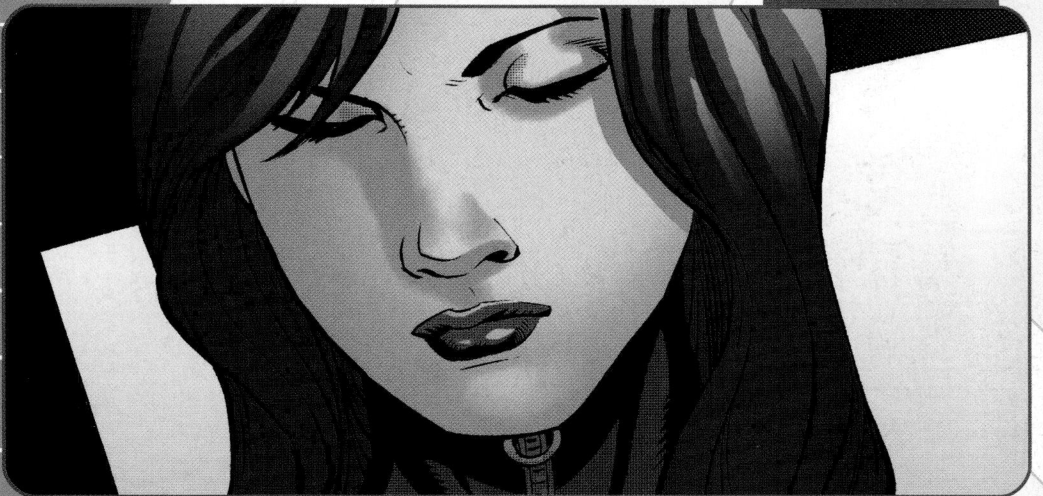

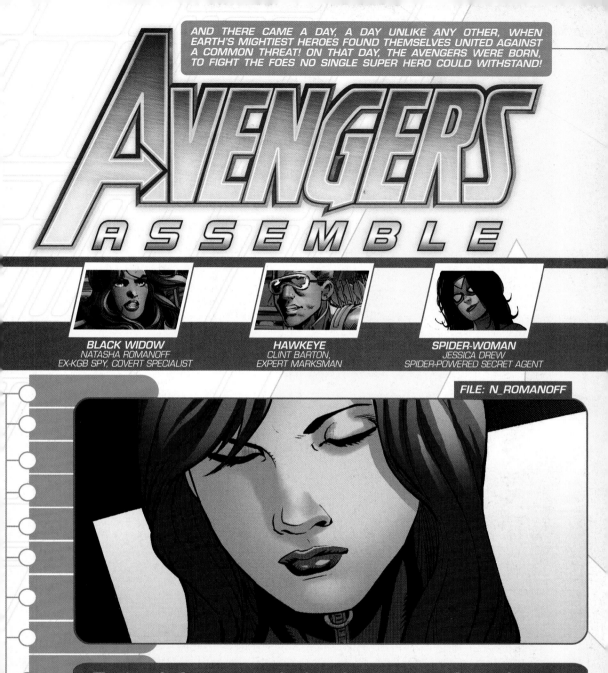

Trained from youth in the ways of espionage and combat, the Black Widow was one of the greatest spies the KGB ever had. They controlled her using false memories and brainwashing, but once she was free of their control she defected and became a strong and faithful ally to her former enemies, the Avengers.

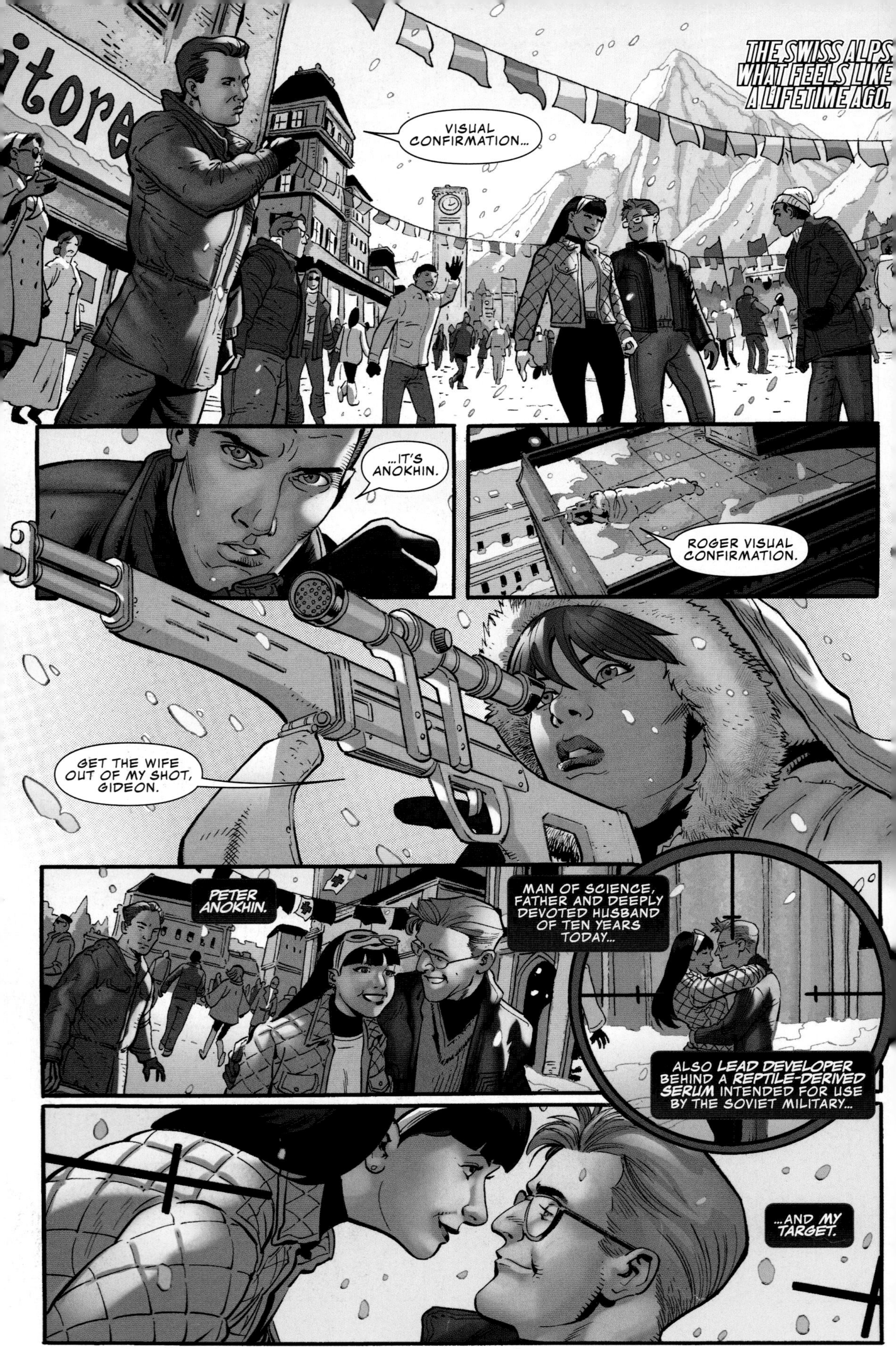

THE SWISS ALPS. WHAT FEELS LIKE A LIFETIME AGO.
VISUAL CONFIRMATION...
...IT'S ANOKHIN.
ROGER VISUAL CONFIRMATION.
GET THE WIFE OUT OF MY SHOT, GIDEON.
PETER ANOKHIN.
MAN OF SCIENCE, FATHER AND DEEPLY DEVOTED HUSBAND OF TEN YEARS TODAY...
ALSO LEAD DEVELOPER BEHIND A REPTILE-DERIVED SERUM INTENDED FOR USE BY THE SOVIET MILITARY...
...AND MY TARGET.

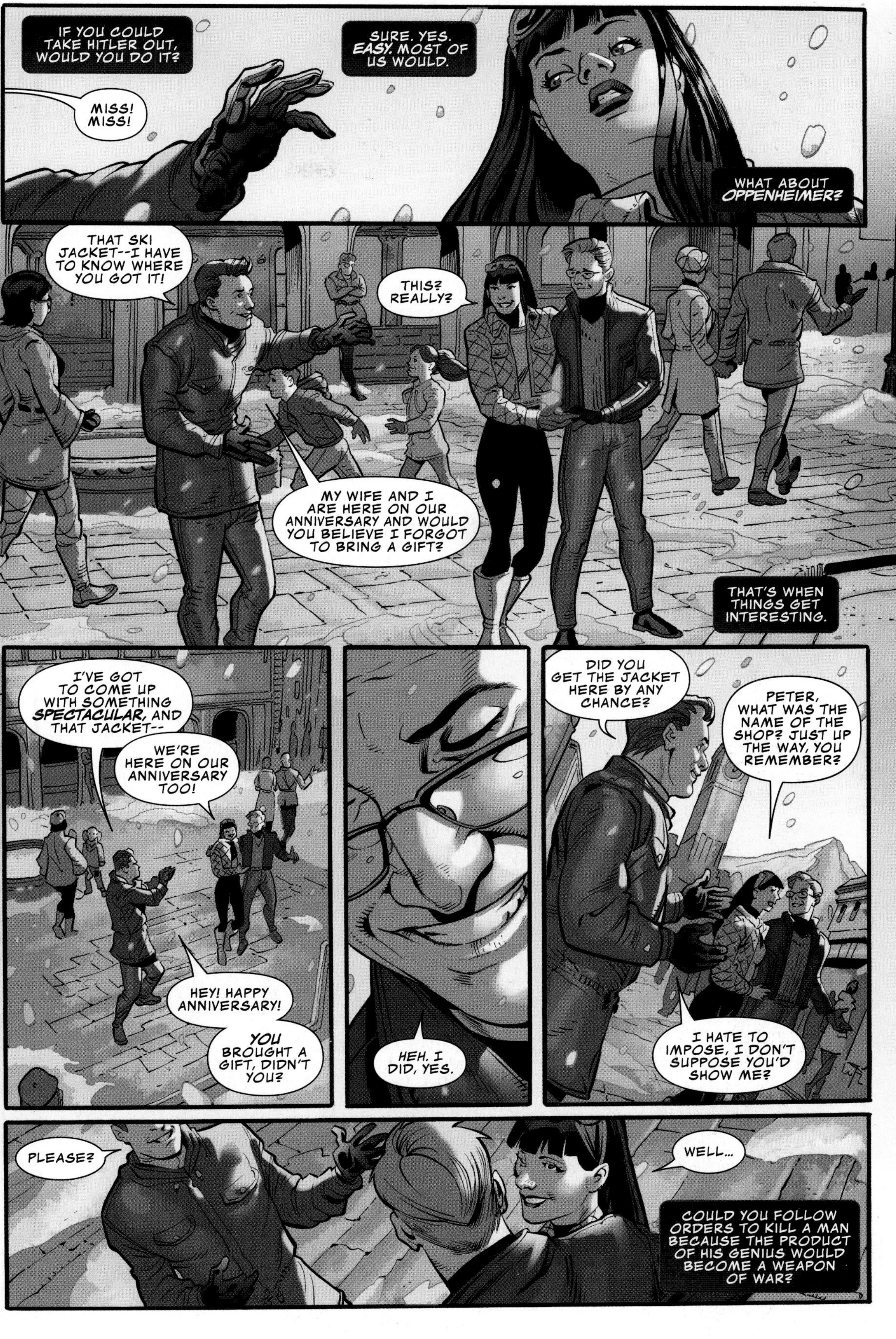
IF YOU COULD TAKE HITLER OUT, WOULD YOU DO IT?
SURE. YES. EASY. MOST OF US WOULD.
MISS! MISS!
WHAT ABOUT OPPENHEIMER?
THAT SKI JACKET--I HAVE TO KNOW WHERE YOU GOT IT!
THIS? REALLY?
MY WIFE AND I ARE HERE ON OUR ANNIVERSARY AND WOULD YOU BELIEVE I FORGOT TO BRING A GIFT?
THAT'S WHEN THINGS GET INTERESTING.
I'VE GOT TO COME UP WITH SOMETHING SPECTACULAR, AND THAT JACKET--
WE'RE HERE ON OUR ANNIVERSARY TOO!
HEY! HAPPY ANNIVERSARY!
YOU BROUGHT A GIFT, DIDN'T YOU?
HEH. I DID, YES.
DID YOU GET THE JACKET HERE BY ANY CHANCE?
PETER, WHAT WAS THE NAME OF THE SHOP? JUST UP THE WAY, YOU REMEMBER?
I HATE TO IMPOSE, I DON'T SUPPOSE YOU'D SHOW ME?
PLEASE?
WELL...
COULD YOU FOLLOW ORDERS TO KILL A MAN BECAUSE THE PRODUCT OF HIS GENIUS WOULD BECOME A WEAPON OF WAR?

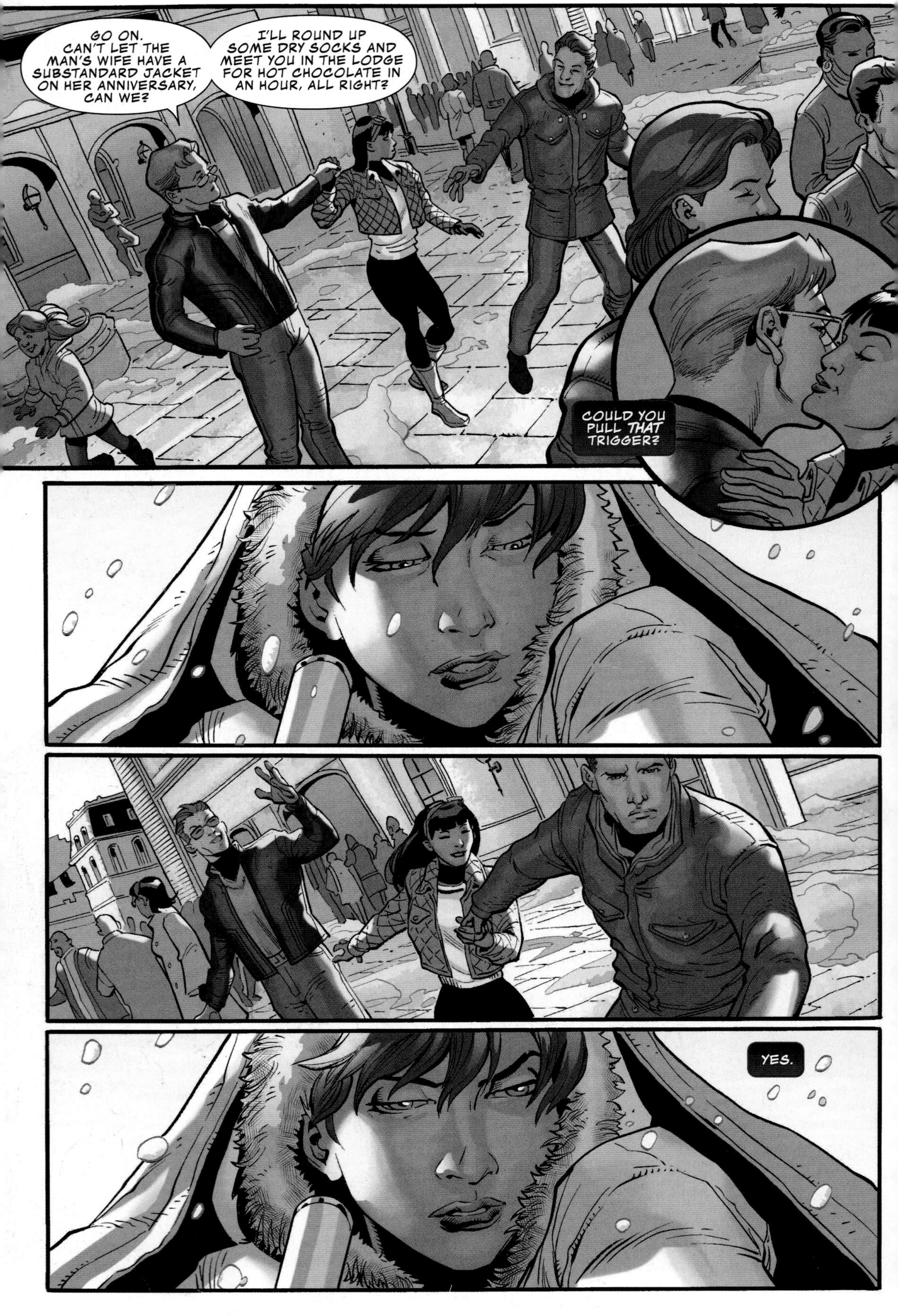
GO ON. CAN'T LET THE MAN'S WIFE HAVE A SUBSTANDARD JACKET ON HER ANNIVERSARY, CAN WE?
I'LL ROUND UP SOME DRY SOCKS AND MEET YOU IN THE LODGE FOR HOT CHOCOLATE IN AN HOUR, ALL RIGHT?
COULD YOU PULL THAT TRIGGER?
YES.

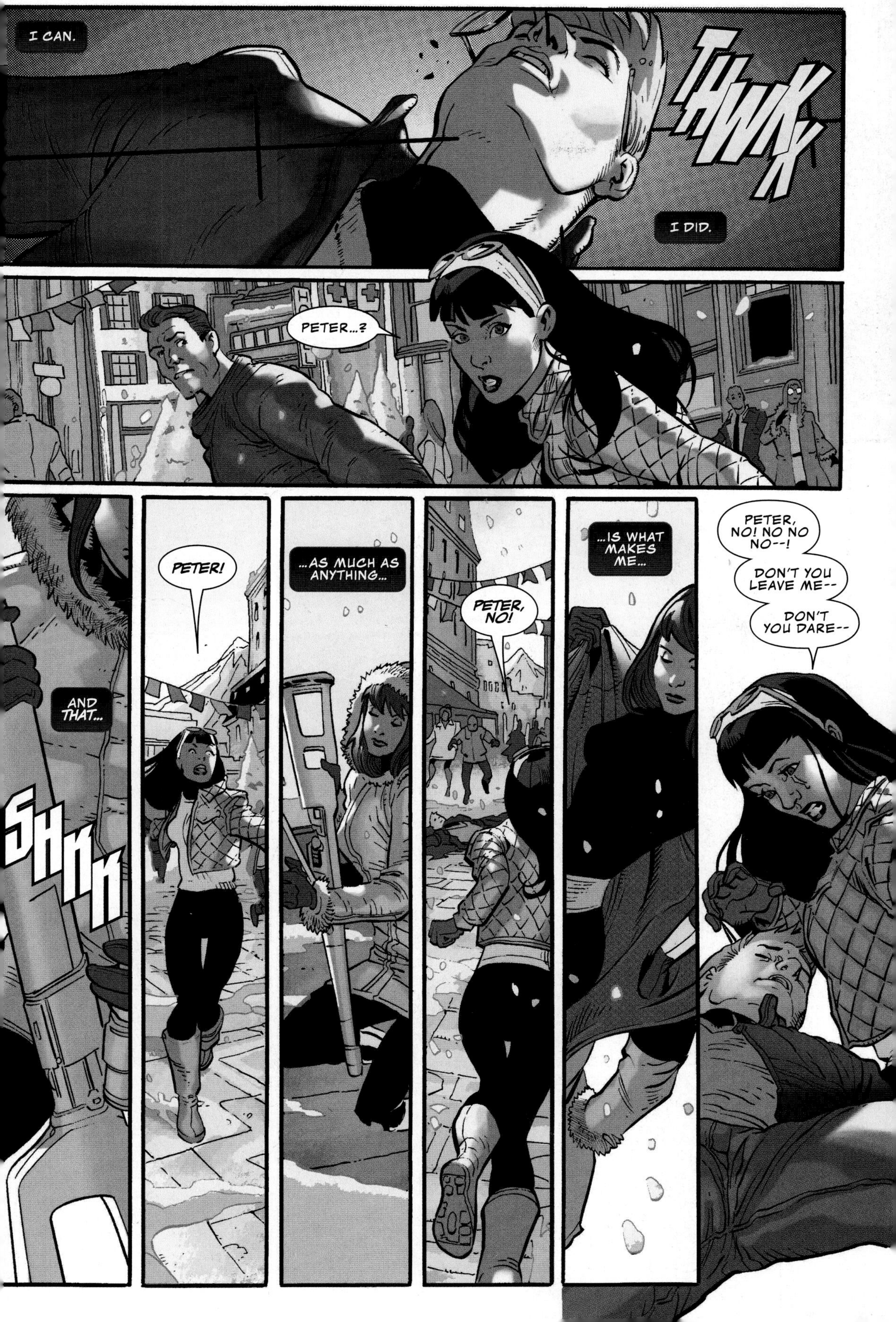
I CAN.
THWKK
I DID.
PETER...?
AND THAT...
SHKK
PETER!
...AS MUCH AS ANYTHING...
PETER, NO!
...IS WHAT MAKES ME...
PETER, NO! NO NO NO--!
DON'T YOU LEAVE ME--
DON'T YOU DARE--

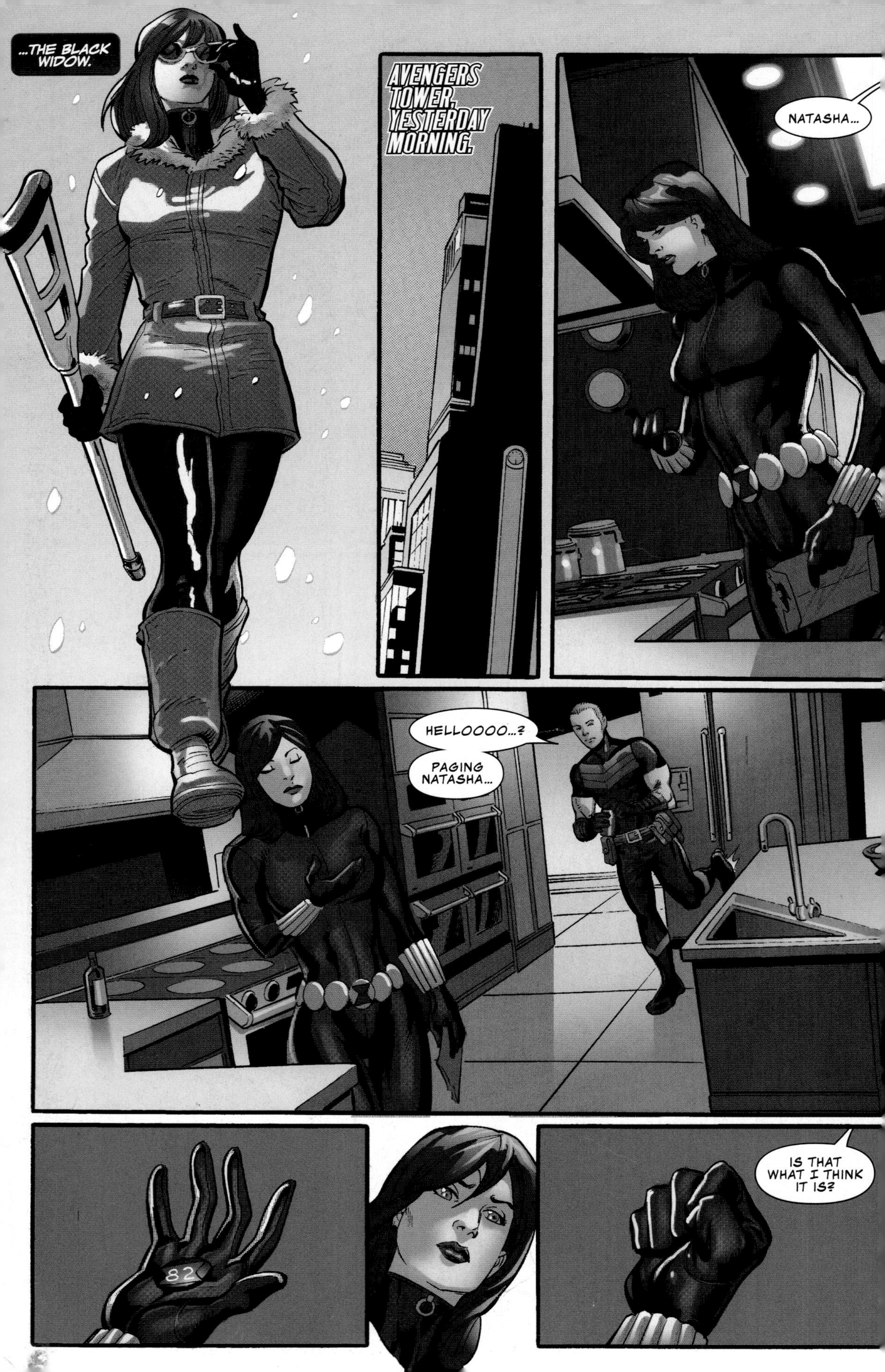
...THE BLACK WIDOW.
AVENGERS TOWER, YESTERDAY MORNING.
NATASHA...
HELLOOOO...?
PAGING NATASHA...
82
IS THAT WHAT I THINK IT IS?

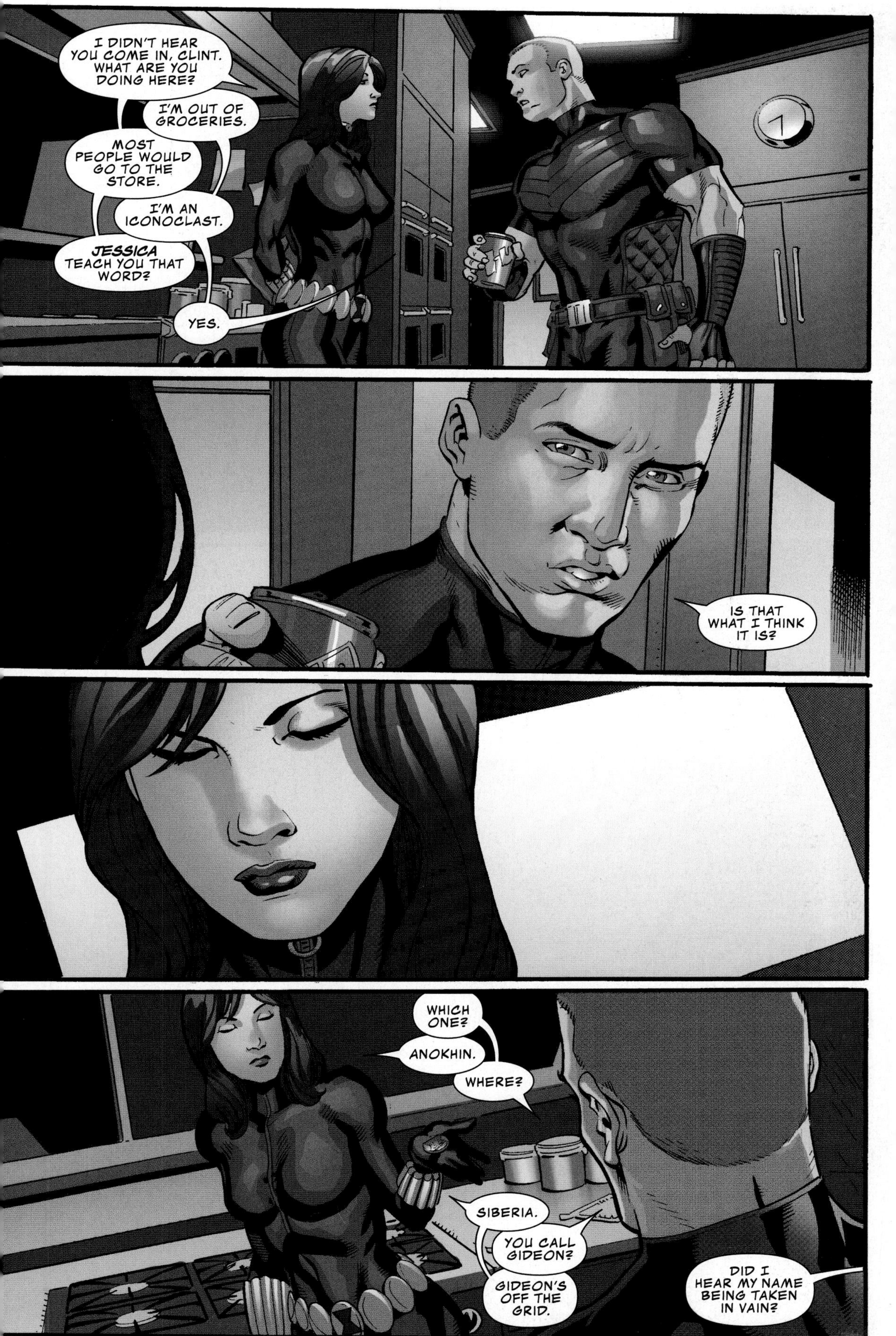
I DIDN'T HEAR YOU COME IN, CLINT. WHAT ARE YOU DOING HERE?
I'M OUT OF GROCERIES.
MOST PEOPLE WOULD GO TO THE STORE.
I'M AN ICONOCLAST.
JESSICA TEACH YOU THAT WORD?
YES.
IS THAT WHAT I THINK IT IS?
WHICH ONE?
ANOKHIN.
WHERE?
SIBERIA.
YOU CALL GIDEON?
GIDEON'S OFF THE GRID.
DID I HEAR MY NAME BEING TAKEN IN VAIN?

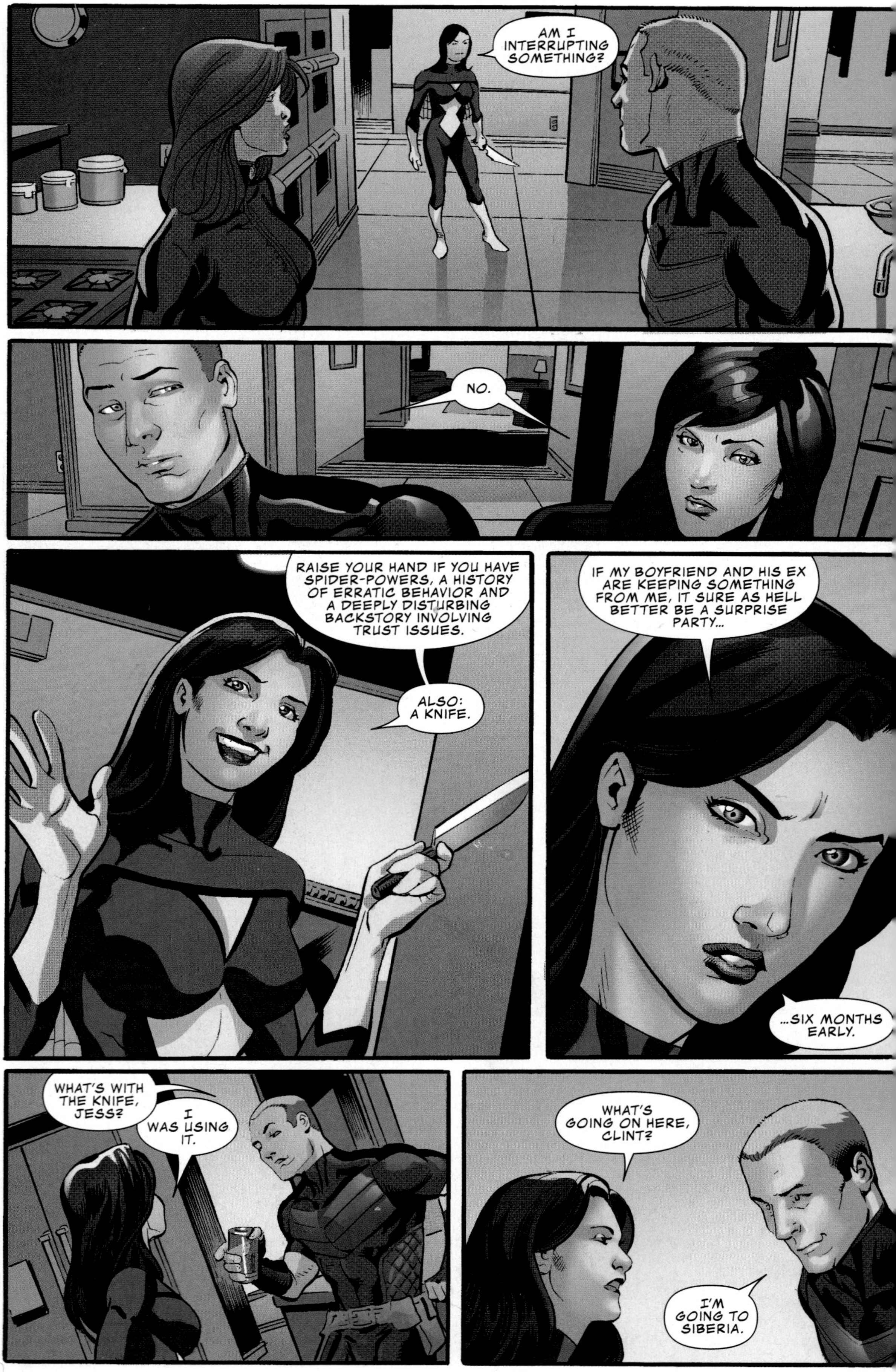

AM I INTERRUPTING SOMETHING?
NO.
RAISE YOUR HAND IF YOU HAVE SPIDER-POWERS, A HISTORY OF ERRATIC BEHAVIOR AND A DEEPLY DISTURBING BACKSTORY INVOLVING TRUST ISSUES.
ALSO: A KNIFE.
IF MY BOYFRIEND AND HIS EX ARE KEEPING SOMETHING FROM ME, IT SURE AS HELL BETTER BE A SURPRISE PARTY...
...SIX MONTHS EARLY.
WHAT'S WITH THE KNIFE, JESS?
I WAS USING IT.
WHAT'S GOING ON HERE, CLINT?
I'M GOING TO SIBERIA.

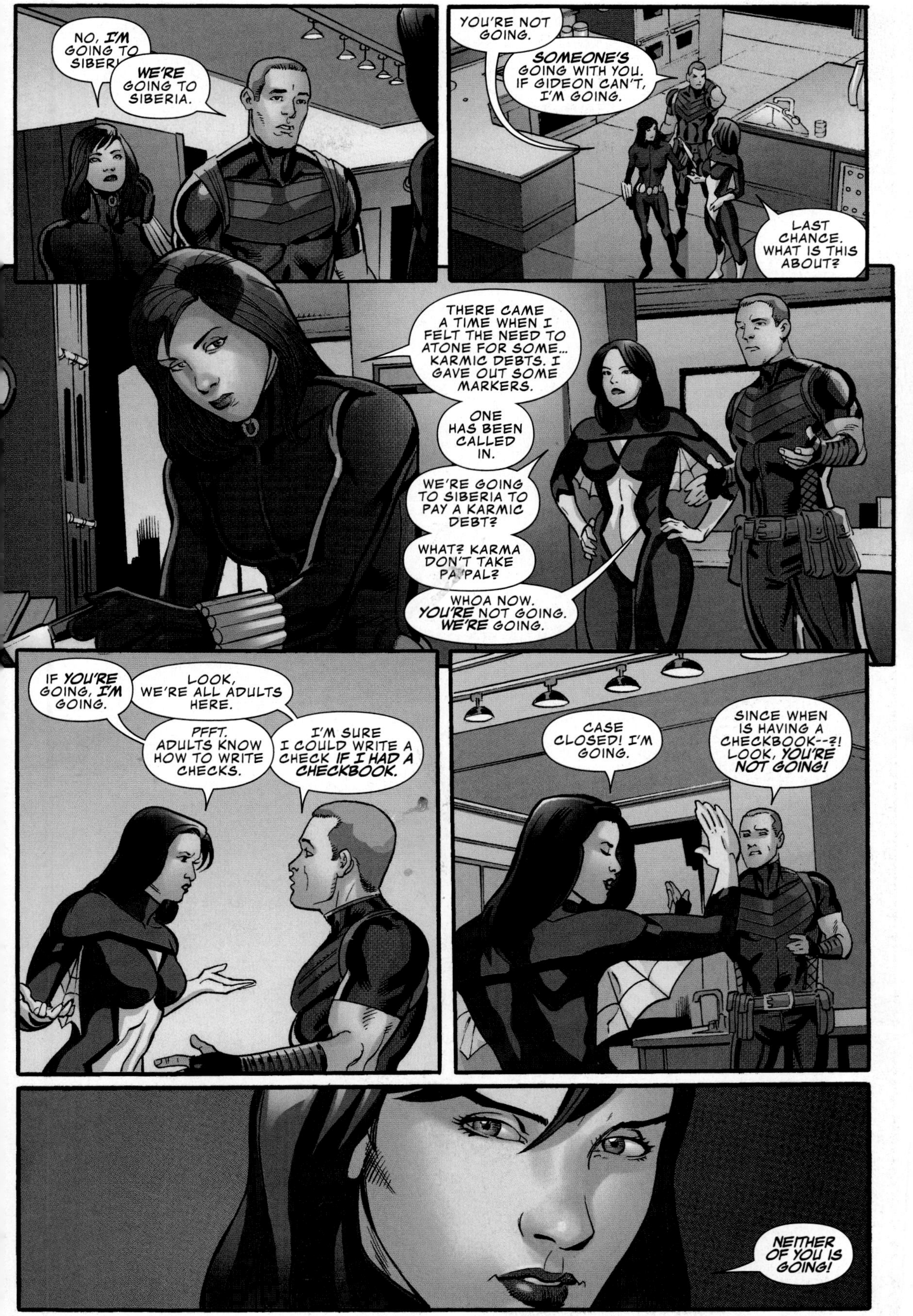
NO, I'M GOING TO SIBERI
WE'RE GOING TO SIBERIA.
YOU'RE NOT GOING.
SOMEONE'S GOING WITH YOU. IF GIDEON CAN'T, I'M GOING.
LAST CHANCE. WHAT IS THIS ABOUT?
THERE CAME A TIME WHEN I FELT THE NEED TO ATONE FOR SOME... KARMIC DEBTS. I GAVE OUT SOME MARKERS.
ONE HAS BEEN CALLED IN.
WE'RE GOING TO SIBERIA TO PAY A KARMIC DEBT?
WHAT? KARMA DON'T TAKE PAYPAL?
WHOA NOW. YOU'RE NOT GOING. WE'RE GOING.
IF YOU'RE GOING, I'M GOING.
LOOK, WE'RE ALL ADULTS HERE.
PFFT. ADULTS KNOW HOW TO WRITE CHECKS.
I'M SURE I COULD WRITE A CHECK IF I HAD A CHECKBOOK.
CASE CLOSED! I'M GOING.
SINCE WHEN IS HAVING A CHECKBOOK--?! LOOK, YOU'RE NOT GOING!
NEITHER OF YOU IS GOING!

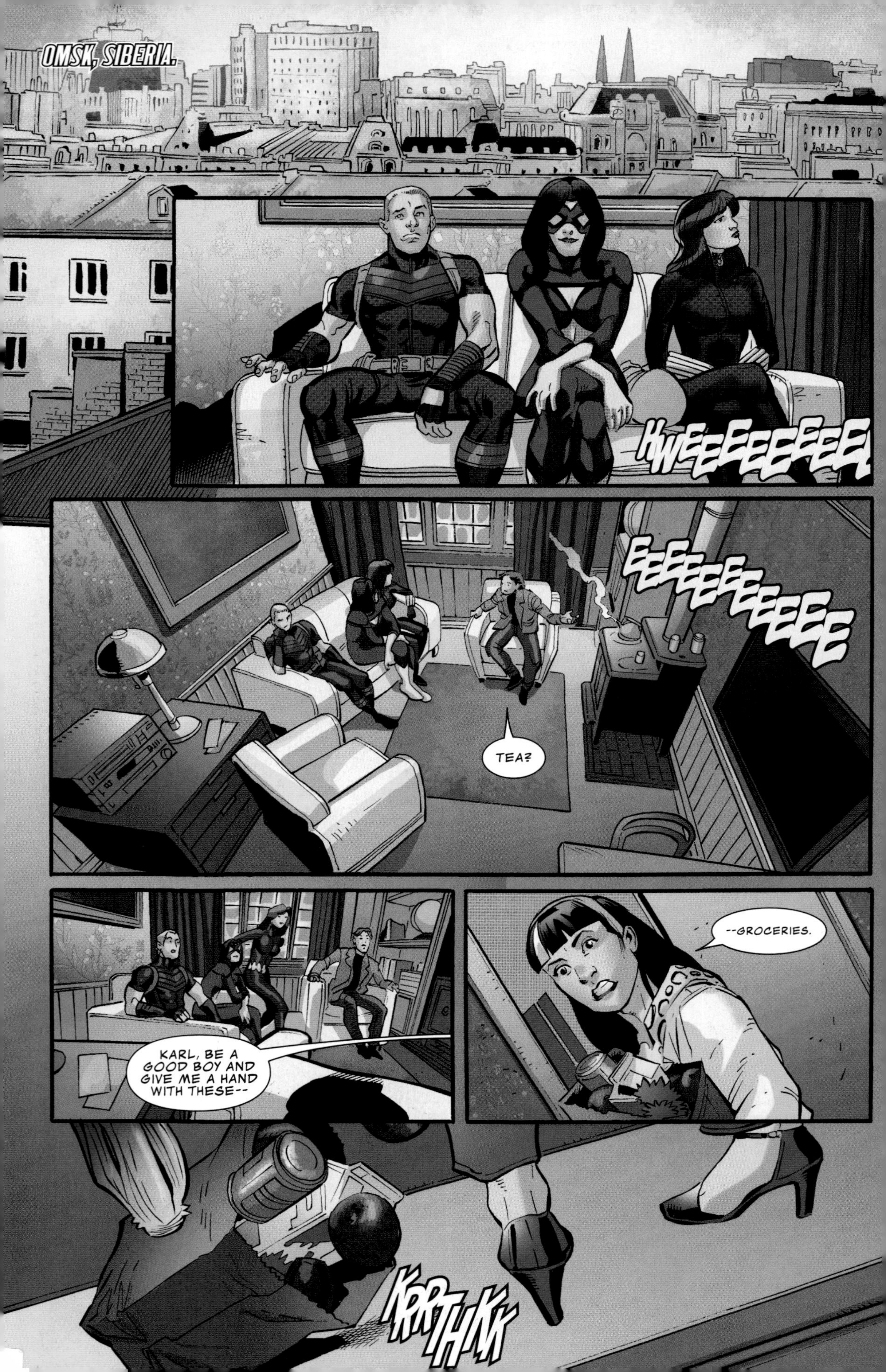
OMSK, SIBERIA.
KWEEEEEEEE
EEEEEEEEEEEE
TEA?
KARL, BE A GOOD BOY AND GIVE ME A HAND WITH THESE--
--GROCERIES.
KRRTHIKK

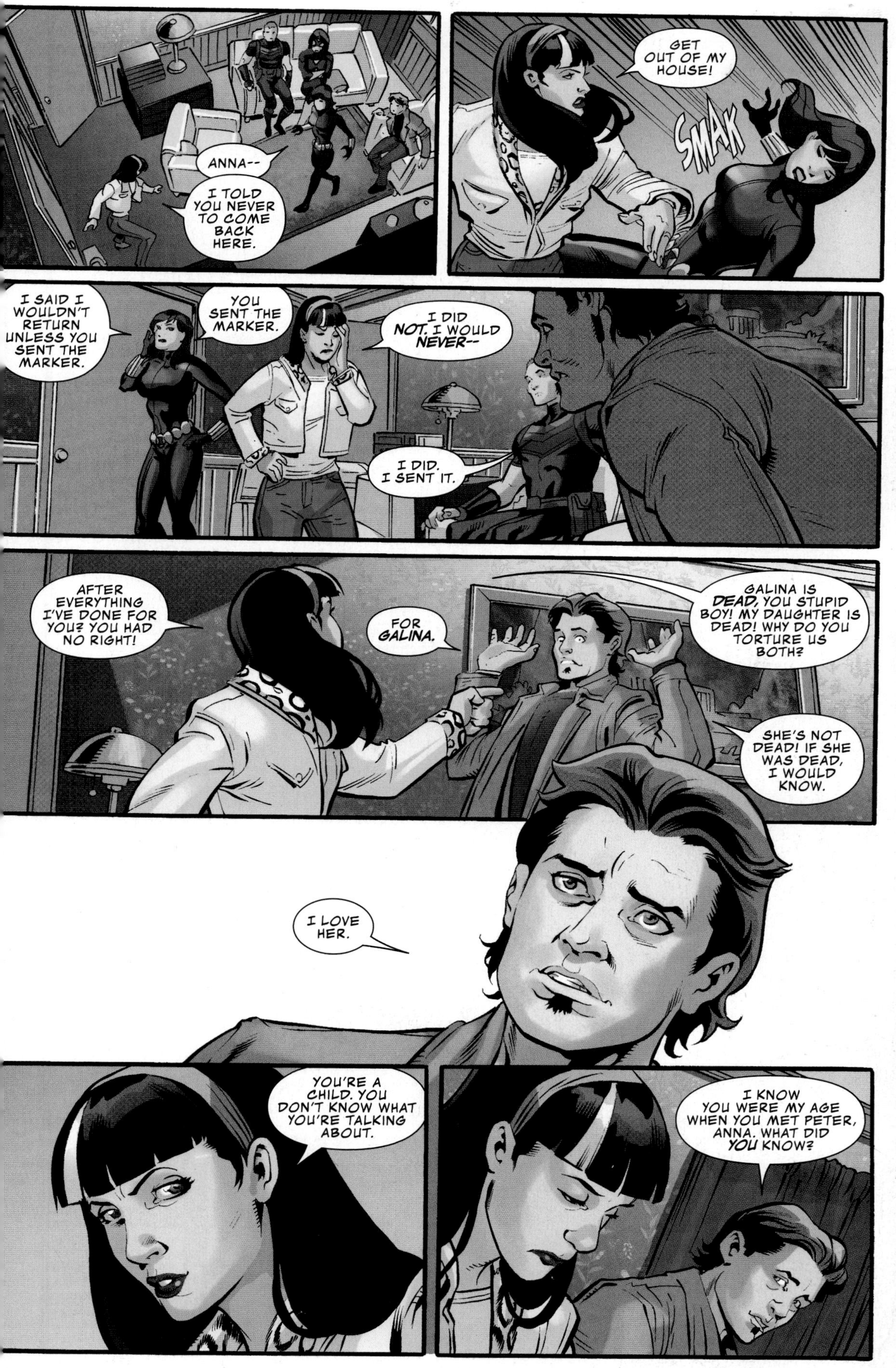
ANNA--
I TOLD YOU NEVER TO COME BACK HERE.
GET OUT OF MY HOUSE!
SMAK
I SAID I WOULDN'T RETURN UNLESS YOU SENT THE MARKER.
YOU SENT THE MARKER.
I DID *NOT.* I WOULD *NEVER*--
I DID. I SENT IT.
AFTER EVERYTHING I'VE DONE FOR YOU? YOU HAD NO RIGHT!
FOR *GALINA.*
GALINA IS *DEAD,* YOU STUPID BOY! MY DAUGHTER IS DEAD! WHY DO YOU TORTURE US BOTH?
SHE'S NOT DEAD! IF SHE WAS DEAD, I WOULD KNOW.
I LOVE HER.
YOU'RE A CHILD. YOU DON'T KNOW WHAT YOU'RE TALKING ABOUT.
I KNOW YOU WERE MY AGE WHEN YOU MET PETER, ANNA. WHAT DID *YOU* KNOW?

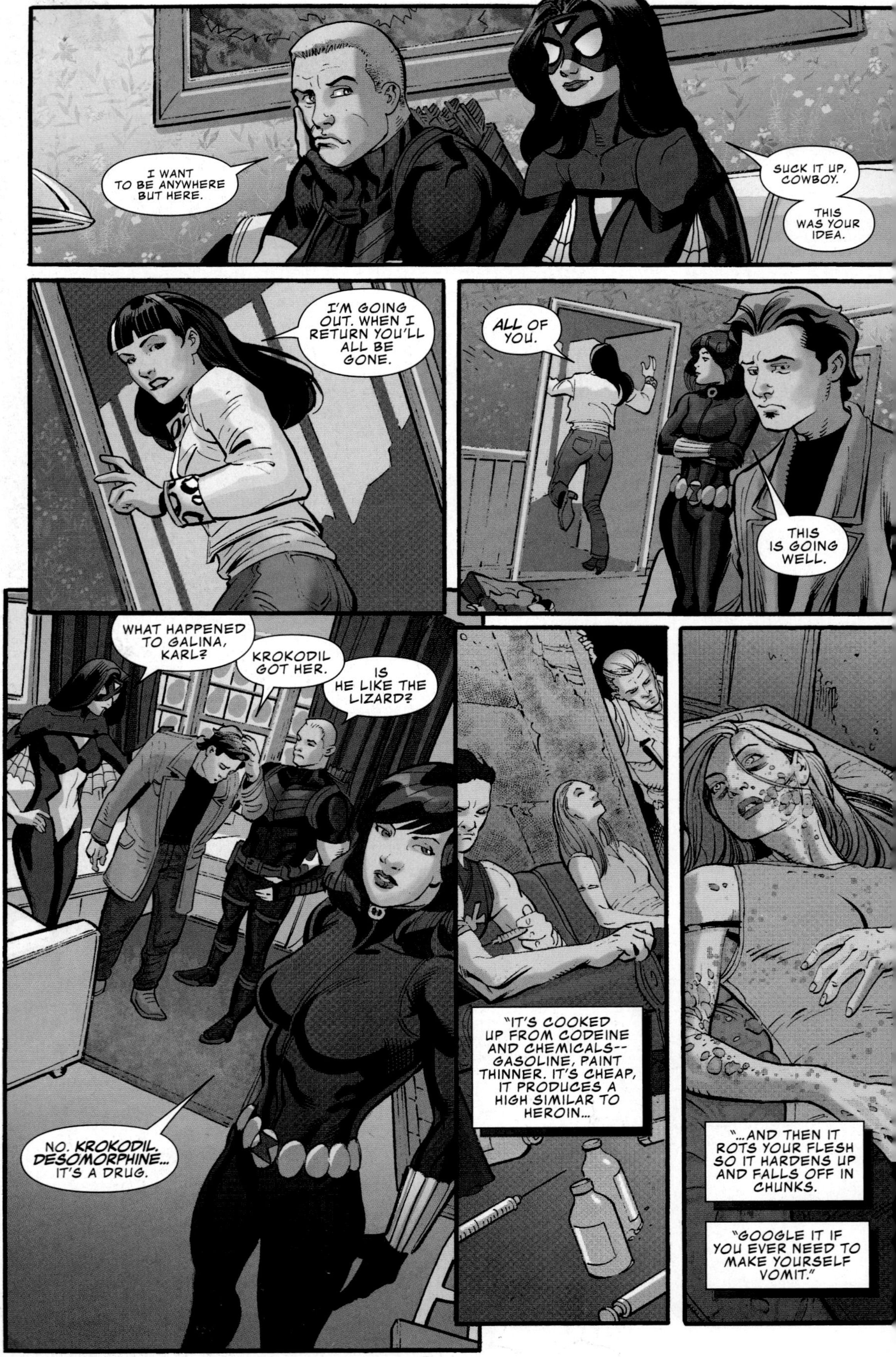

I WANT TO BE ANYWHERE BUT HERE.
SUCK IT UP, COWBOY.
THIS WAS YOUR IDEA.
I'M GOING OUT. WHEN I RETURN YOU'LL ALL BE GONE.
ALL OF YOU.
THIS IS GOING WELL.
WHAT HAPPENED TO GALINA, KARL?
KROKODIL GOT HER.
IS HE LIKE THE LIZARD?
NO. KROKODIL. DESOMORPHINE... IT'S A DRUG.
"IT'S COOKED UP FROM CODEINE AND CHEMICALS-- GASOLINE, PAINT THINNER. IT'S CHEAP, IT PRODUCES A HIGH SIMILAR TO HEROIN...
"...AND THEN IT ROTS YOUR FLESH SO IT HARDENS UP AND FALLS OFF IN CHUNKS.
"GOOGLE IT IF YOU EVER NEED TO MAKE YOURSELF VOMIT."

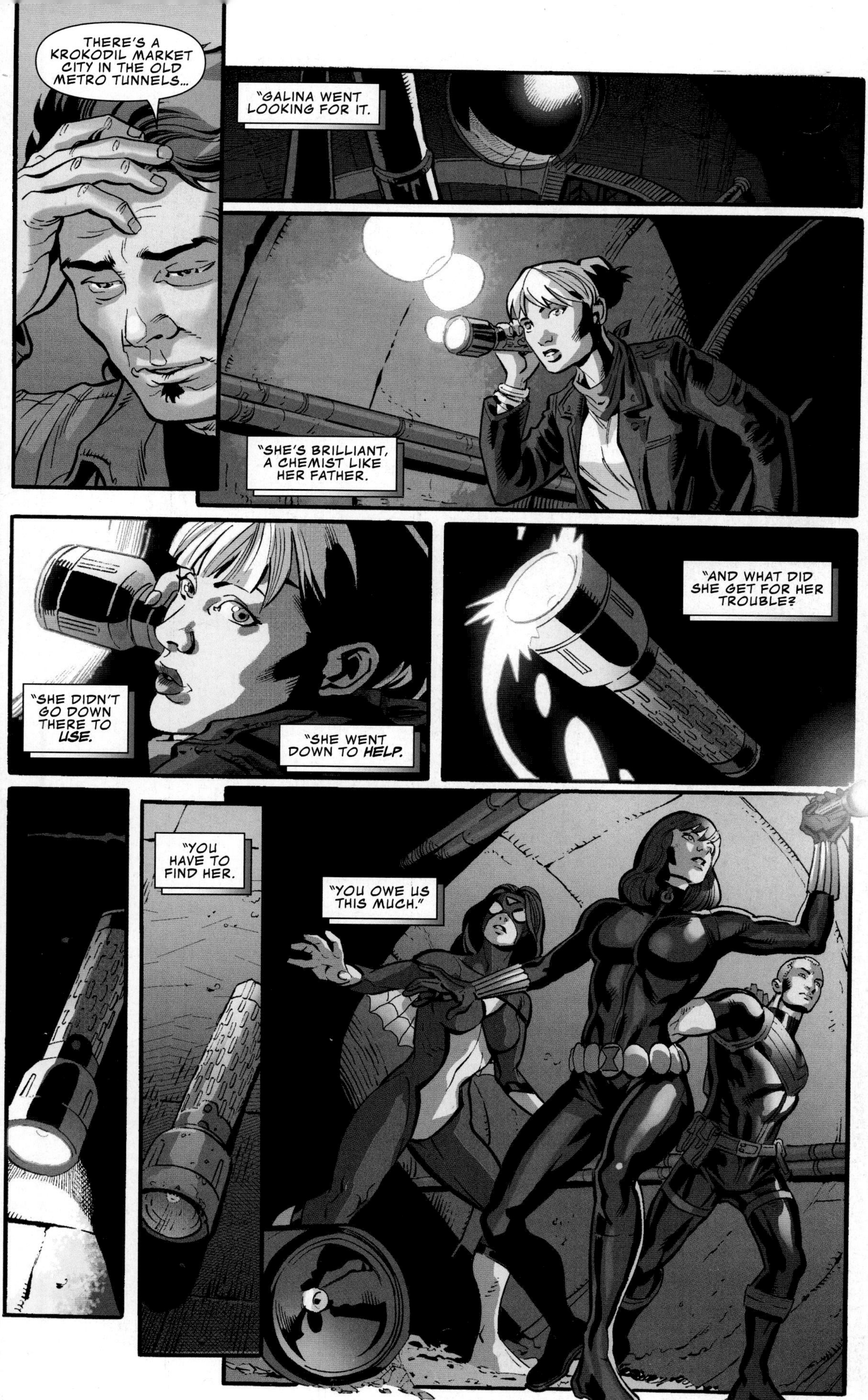
THERE'S A KROKODIL MARKET CITY IN THE OLD METRO TUNNELS...
"GALINA WENT LOOKING FOR IT.
"SHE'S BRILLIANT, A CHEMIST LIKE HER FATHER.
"SHE DIDN'T GO DOWN THERE TO USE.
"SHE WENT DOWN TO HELP.
"AND WHAT DID SHE GET FOR HER TROUBLE?
"YOU HAVE TO FIND HER.
"YOU OWE US THIS MUCH."

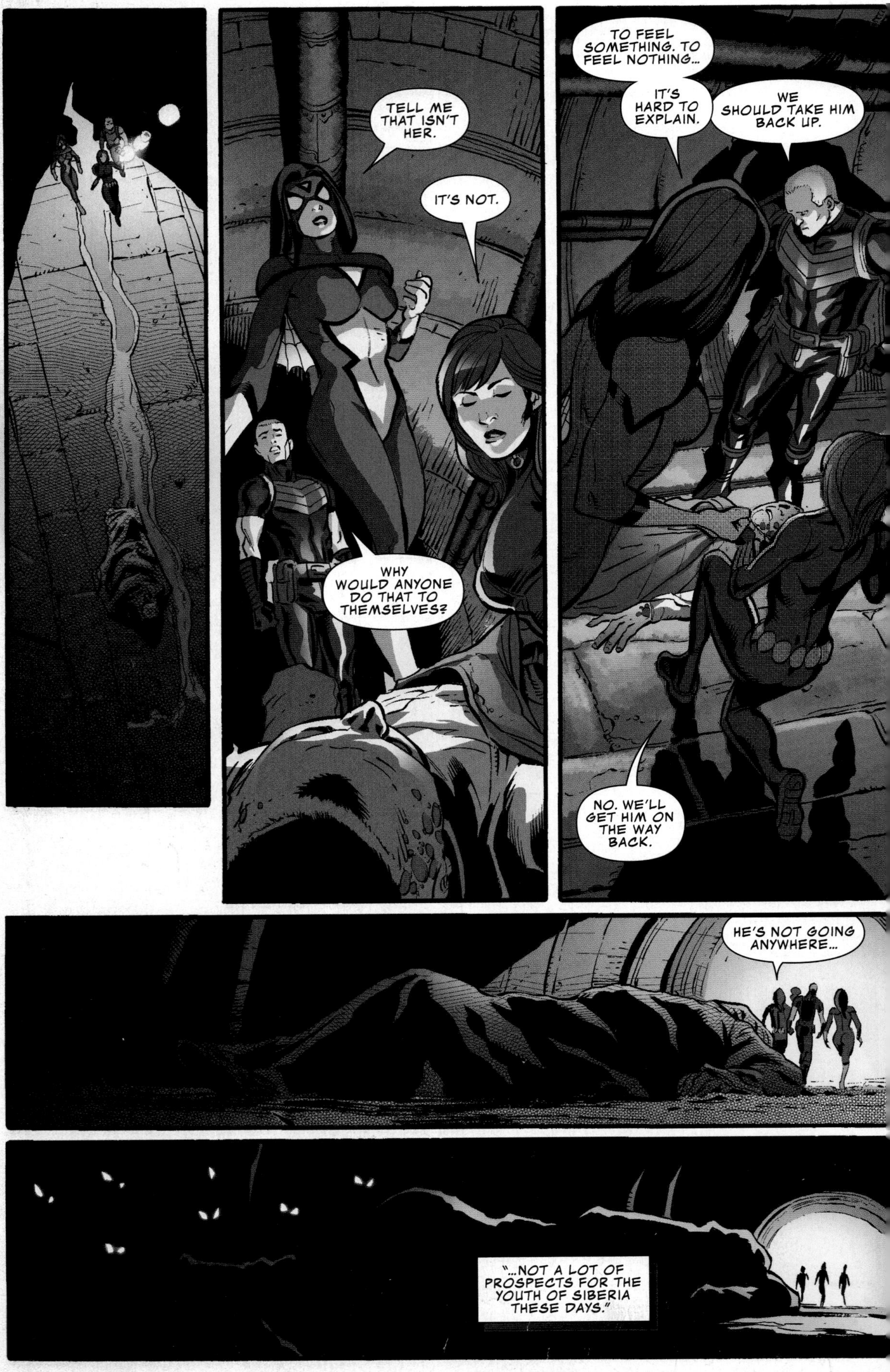
TELL ME THAT ISN'T HER.
IT'S NOT.
WHY WOULD ANYONE DO THAT TO THEMSELVES?
TO FEEL SOMETHING. TO FEEL NOTHING...
IT'S HARD TO EXPLAIN.
WE SHOULD TAKE HIM BACK UP.
NO. WE'LL GET HIM ON THE WAY BACK.
HE'S NOT GOING ANYWHERE...
"...NOT A LOT OF PROSPECTS FOR THE YOUTH OF SIBERIA THESE DAYS."

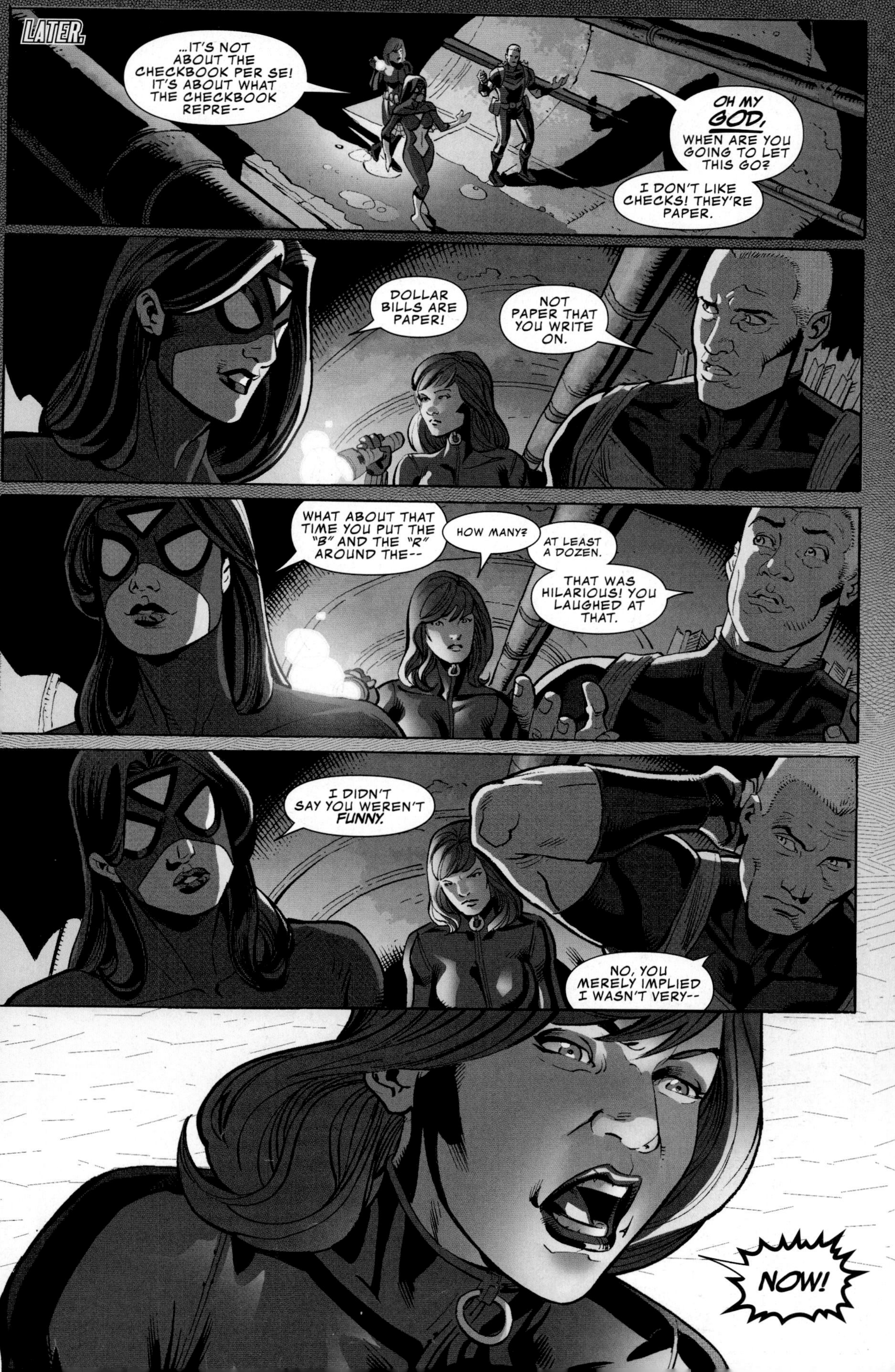
LATER.
...IT'S NOT ABOUT THE CHECKBOOK PER SE! IT'S ABOUT WHAT THE CHECKBOOK REPRE--
OH MY GOD, WHEN ARE YOU GOING TO LET THIS GO?
I DON'T LIKE CHECKS! THEY'RE PAPER.
DOLLAR BILLS ARE PAPER!
NOT PAPER THAT YOU WRITE ON.
WHAT ABOUT THAT TIME YOU PUT THE "B" AND THE "R" AROUND THE--
HOW MANY?
AT LEAST A DOZEN.
THAT WAS HILARIOUS! YOU LAUGHED AT THAT.
I DIDN'T SAY YOU WEREN'T FUNNY.
NO, YOU MERELY IMPLIED I WASN'T VERY--
NOW!

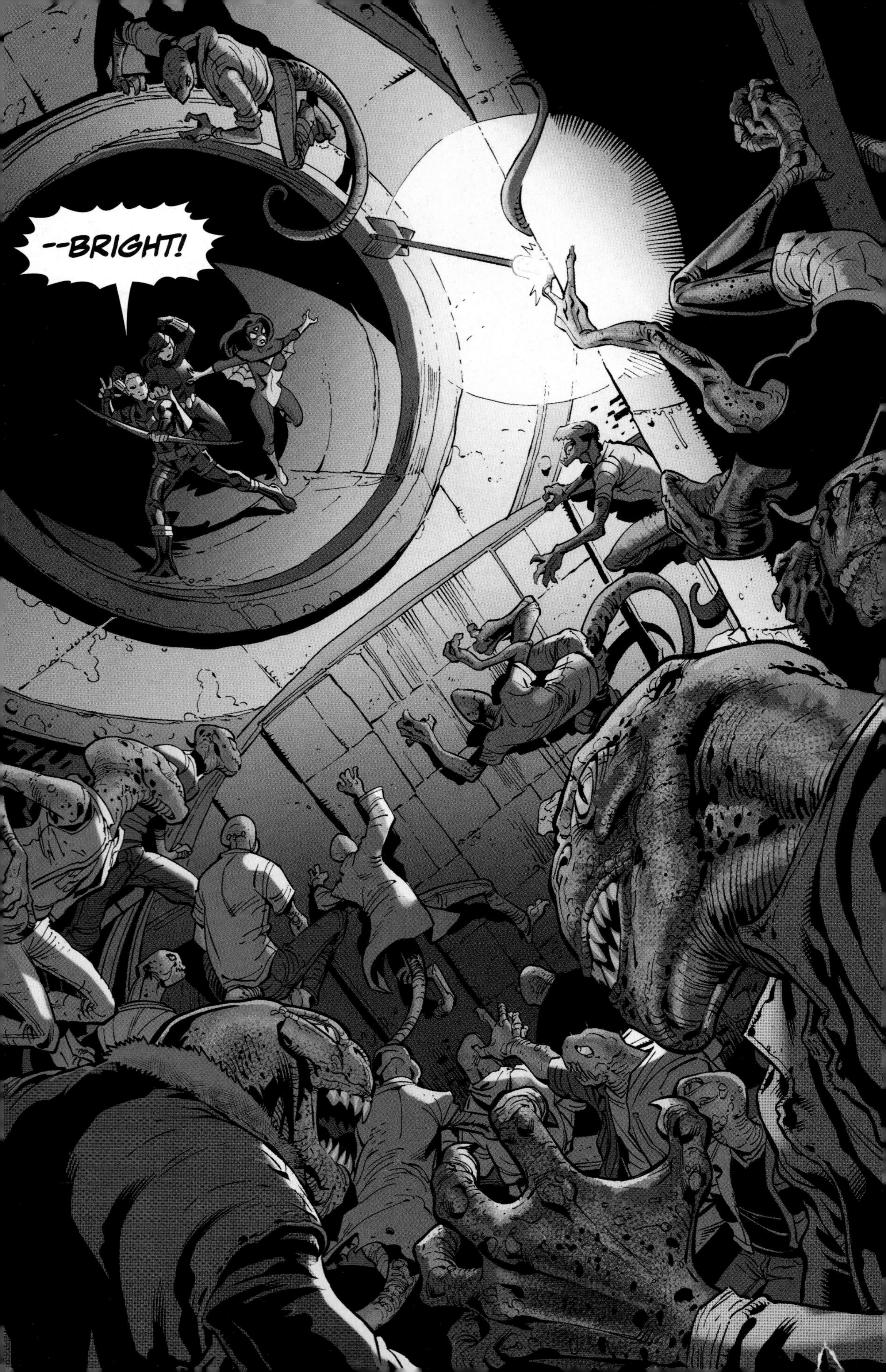
--BRIGHT!

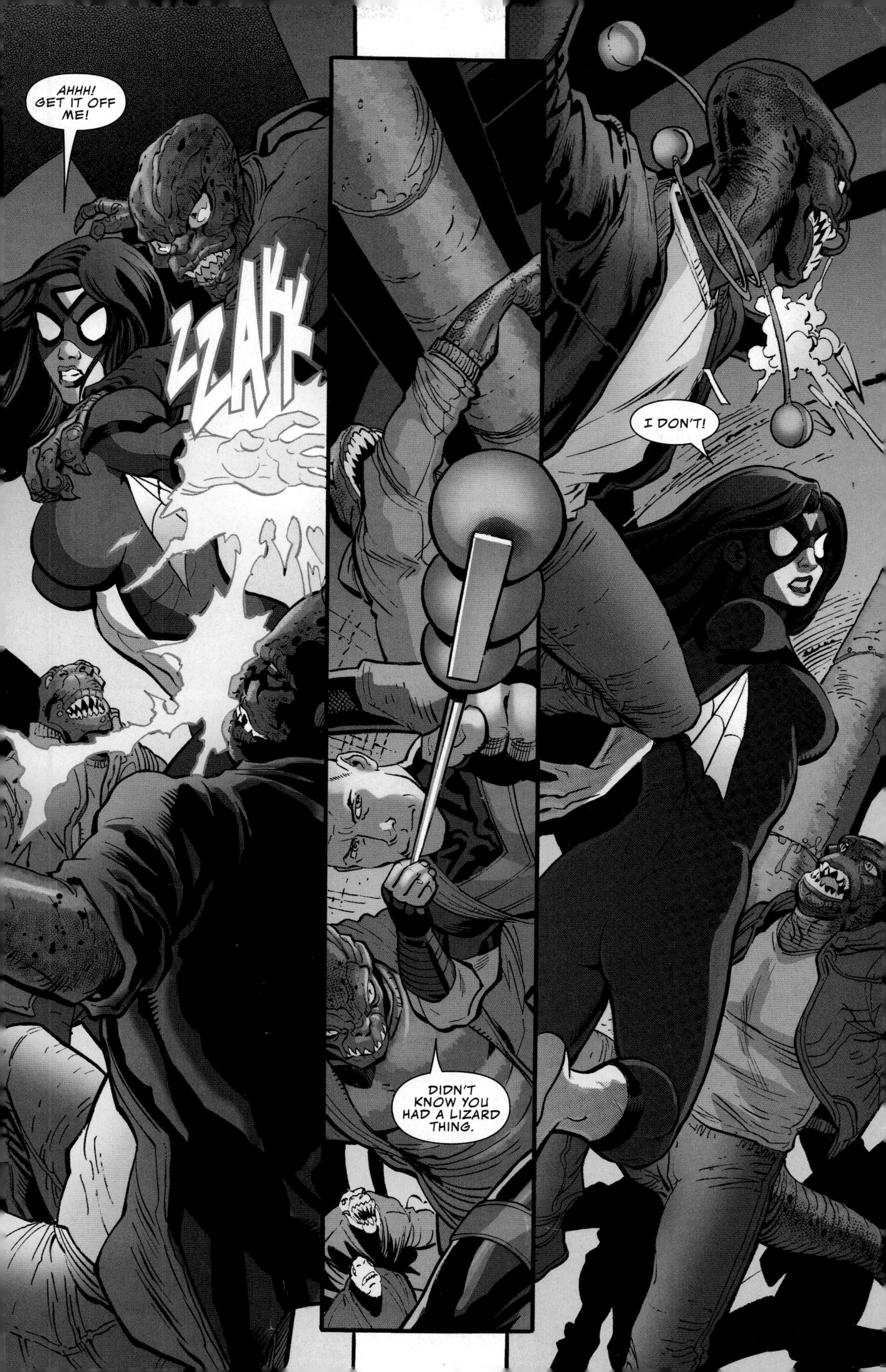
AHHH! GET IT OFF ME!
ZZAKK
I DON'T!
DIDN'T KNOW YOU HAD A LIZARD THING.

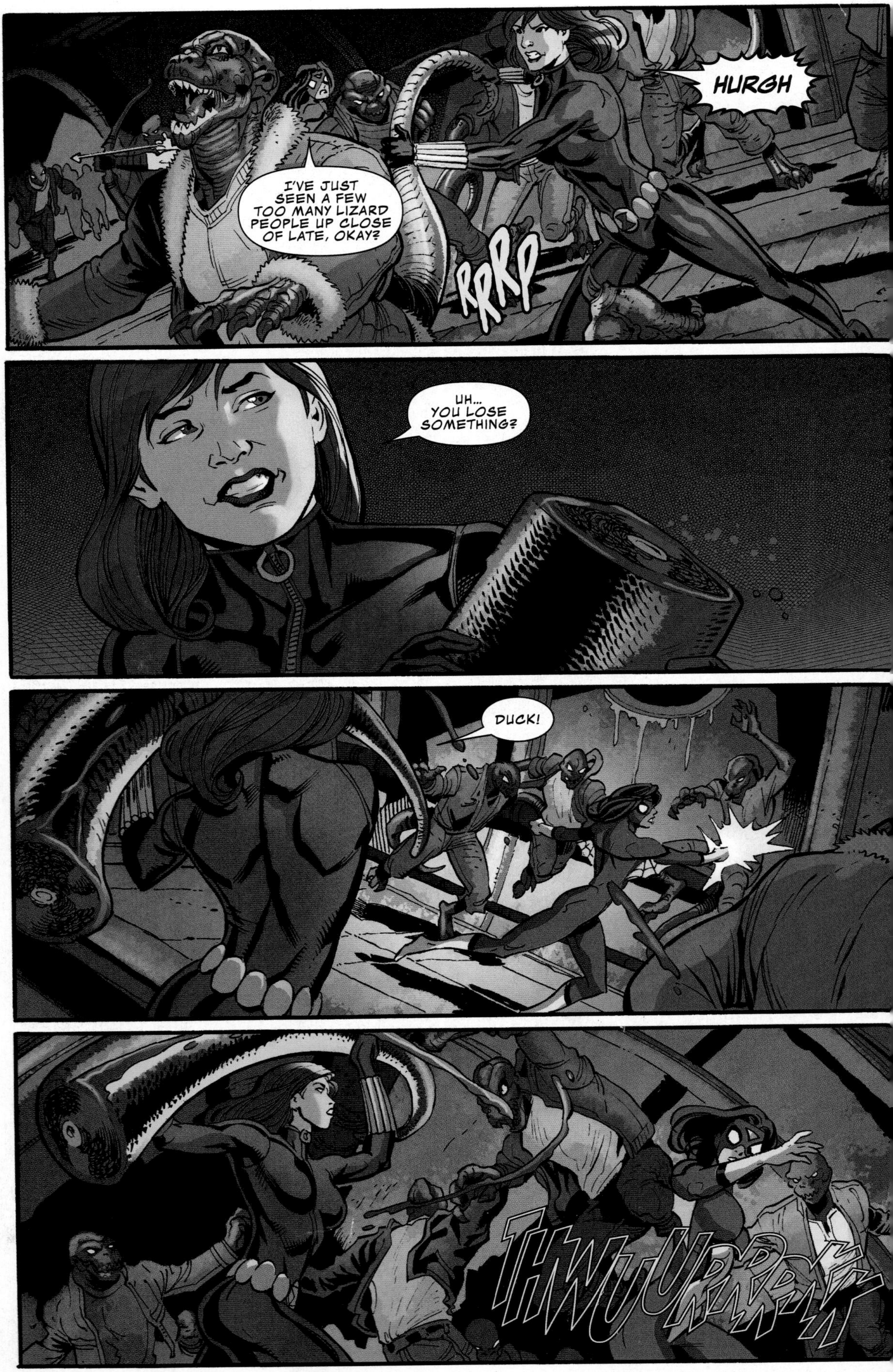
HURGH
I'VE JUST SEEN A FEW TOO MANY LIZARD PEOPLE UP CLOSE OF LATE, OKAY?
RRRP
UH... YOU LOSE SOMETHING?
DUCK!
THWURRRK

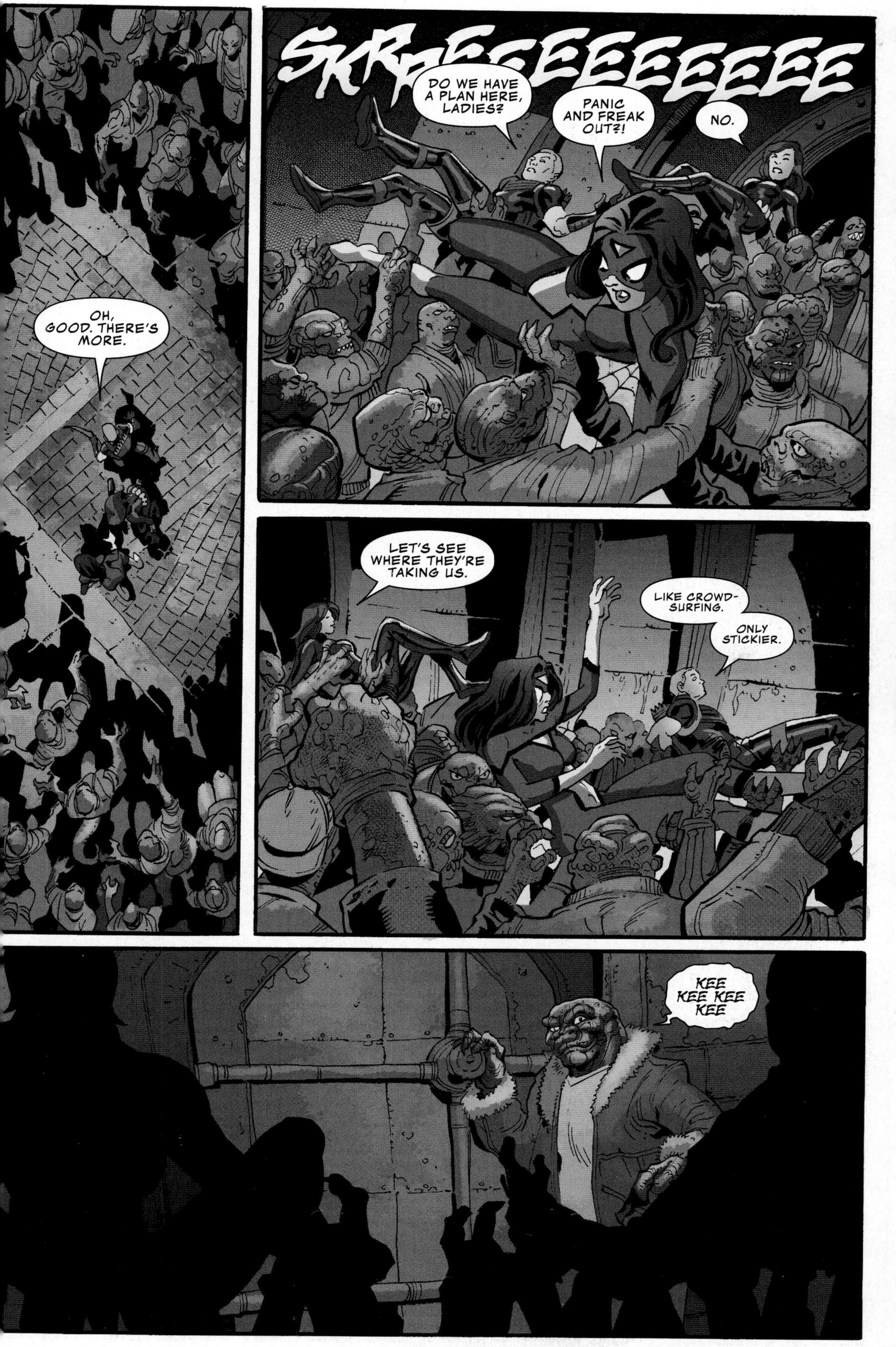
OH, GOOD. THERE'S MORE.
SKREEEEEEEEEEEE
DO WE HAVE A PLAN HERE, LADIES?
PANIC AND FREAK OUT?!
NO.
LET'S SEE WHERE THEY'RE TAKING US.
LIKE CROWD-SURFING.
ONLY STICKIER.
KEE KEE KEE KEE

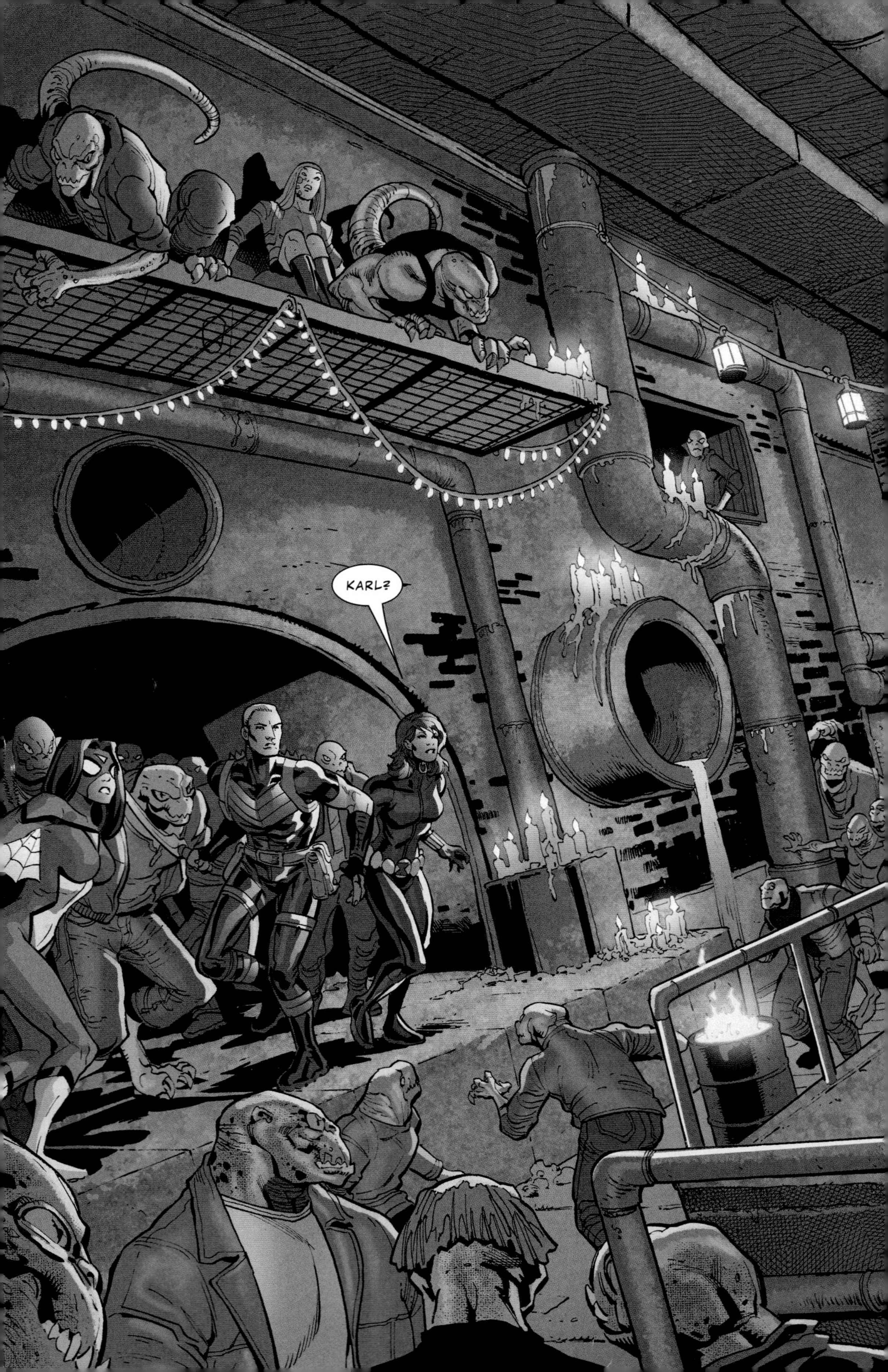
KARL?

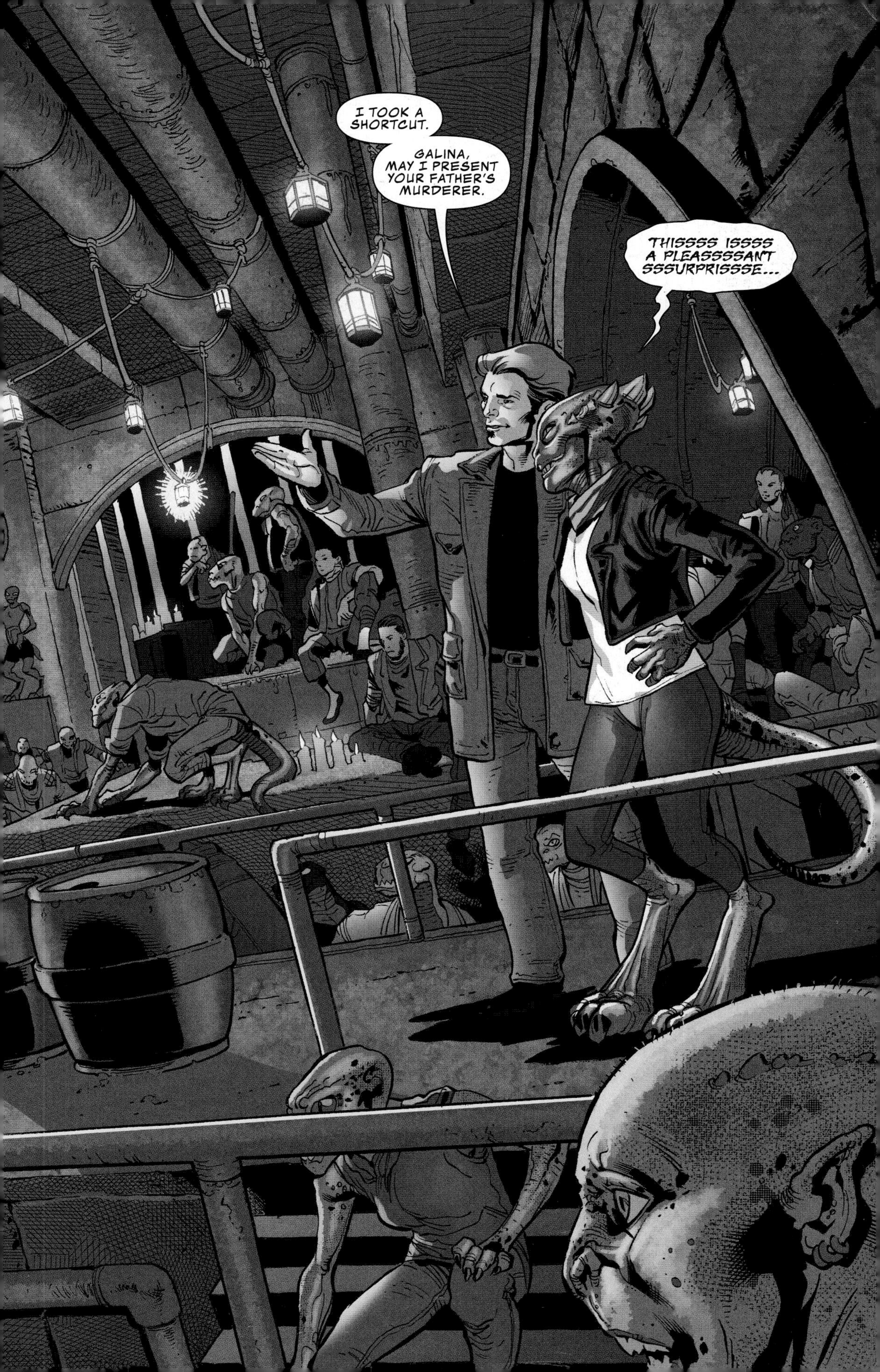
I TOOK A SHORTCUT.
GALINA, MAY I PRESENT YOUR FATHER'S MURDERER.
THISSSS ISSSS A PLEASSSSANT SSSURPRISSSE...

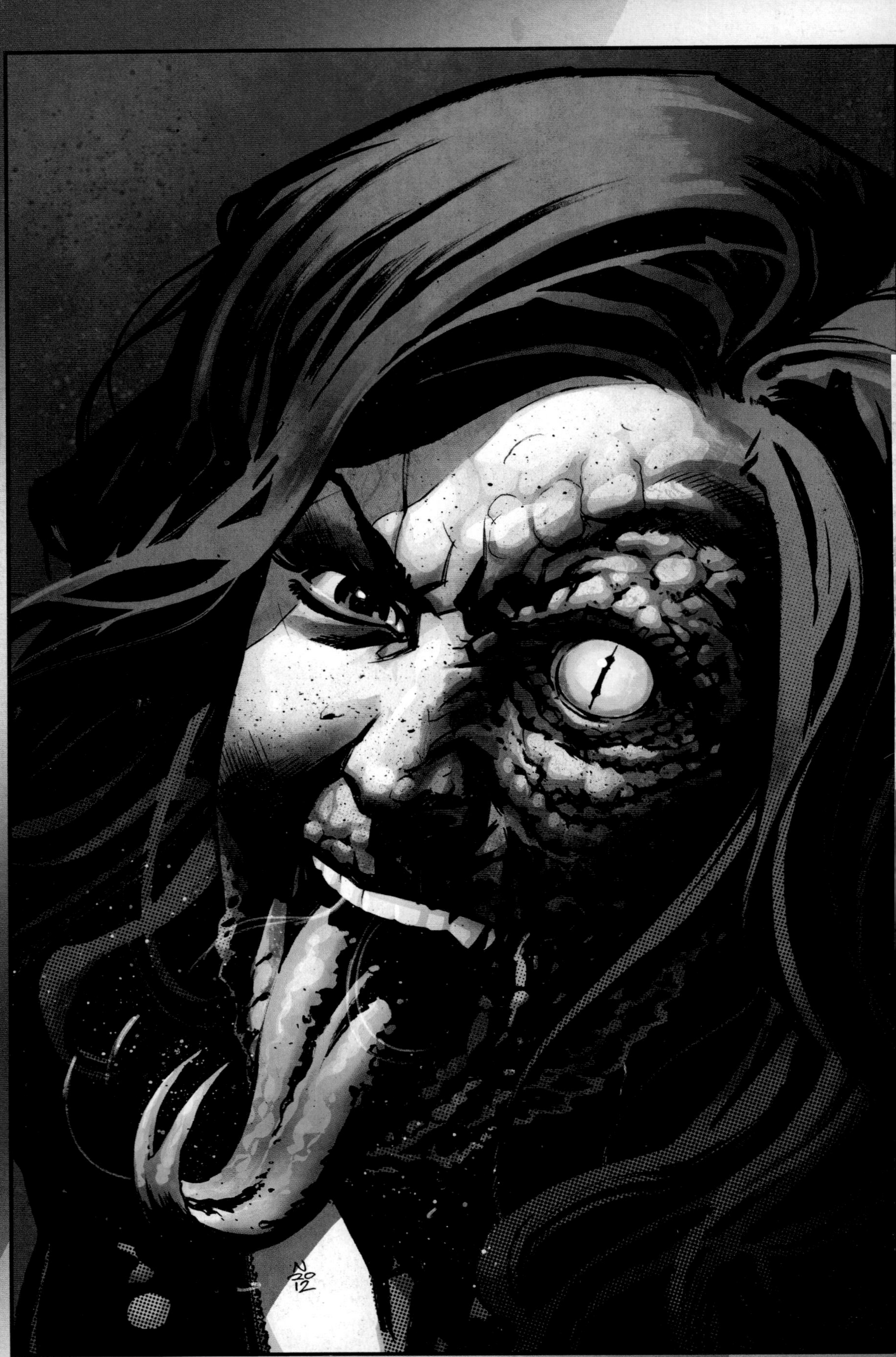

THIRTEEN

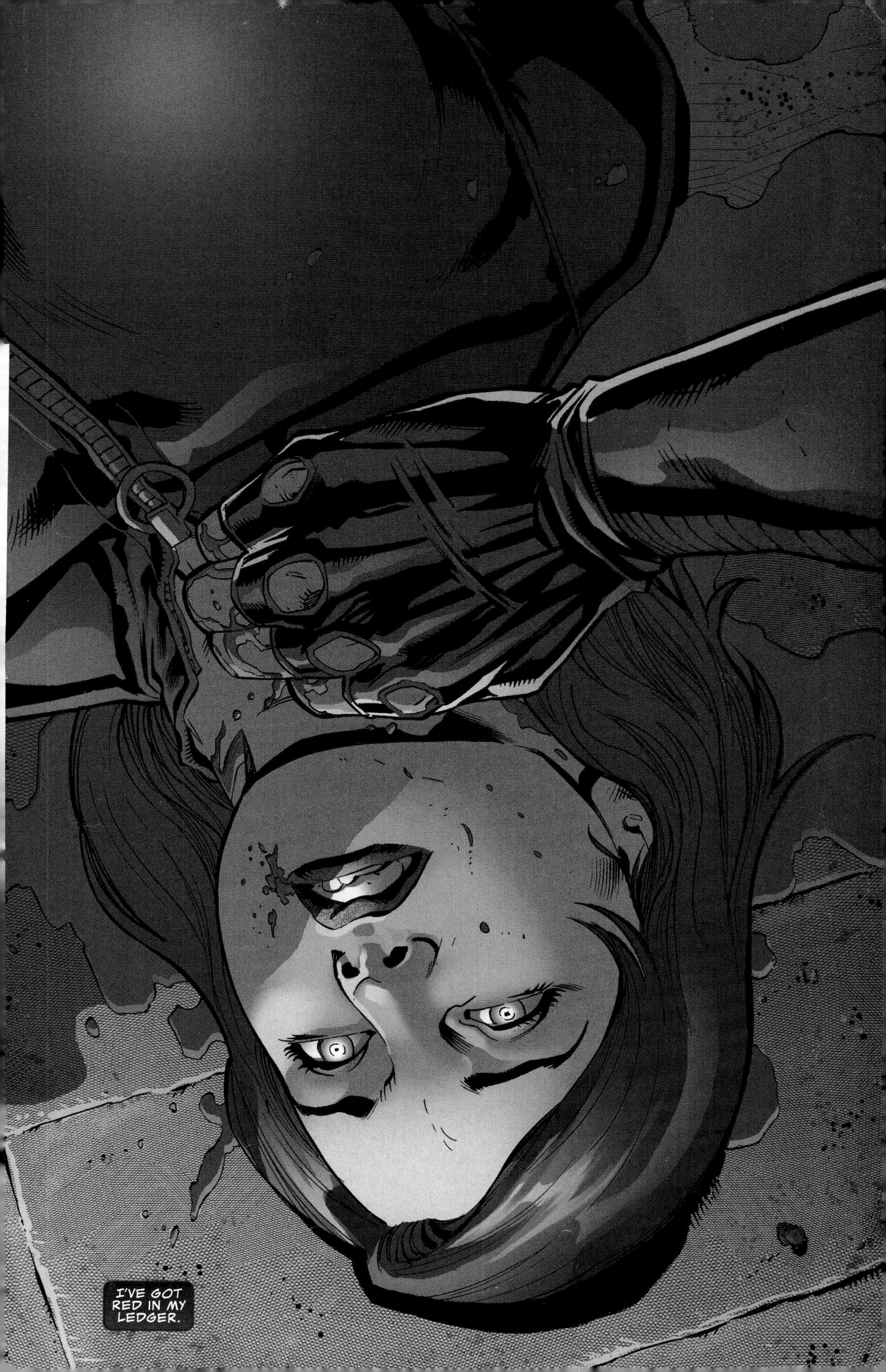
I'VE GOT RED IN MY LEDGER.

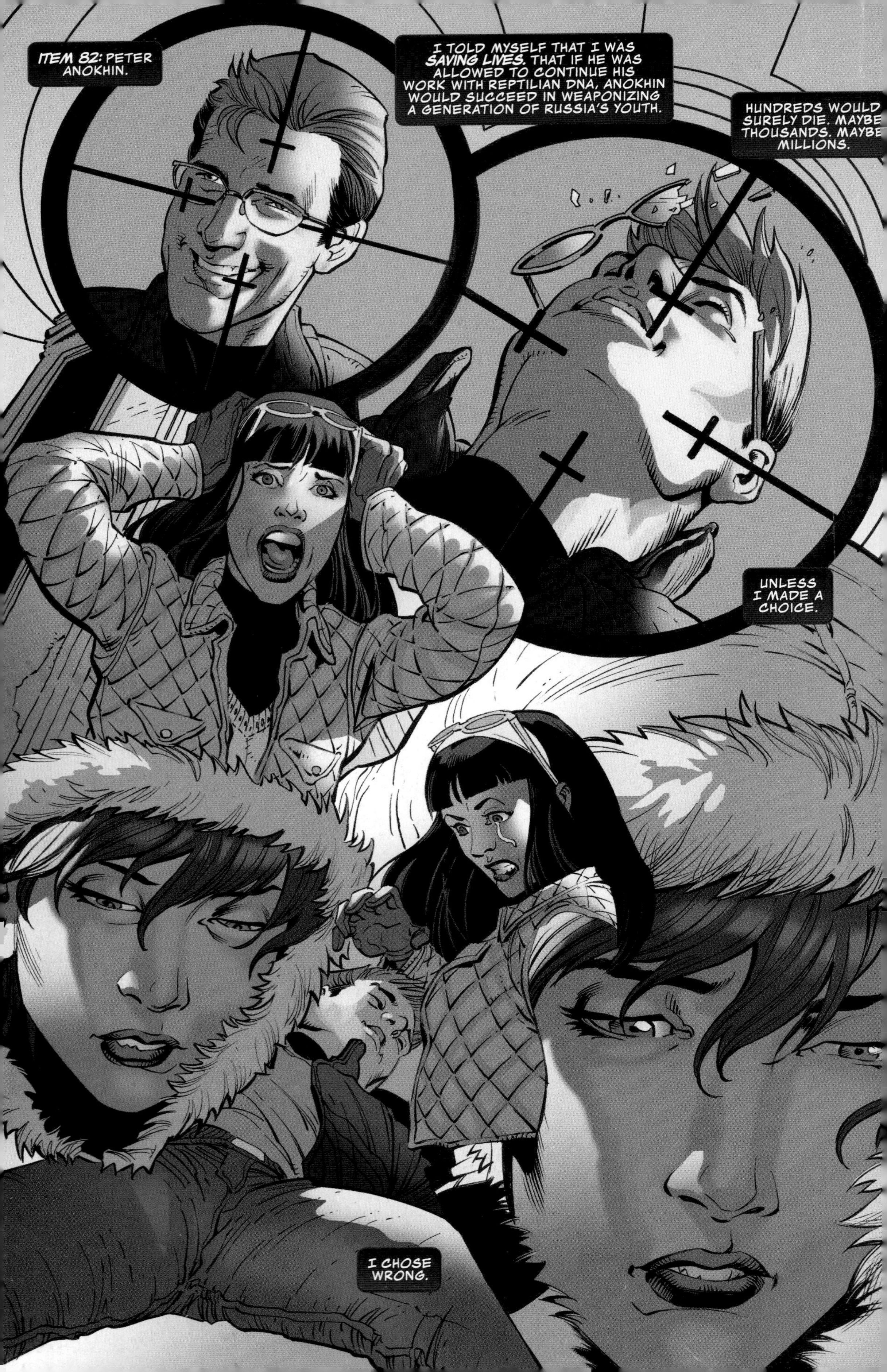
ITEM 82: PETER ANOKHIN.
I TOLD MYSELF THAT I WAS SAVING LIVES. THAT IF HE WAS ALLOWED TO CONTINUE HIS WORK WITH REPTILIAN DNA, ANOKHIN WOULD SUCCEED IN WEAPONIZING A GENERATION OF RUSSIA'S YOUTH.
HUNDREDS WOULD SURELY DIE. MAYBE THOUSANDS. MAYBE MILLIONS.
UNLESS I MADE A CHOICE.
I CHOSE WRONG.

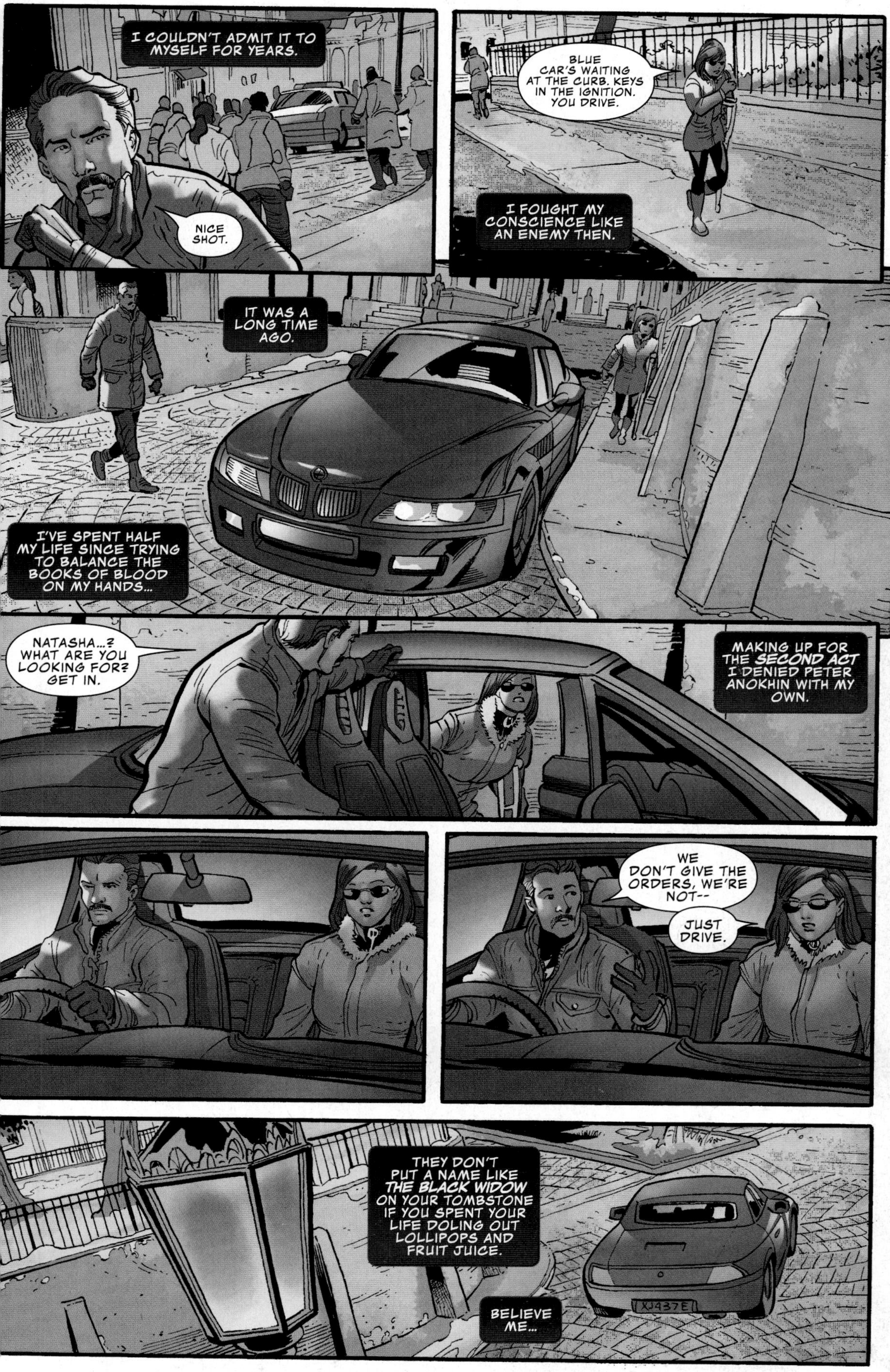
I COULDN'T ADMIT IT TO MYSELF FOR YEARS.
NICE SHOT.
BLUE CAR'S WAITING AT THE CURB. KEYS IN THE IGNITION. YOU DRIVE.
I FOUGHT MY CONSCIENCE LIKE AN ENEMY THEN.
IT WAS A LONG TIME AGO.
I'VE SPENT HALF MY LIFE SINCE TRYING TO BALANCE THE BOOKS OF BLOOD ON MY HANDS...
NATASHA...? WHAT ARE YOU LOOKING FOR? GET IN.
MAKING UP FOR THE SECOND ACT I DENIED PETER ANOKHIN WITH MY OWN.
WE DON'T GIVE THE ORDERS, WE'RE NOT--
JUST DRIVE.
THEY DON'T PUT A NAME LIKE THE BLACK WIDOW ON YOUR TOMBSTONE IF YOU SPENT YOUR LIFE DOLING OUT LOLLIPOPS AND FRUIT JUICE.
XJ437E
BELIEVE ME...

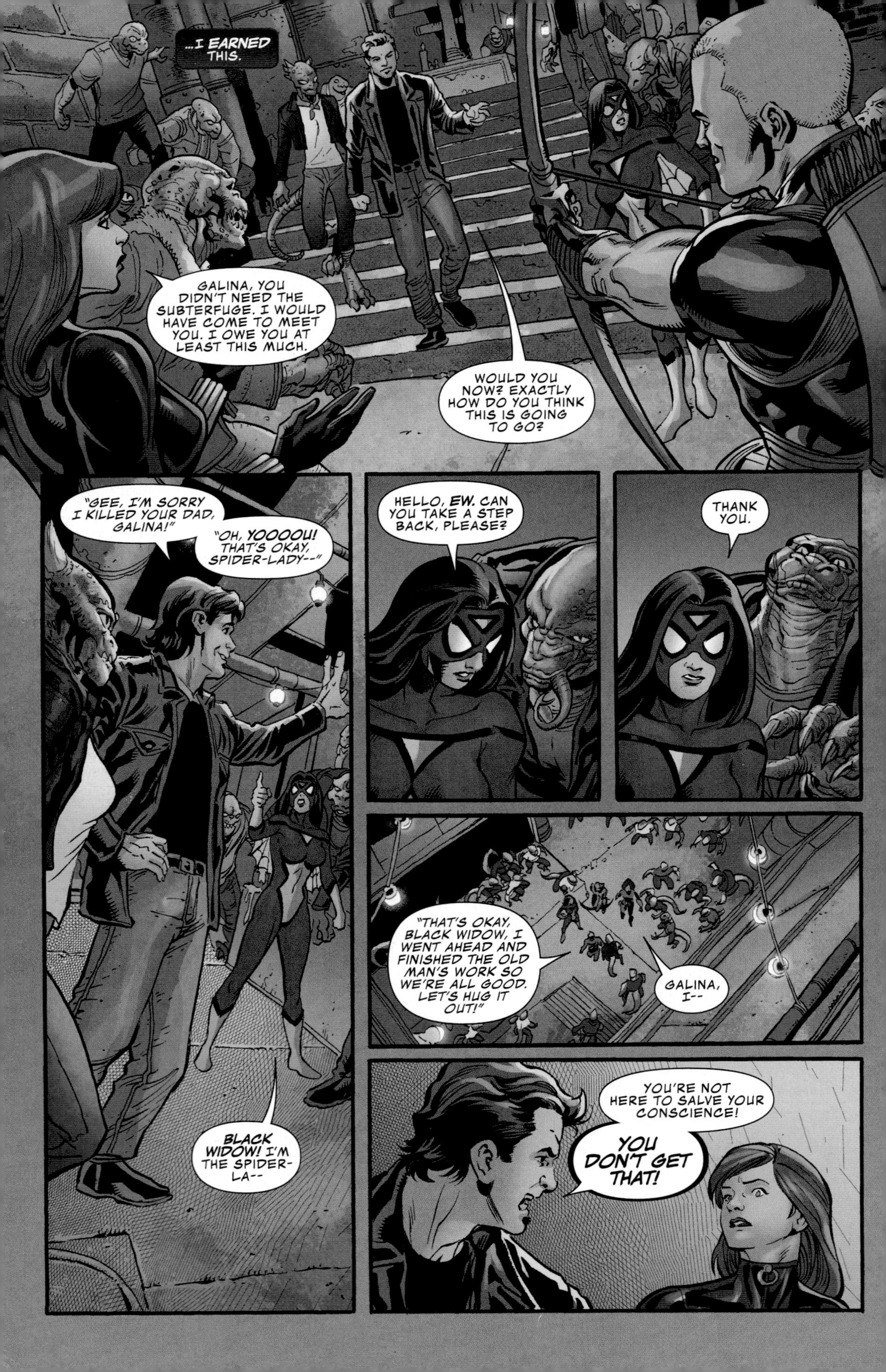
...I EARNED THIS.
GALINA, YOU DIDN'T NEED THE SUBTERFUGE. I WOULD HAVE COME TO MEET YOU. I OWE YOU AT LEAST THIS MUCH.
WOULD YOU NOW? EXACTLY HOW DO YOU THINK THIS IS GOING TO GO?
"GEE, I'M SORRY I KILLED YOUR DAD, GALINA!"
"OH, YOOOOU! THAT'S OKAY, SPIDER-LADY--"
BLACK WIDOW! I'M THE SPIDER-LA--
HELLO, EW. CAN YOU TAKE A STEP BACK, PLEASE?
THANK YOU.
"THAT'S OKAY, BLACK WIDOW, I WENT AHEAD AND FINISHED THE OLD MAN'S WORK SO WE'RE ALL GOOD. LET'S HUG IT OUT!"
GALINA, I--
YOU'RE NOT HERE TO SALVE YOUR CONSCIENCE!
YOU DON'T GET THAT!

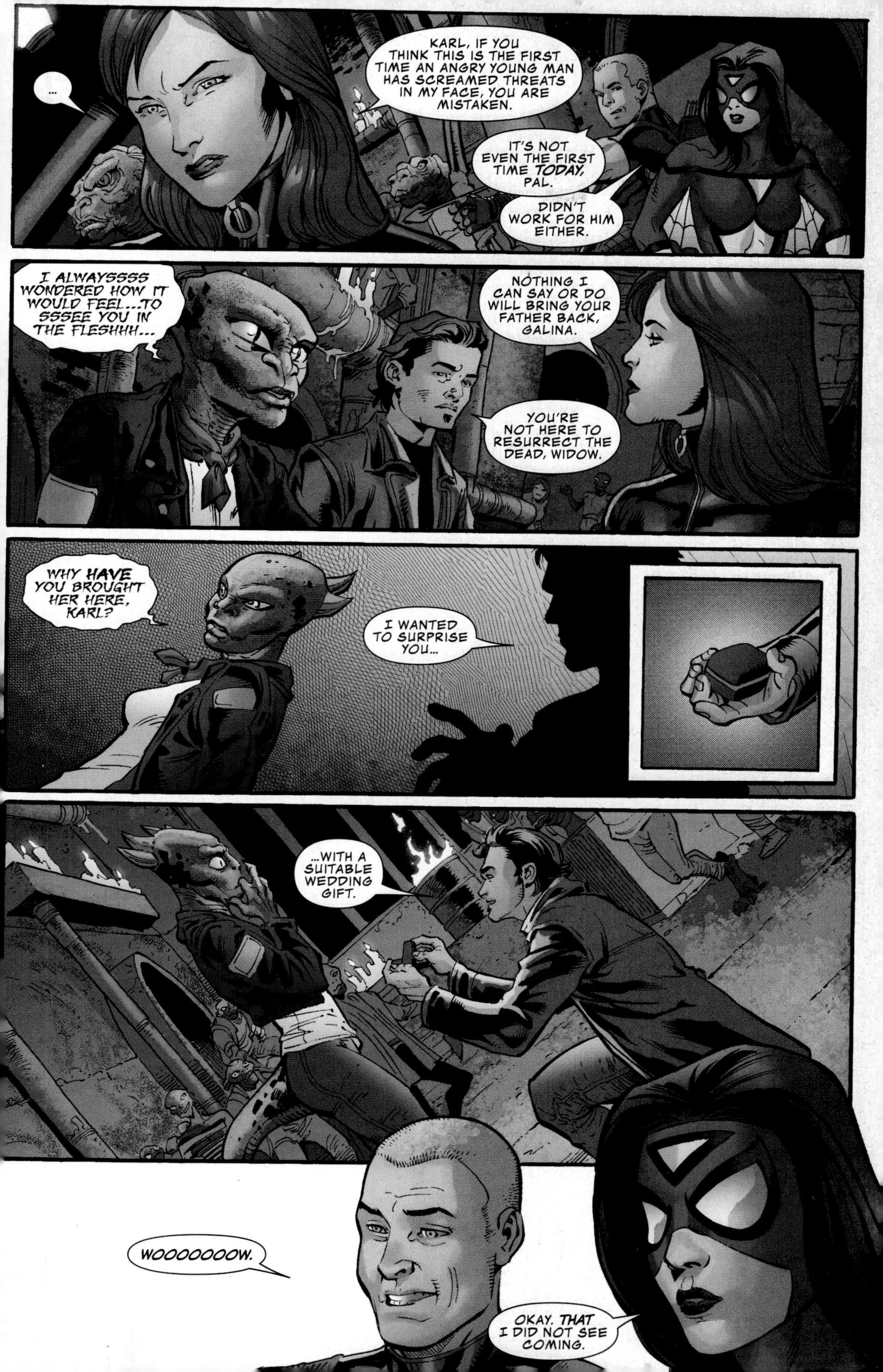
...
KARL, IF YOU THINK THIS IS THE FIRST TIME AN ANGRY YOUNG MAN HAS SCREAMED THREATS IN MY FACE, YOU ARE MISTAKEN.
IT'S NOT EVEN THE FIRST TIME TODAY, PAL.
DIDN'T WORK FOR HIM EITHER.
I ALWAYSSSS WONDERED HOW IT WOULD FEEL...TO SSSEE YOU IN THE FLESHHH...
NOTHING I CAN SAY OR DO WILL BRING YOUR FATHER BACK, GALINA.
YOU'RE NOT HERE TO RESURRECT THE DEAD, WIDOW.
WHY HAVE YOU BROUGHT HER HERE, KARL?
I WANTED TO SURPRISE YOU...
...WITH A SUITABLE WEDDING GIFT.
WOOOOOOOW.
OKAY. THAT I DID NOT SEE COMING.

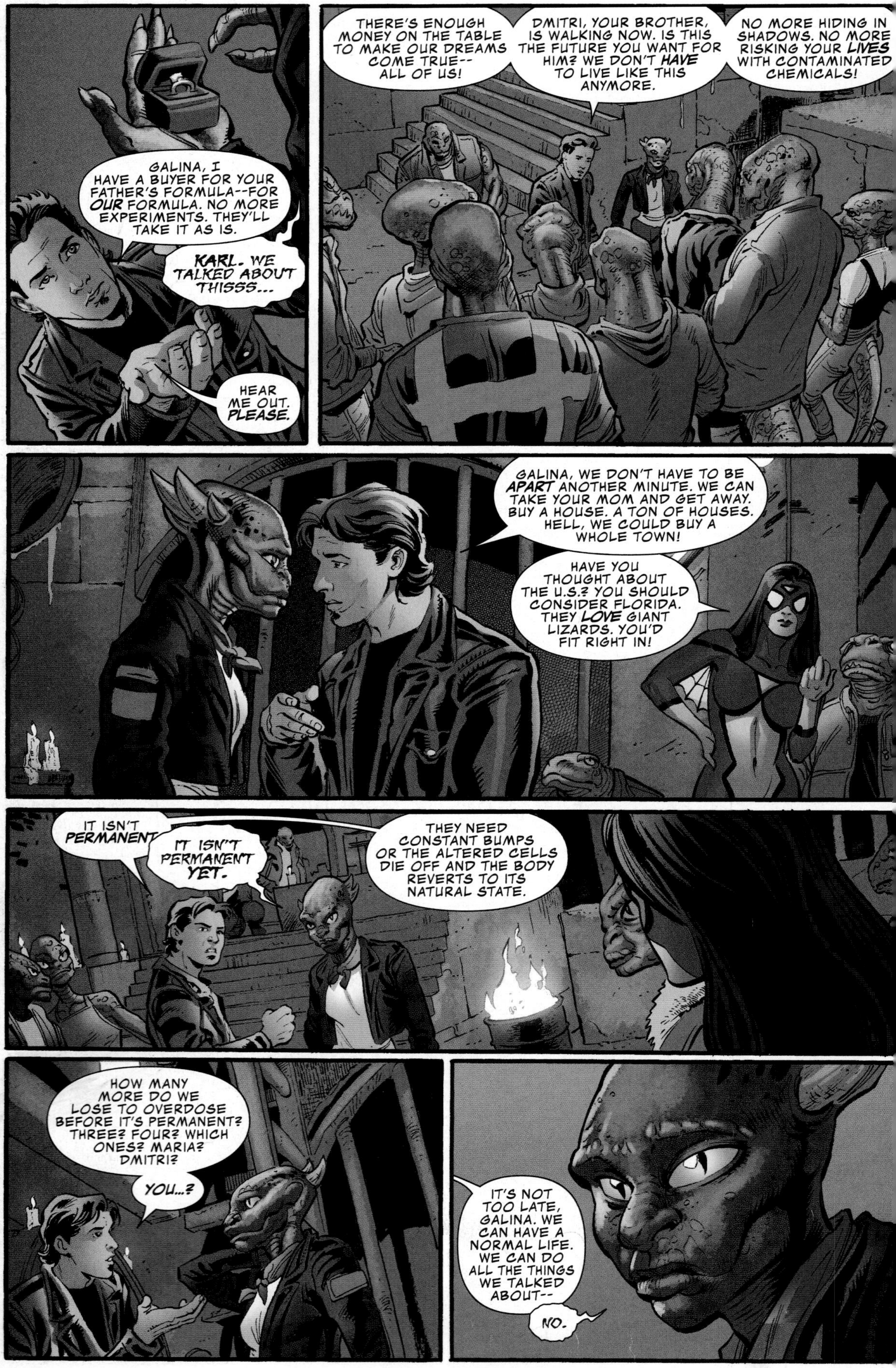
GALINA, I HAVE A BUYER FOR YOUR FATHER'S FORMULA--FOR OUR FORMULA. NO MORE EXPERIMENTS. THEY'LL TAKE IT AS IS.
KARL. WE TALKED ABOUT THISSS...
HEAR ME OUT. PLEASE.
THERE'S ENOUGH MONEY ON THE TABLE TO MAKE OUR DREAMS COME TRUE-- ALL OF US!
DMITRI, YOUR BROTHER, IS WALKING NOW. IS THIS THE FUTURE YOU WANT FOR HIM? WE DON'T HAVE TO LIVE LIKE THIS ANYMORE.
NO MORE HIDING IN SHADOWS. NO MORE RISKING YOUR LIVES WITH CONTAMINATED CHEMICALS!
GALINA, WE DON'T HAVE TO BE APART ANOTHER MINUTE. WE CAN TAKE YOUR MOM AND GET AWAY. BUY A HOUSE. A TON OF HOUSES. HELL, WE COULD BUY A WHOLE TOWN!
HAVE YOU THOUGHT ABOUT THE U.S.? YOU SHOULD CONSIDER FLORIDA. THEY LOVE GIANT LIZARDS. YOU'D FIT RIGHT IN!
IT ISN'T PERMANENT.
IT ISN'T PERMANENT YET.
THEY NEED CONSTANT BUMPS OR THE ALTERED CELLS DIE OFF AND THE BODY REVERTS TO ITS NATURAL STATE.
HOW MANY MORE DO WE LOSE TO OVERDOSE BEFORE IT'S PERMANENT? THREE? FOUR? WHICH ONES? MARIA? DMITRI?
YOU...?
IT'S NOT TOO LATE, GALINA. WE CAN HAVE A NORMAL LIFE. WE CAN DO ALL THE THINGS WE TALKED ABOUT--
NO.

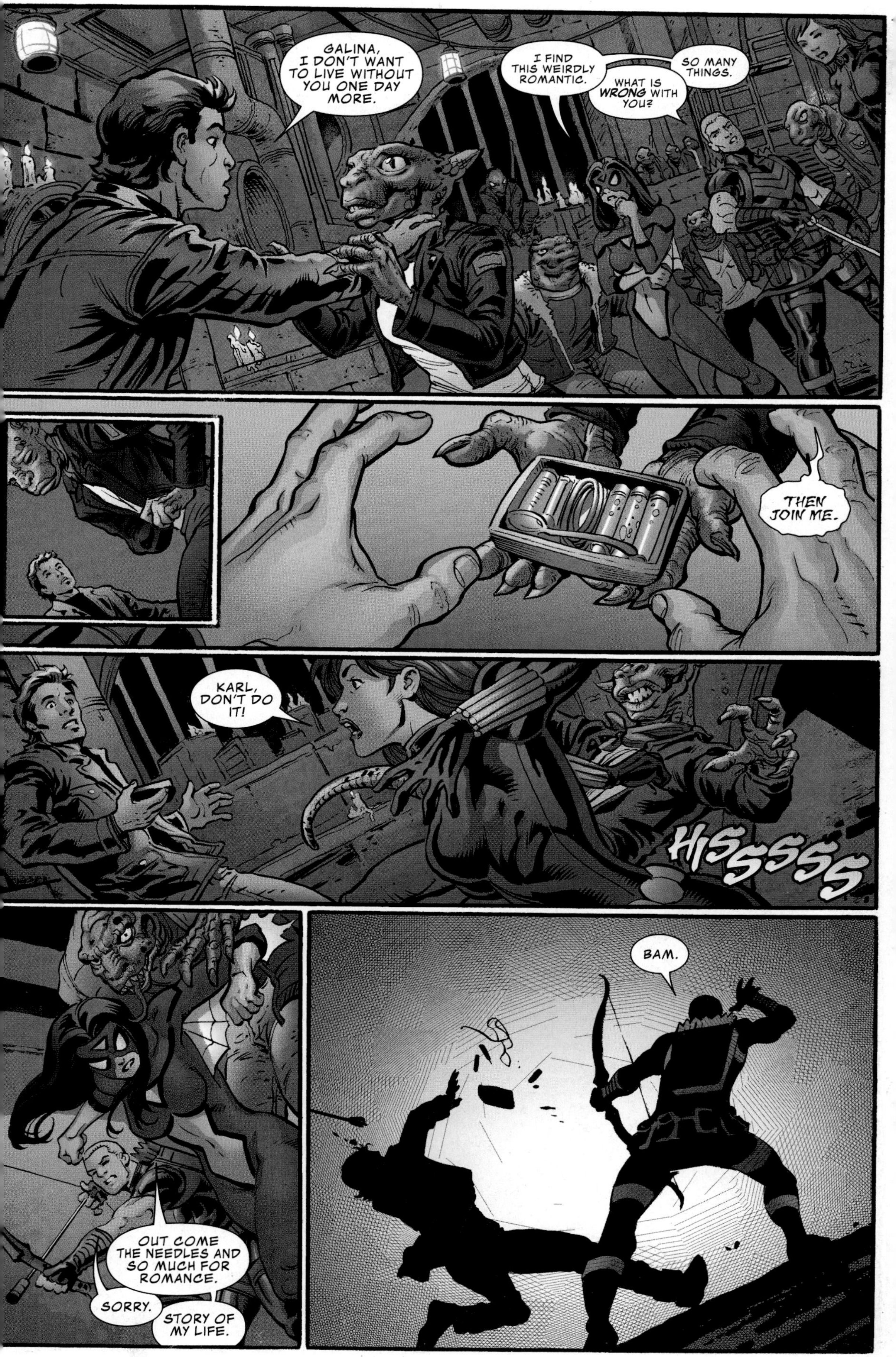

GALINA, I DON'T WANT TO LIVE WITHOUT YOU ONE DAY MORE.
I FIND THIS WEIRDLY ROMANTIC.
WHAT IS WRONG WITH YOU?
SO MANY THINGS.
THEN JOIN ME.
KARL, DON'T DO IT!
HISSSSS
OUT COME THE NEEDLES AND SO MUCH FOR ROMANCE.
SORRY.
STORY OF MY LIFE.
BAM.

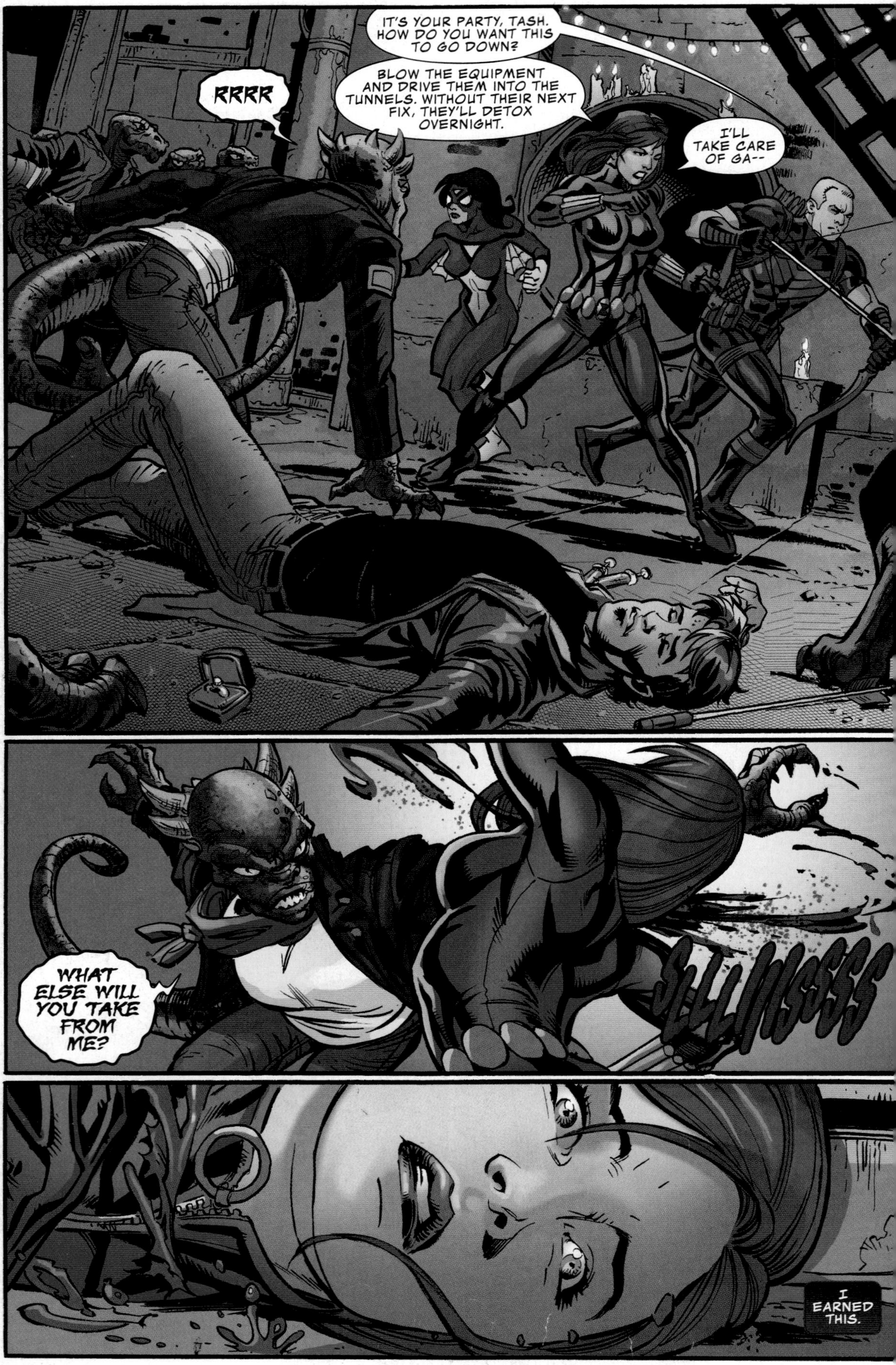
IT'S YOUR PARTY, TASH. HOW DO YOU WANT THIS TO GO DOWN?
RRRR
BLOW THE EQUIPMENT AND DRIVE THEM INTO THE TUNNELS. WITHOUT THEIR NEXT FIX, THEY'LL DETOX OVERNIGHT.
I'LL TAKE CARE OF GA--
WHAT ELSE WILL YOU TAKE FROM ME?
SLLLNSSSS
I EARNED THIS.

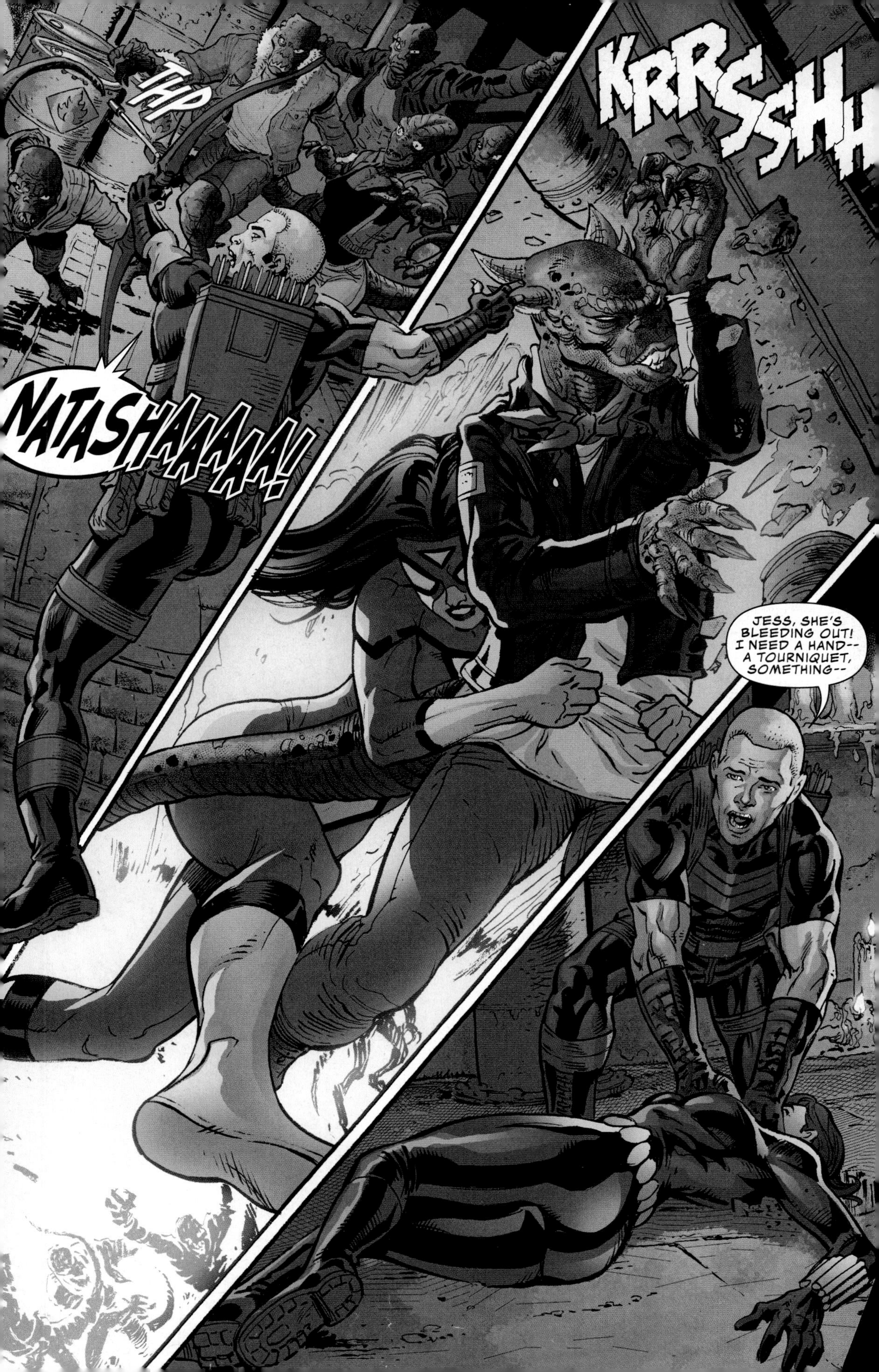
THP
NATASHAAAAAA!
KRRSSHH
JESS, SHE'S BLEEDING OUT! I NEED A HAND-- A TOURNIQUET, SOMETHING--

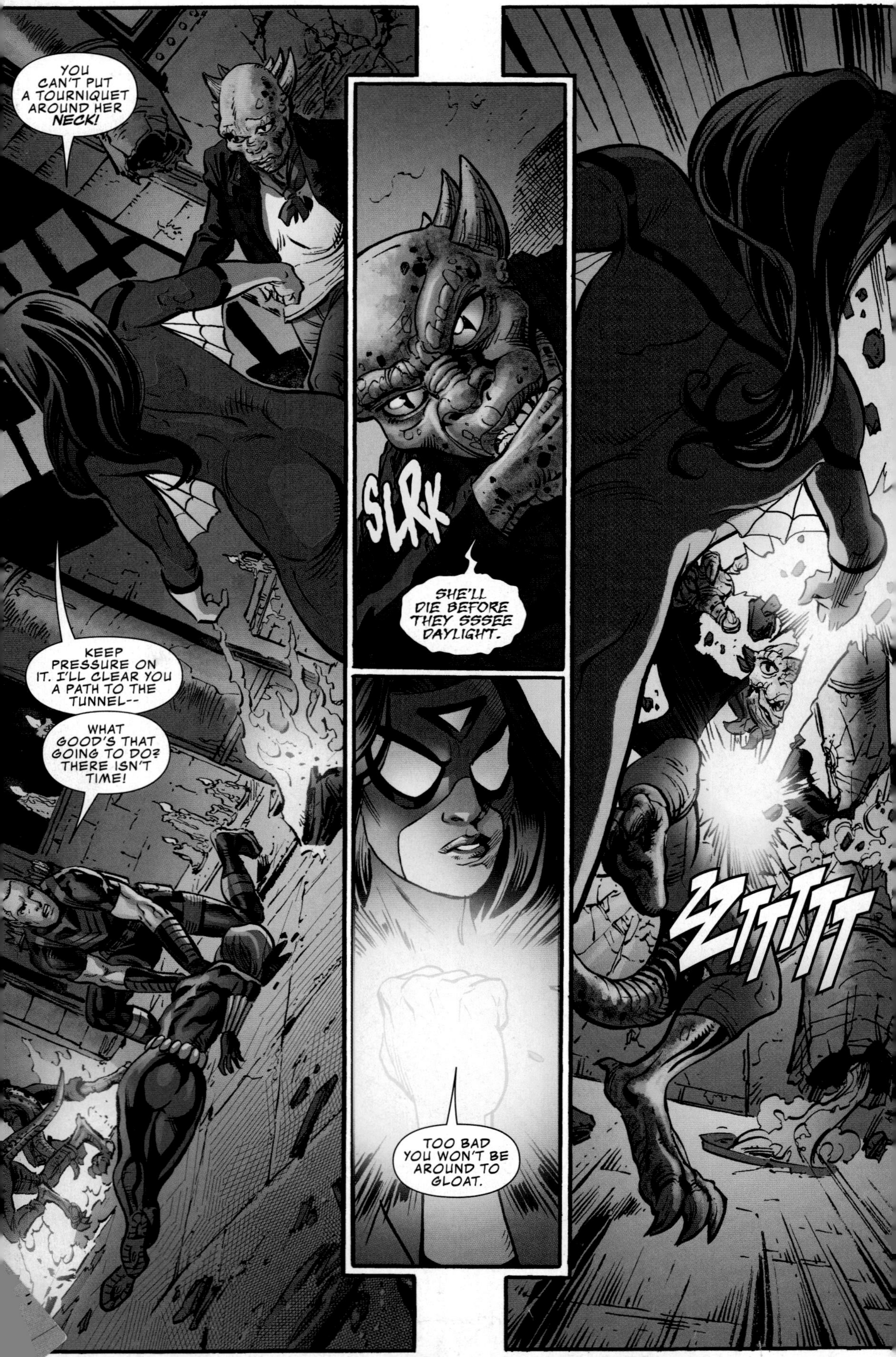
YOU CAN'T PUT A TOURNIQUET AROUND HER NECK!
KEEP PRESSURE ON IT. I'LL CLEAR YOU A PATH TO THE TUNNEL--
WHAT GOOD'S THAT GOING TO DO? THERE ISN'T TIME!
SLRK
SHE'LL DIE BEFORE THEY SSSEE DAYLIGHT.
TOO BAD YOU WON'T BE AROUND TO GLOAT.
ZZTTTTT

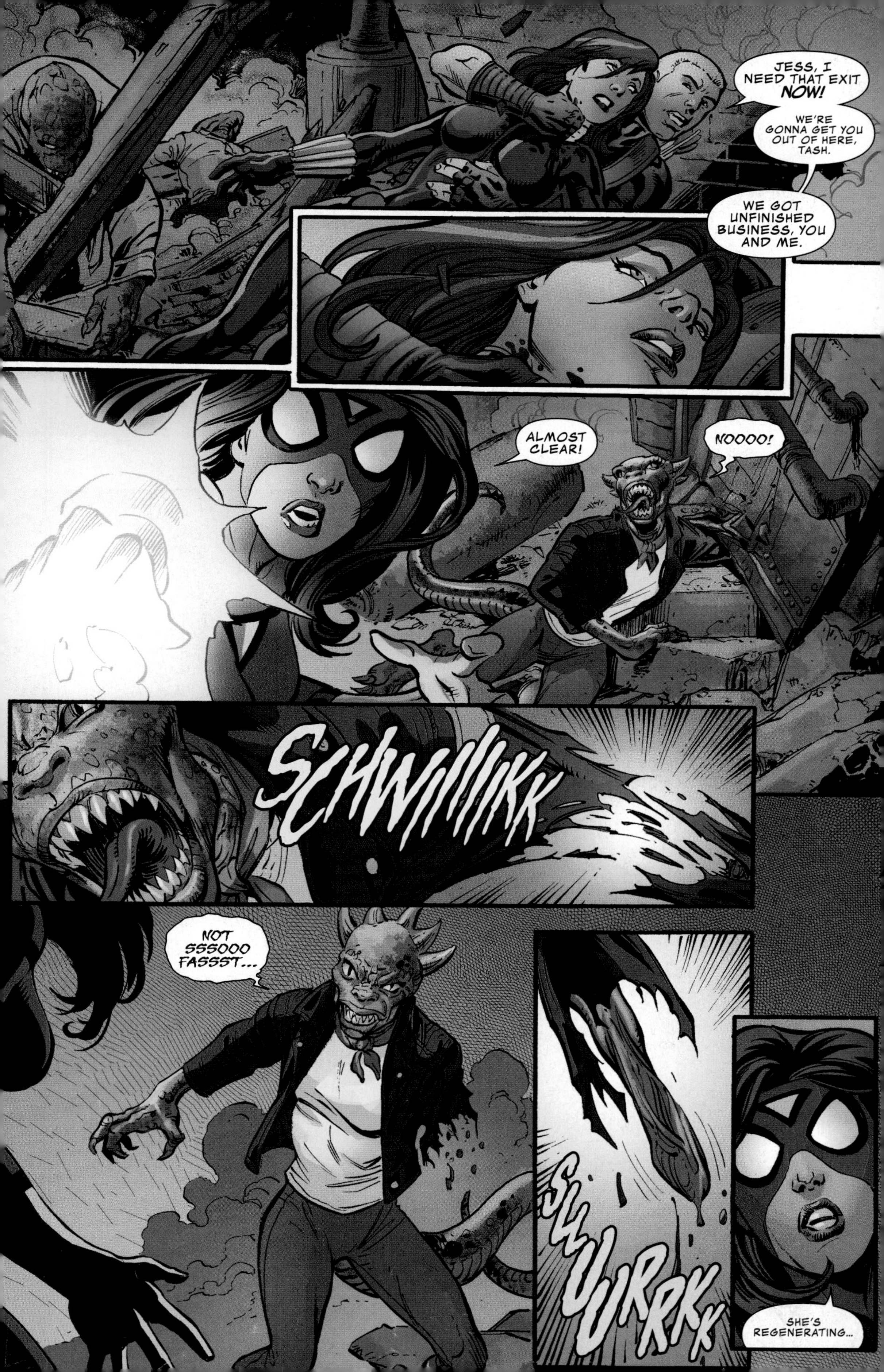
JESS, I NEED THAT EXIT NOW!
WE'RE GONNA GET YOU OUT OF HERE, TASH.
WE GOT UNFINISHED BUSINESS, YOU AND ME.
ALMOST CLEAR!
NOOOO!
SCHWIIIIKK
NOT SSSOOO FASSST...
SHWURRKK
SHE'S REGENERATING...

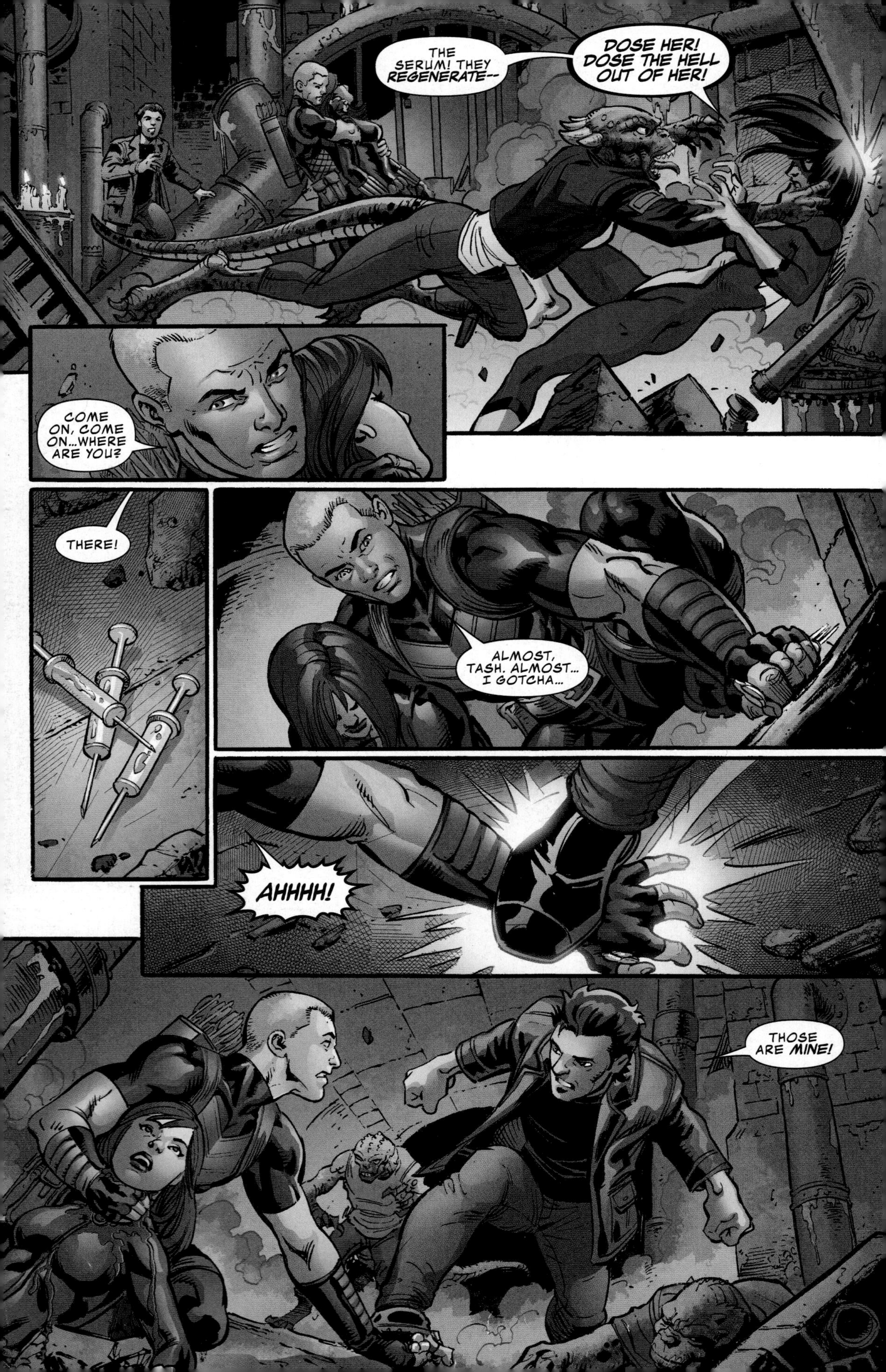
THE SERUM! THEY REGENERATE--
DOSE HER! DOSE THE HELL OUT OF HER!
COME ON, COME ON...WHERE ARE YOU?
THERE!
ALMOST, TASH. ALMOST... I GOTCHA...
AHHHH!
THOSE ARE MINE!

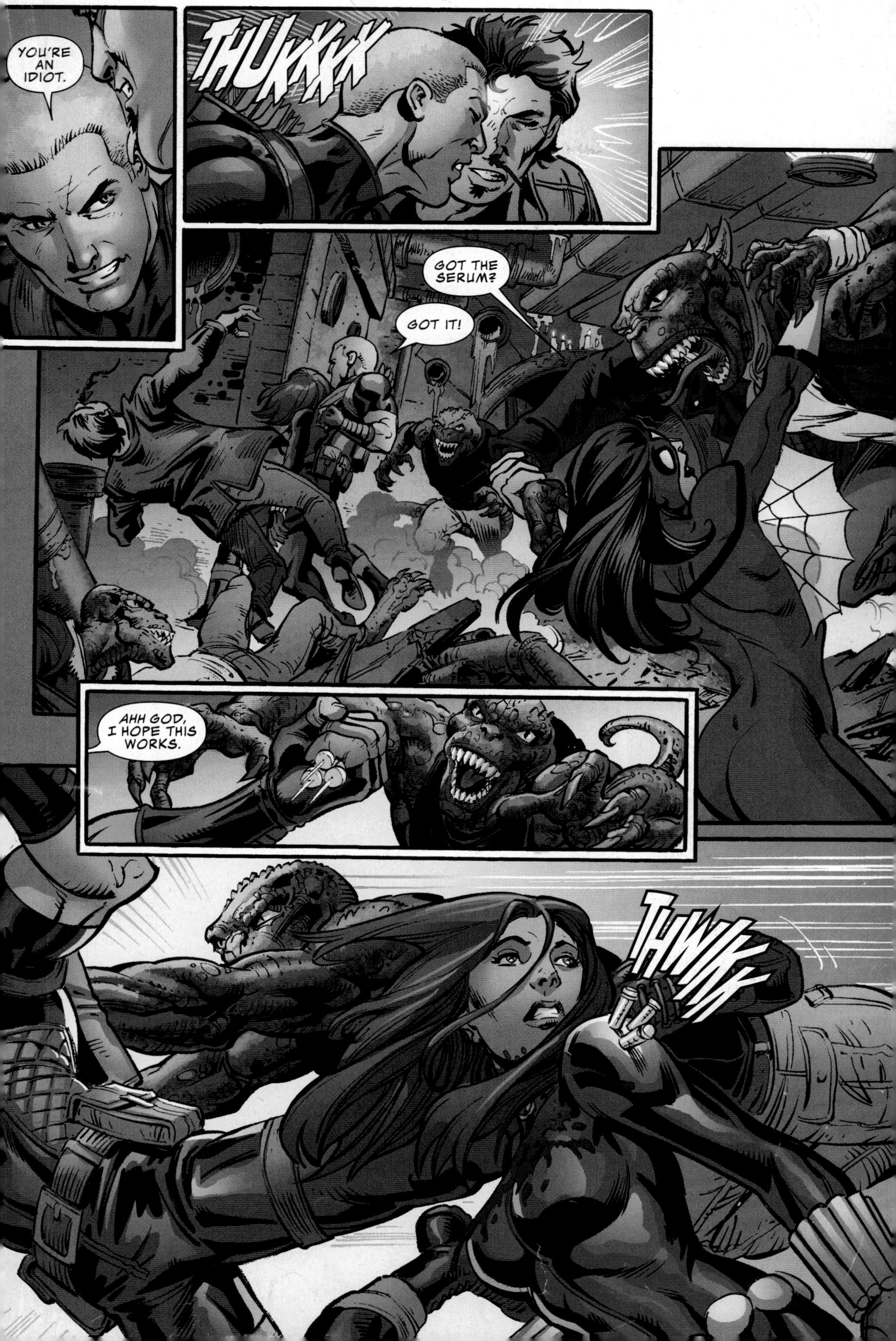
YOU'RE AN IDIOT.
THUKKKK
GOT THE SERUM?
GOT IT!
AHH GOD, I HOPE THIS WORKS.
THWKK

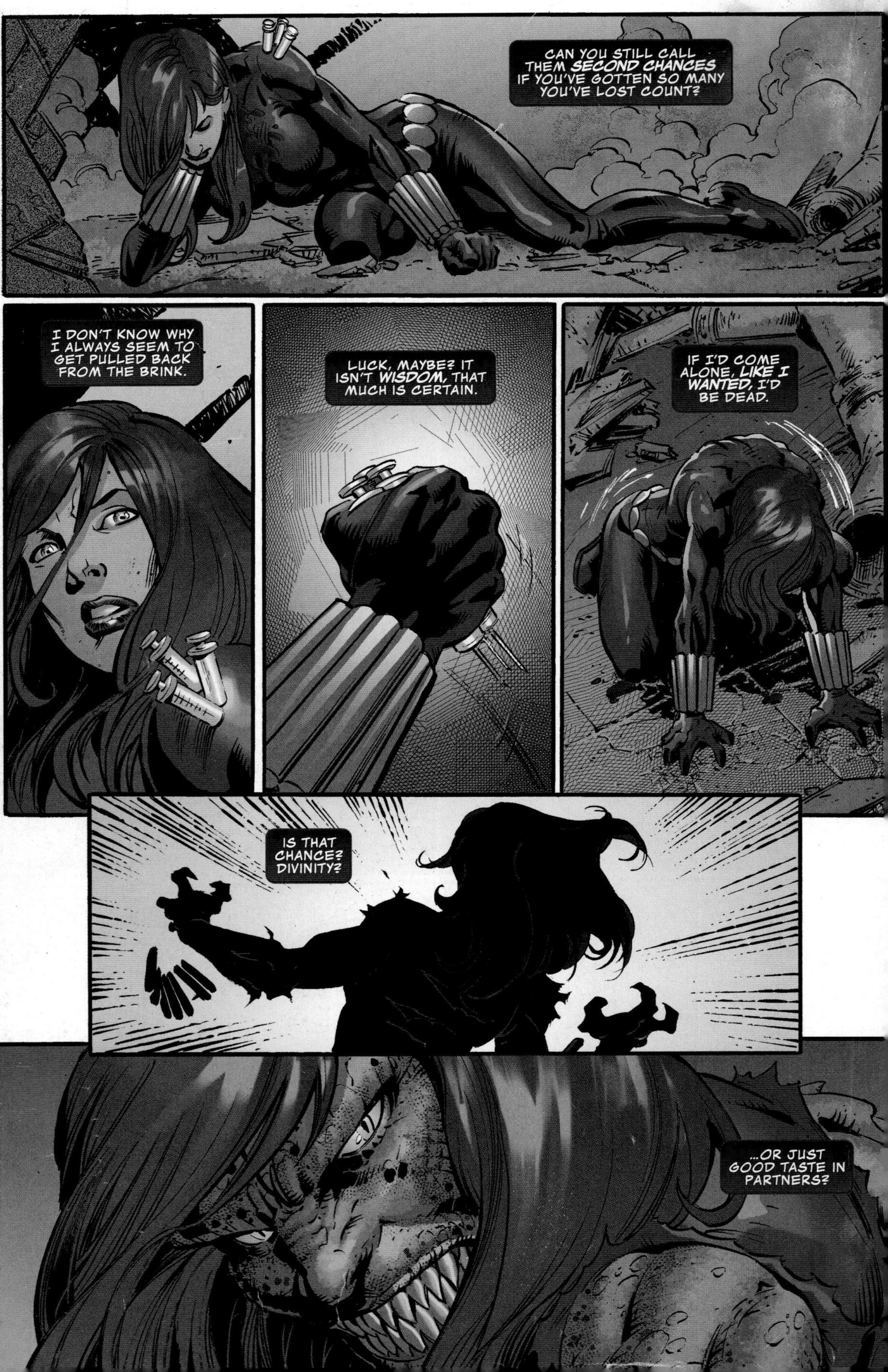
CAN YOU STILL CALL THEM SECOND CHANCES IF YOU'VE GOTTEN SO MANY YOU'VE LOST COUNT?
I DON'T KNOW WHY I ALWAYS SEEM TO GET PULLED BACK FROM THE BRINK.
LUCK, MAYBE? IT ISN'T WISDOM, THAT MUCH IS CERTAIN.
IF I'D COME ALONE, LIKE I WANTED, I'D BE DEAD.
IS THAT CHANCE? DIVINITY?
...OR JUST GOOD TASTE IN PARTNERS?

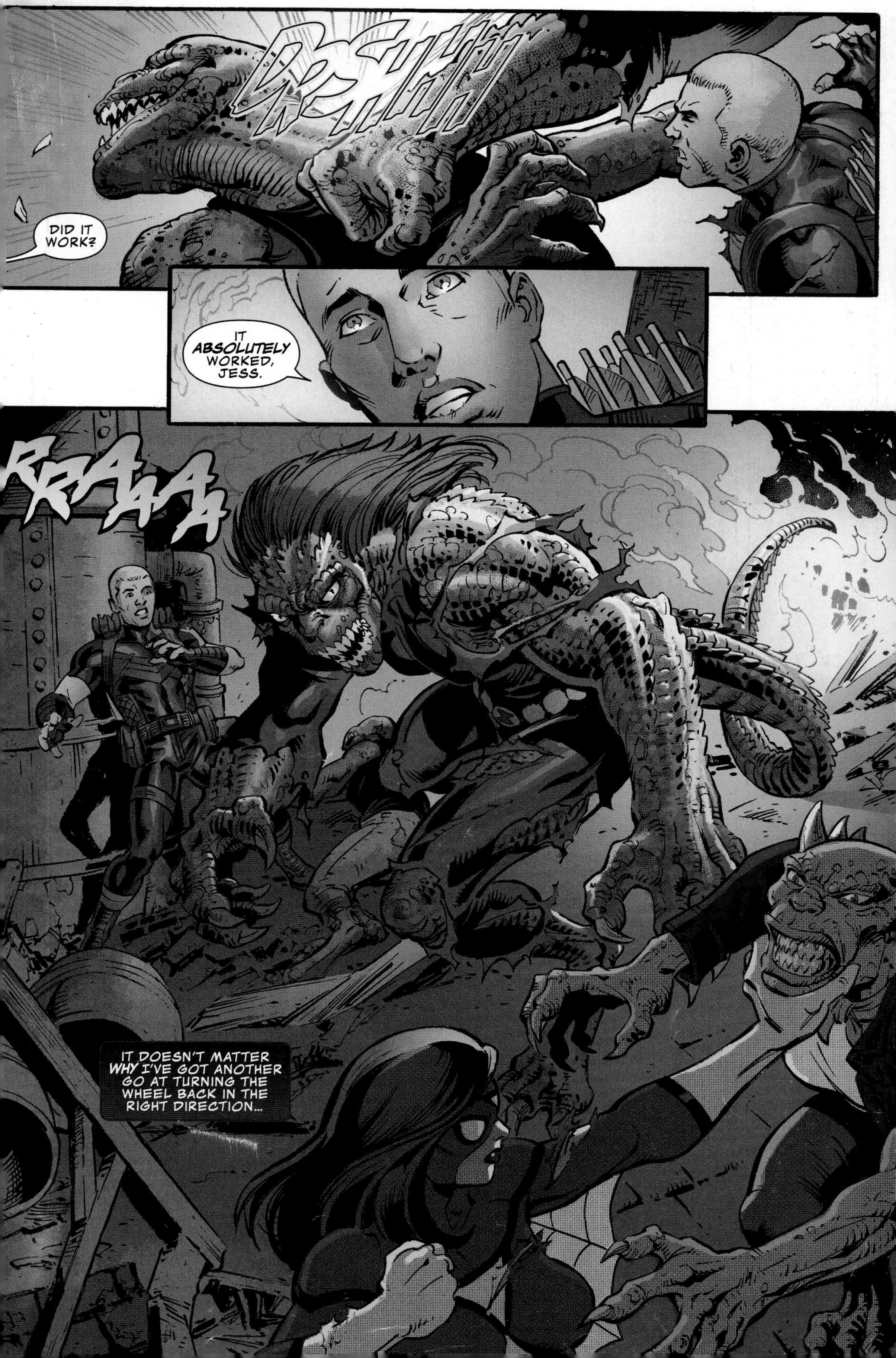
DID IT WORK?
IT **ABSOLUTELY** WORKED, JESS.
IT DOESN'T MATTER ***WHY*** I'VE GOT ANOTHER GO AT TURNING THE WHEEL BACK IN THE RIGHT DIRECTION...

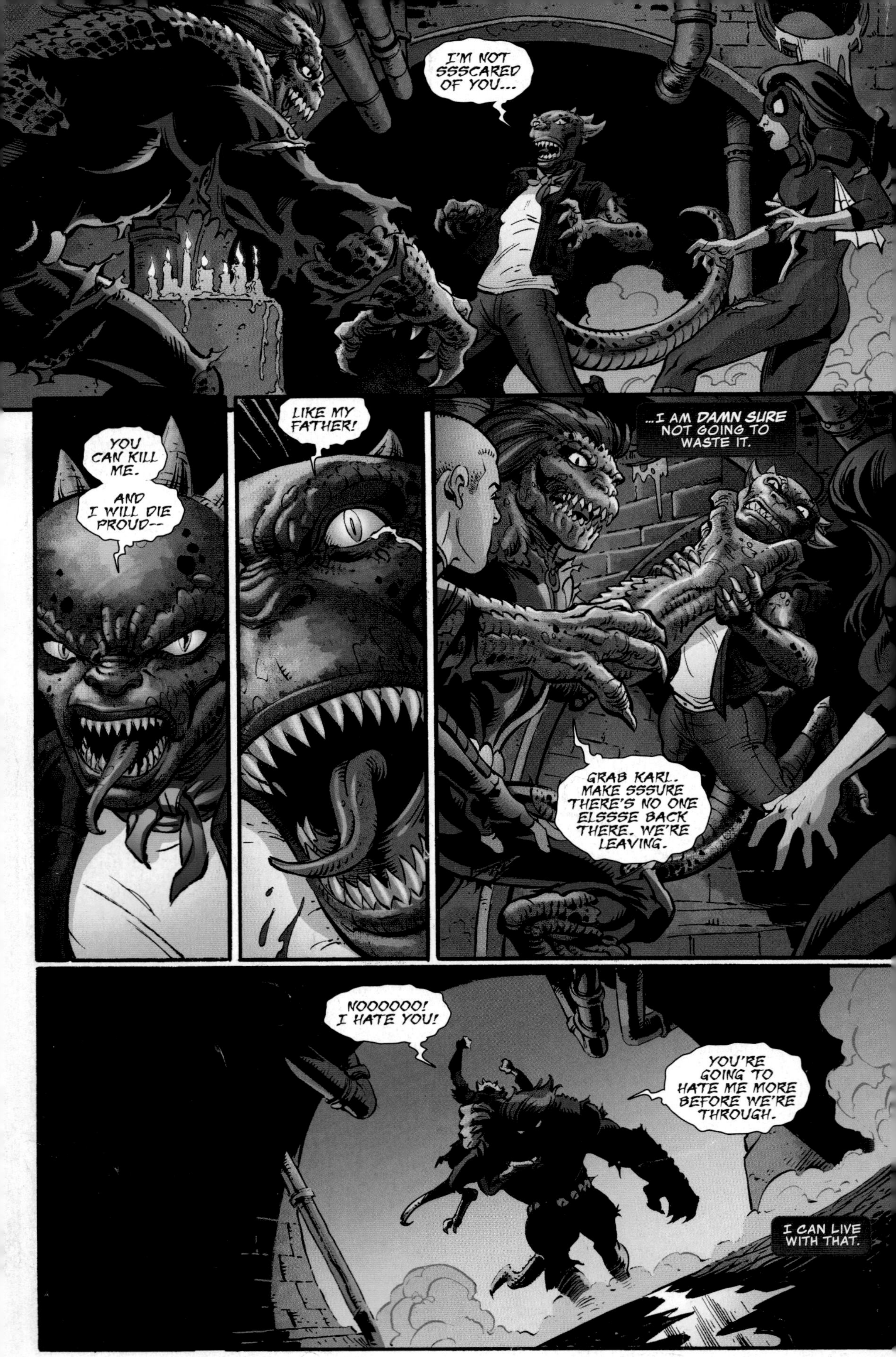

I'M NOT SSSCARED OF YOU...
YOU CAN KILL ME.
AND I WILL DIE PROUD--
LIKE MY FATHER!
...I AM DAMN SURE NOT GOING TO WASTE IT.
GRAB KARL. MAKE SSSURE THERE'S NO ONE ELSSSE BACK THERE. WE'RE LEAVING.
NOOOOOO! I HATE YOU!
YOU'RE GOING TO HATE ME MORE BEFORE WE'RE THROUGH.
I CAN LIVE WITH THAT.

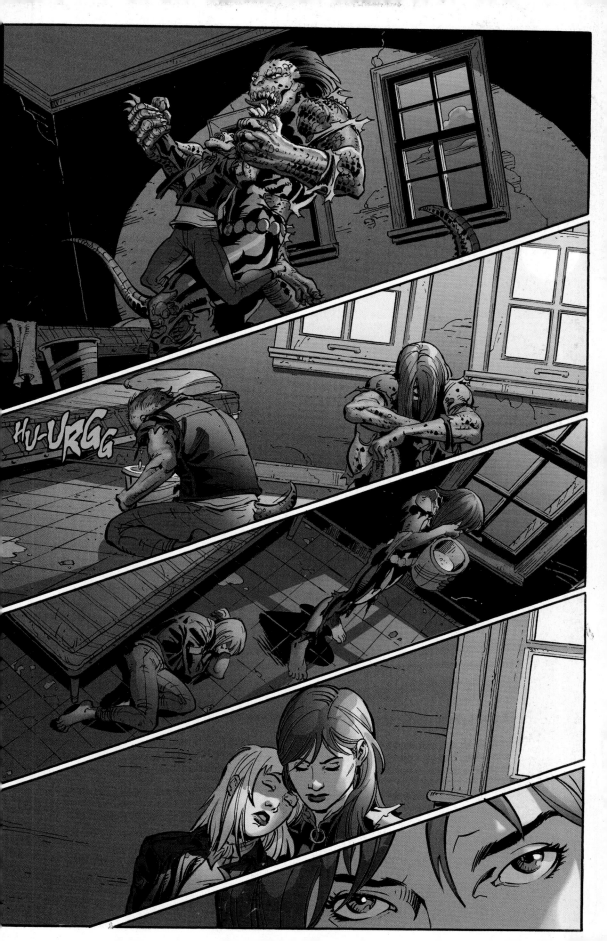

HU-URGG

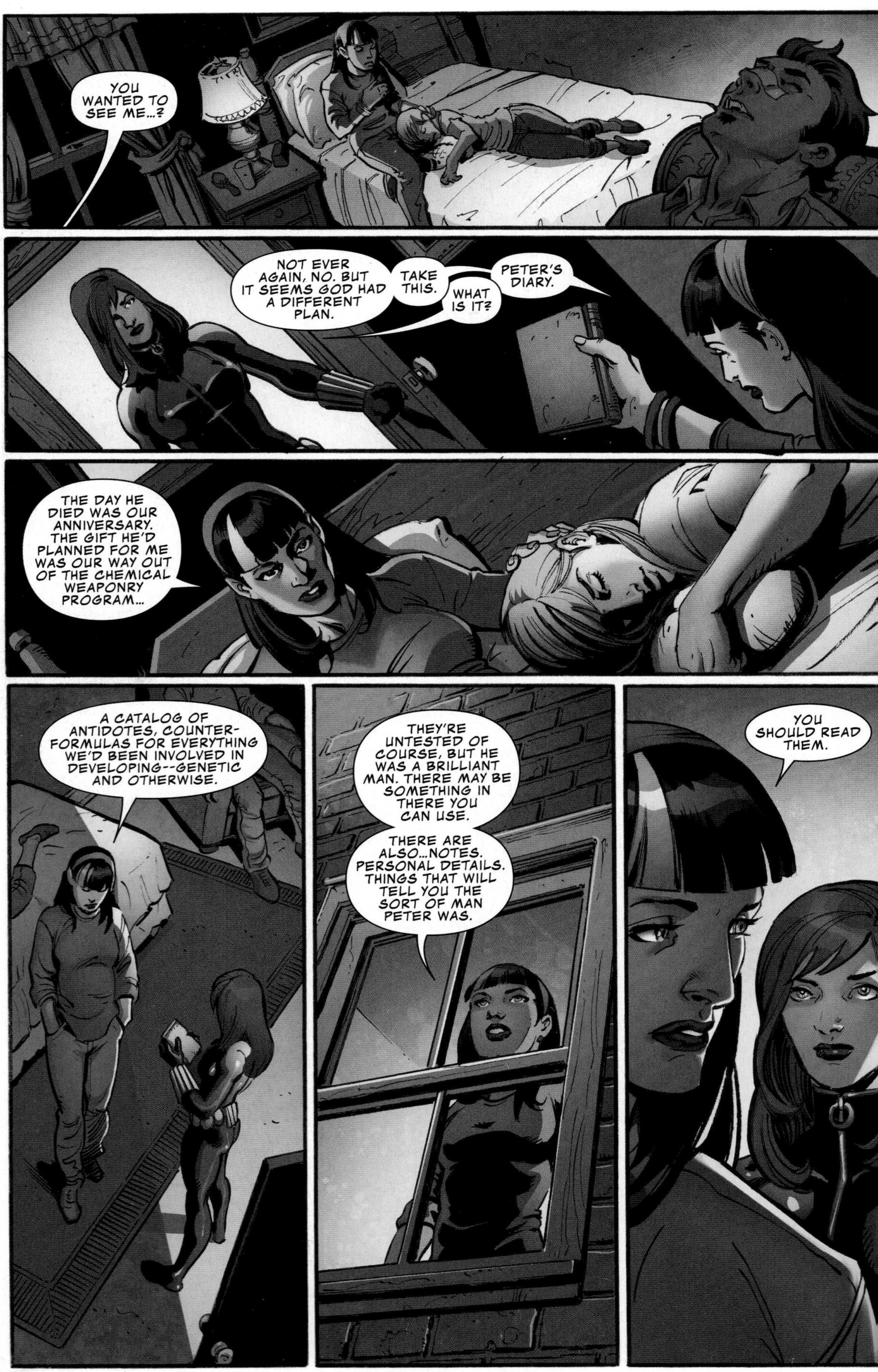
YOU WANTED TO SEE ME...?
NOT EVER AGAIN, NO. BUT IT SEEMS GOD HAD A DIFFERENT PLAN.
TAKE THIS.
WHAT IS IT?
PETER'S DIARY.
THE DAY HE DIED WAS OUR ANNIVERSARY. THE GIFT HE'D PLANNED FOR ME WAS OUR WAY OUT OF THE CHEMICAL WEAPONRY PROGRAM...
A CATALOG OF ANTIDOTES, COUNTER-FORMULAS FOR EVERYTHING WE'D BEEN INVOLVED IN DEVELOPING--GENETIC AND OTHERWISE.
THEY'RE UNTESTED OF COURSE, BUT HE WAS A BRILLIANT MAN. THERE MAY BE SOMETHING IN THERE YOU CAN USE.
THERE ARE ALSO...NOTES. PERSONAL DETAILS. THINGS THAT WILL TELL YOU THE SORT OF MAN PETER WAS.
YOU SHOULD READ THEM.

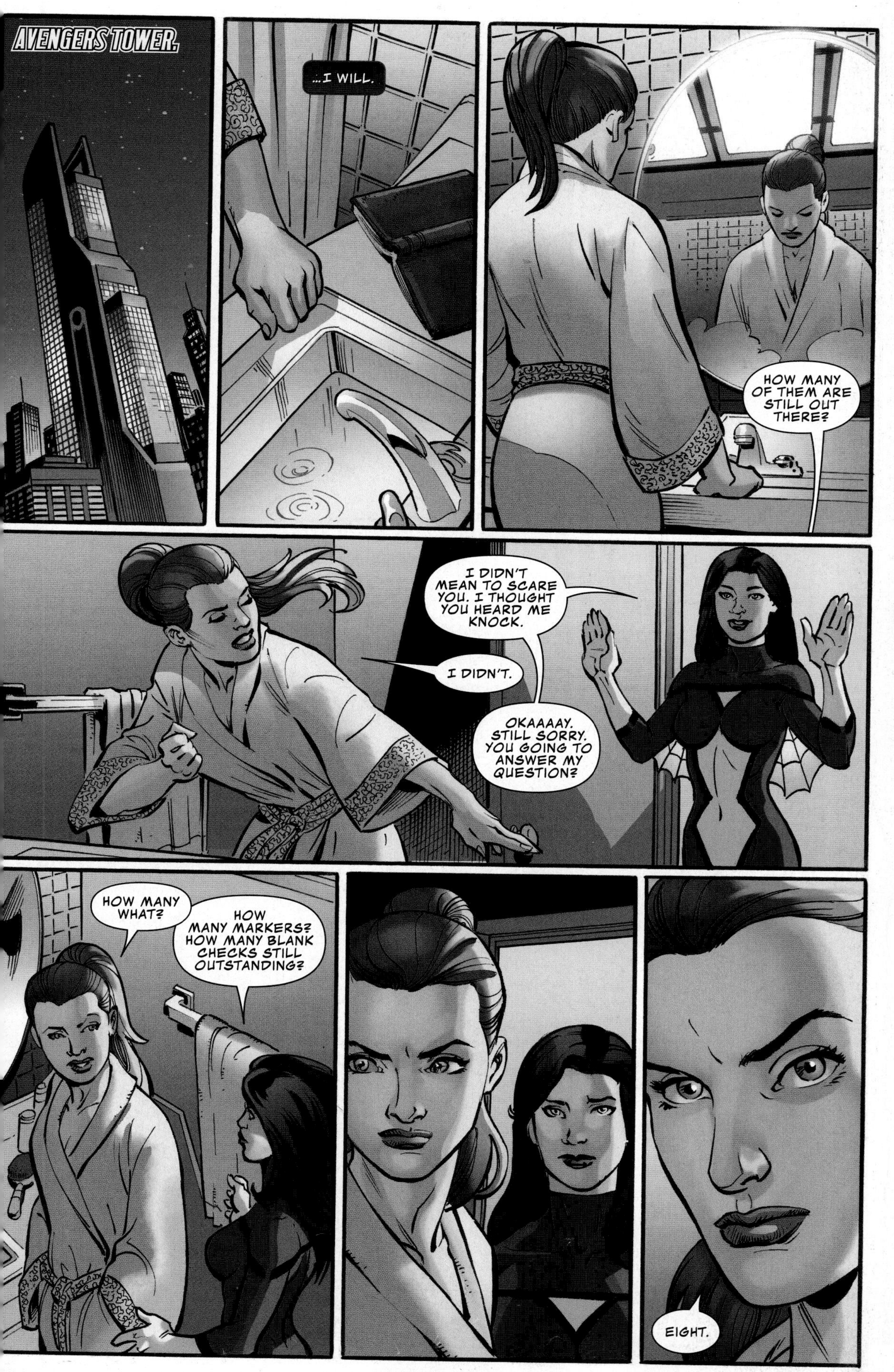
AVENGERS TOWER.
...I WILL.
HOW MANY OF THEM ARE STILL OUT THERE?
I DIDN'T MEAN TO SCARE YOU. I THOUGHT YOU HEARD ME KNOCK.
I DIDN'T.
OKAAAAY. STILL SORRY. YOU GOING TO ANSWER MY QUESTION?
HOW MANY WHAT?
HOW MANY MARKERS? HOW MANY BLANK CHECKS STILL OUTSTANDING?
EIGHT.

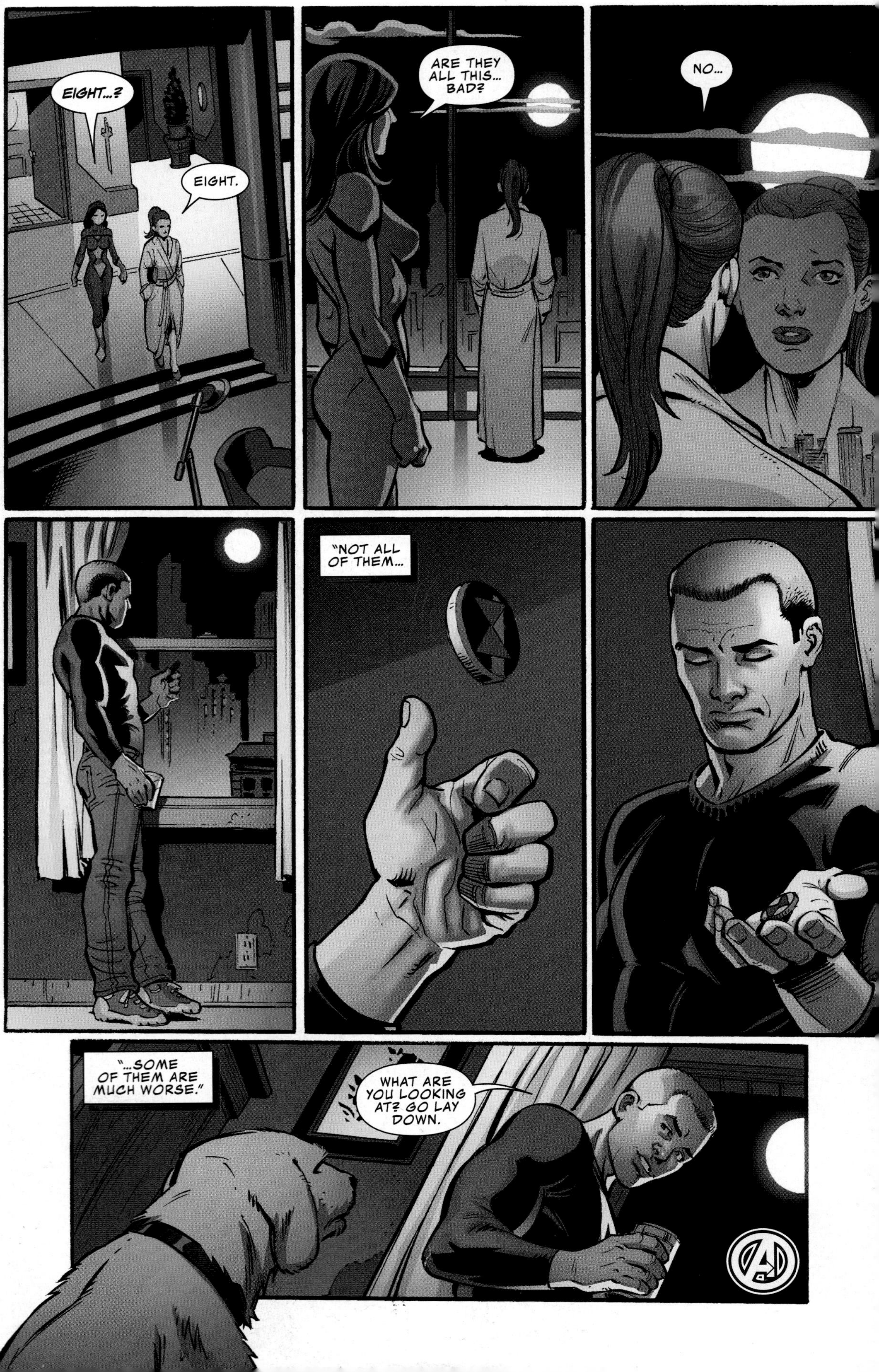
EIGHT...?
EIGHT.
ARE THEY ALL THIS... BAD?
NO...
"NOT ALL OF THEM...
"...SOME OF THEM ARE MUCH WORSE."
WHAT ARE YOU LOOKING AT? GO LAY DOWN.

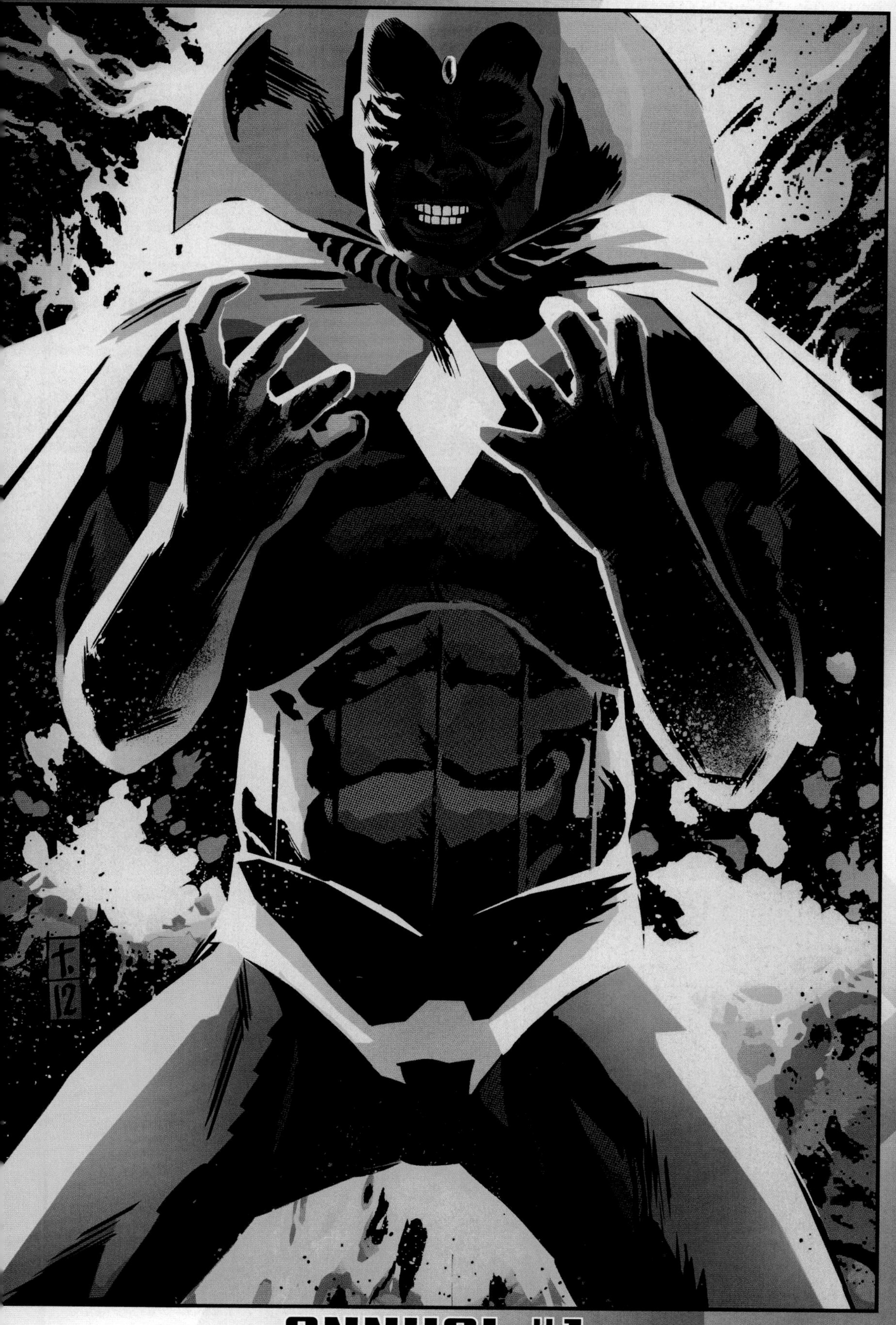

ANNUAL #1

AND THERE CAME A DAY, A DAY UNLIKE ANY OTHER, WHEN EARTH'S MIGHTIEST HEROES FOUND THEMSELVES UNITED AGAINST A COMMON THREAT! ON THAT DAY, THE AVENGERS WERE BORN, TO FIGHT THE FOES NO SINGLE SUPER HERO COULD WITHSTAND!

AVENGERS ASSEMBLE

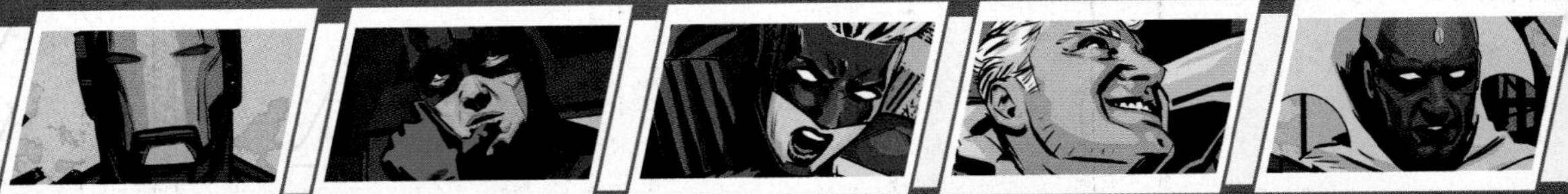

IRON MAN
TONY STARK
BILLIONAIRE TECHNOLOGIST,
HIGH-TECH ARMOR

GIANT-MAN
HANK PYM
DOCTOR OF SCIENCE.
GROWS. SHRINKS.

CAPTAIN MARVEL
CAROL DANVERS
FIGHTER PILOT,
FLIES, ZAPS, PUNCHES

QUICKSILVER
PIETRO MAXIMOFF
QUICK-TEMPERED
SUPER-SPEEDSTER

THE VISION
DENSITY MANIPULATION,
THERMOSCOPIC
VISION

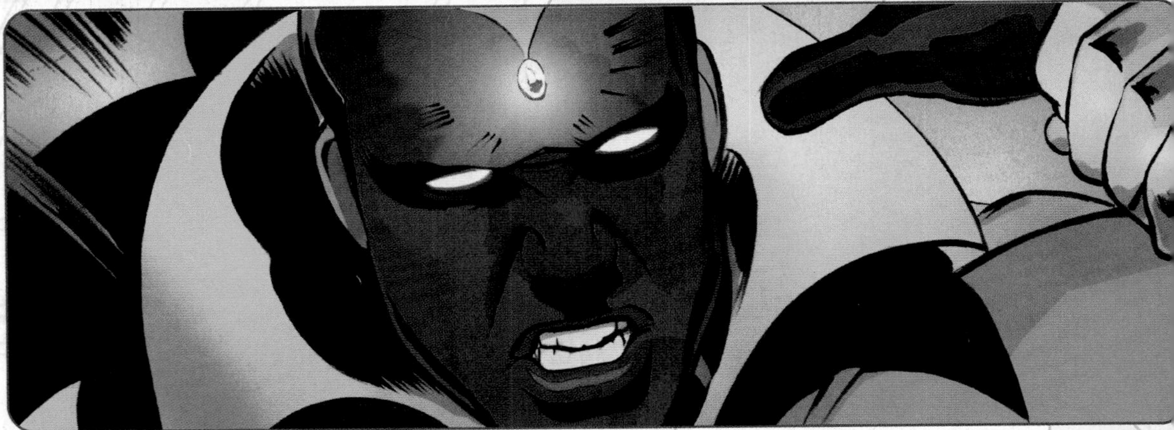

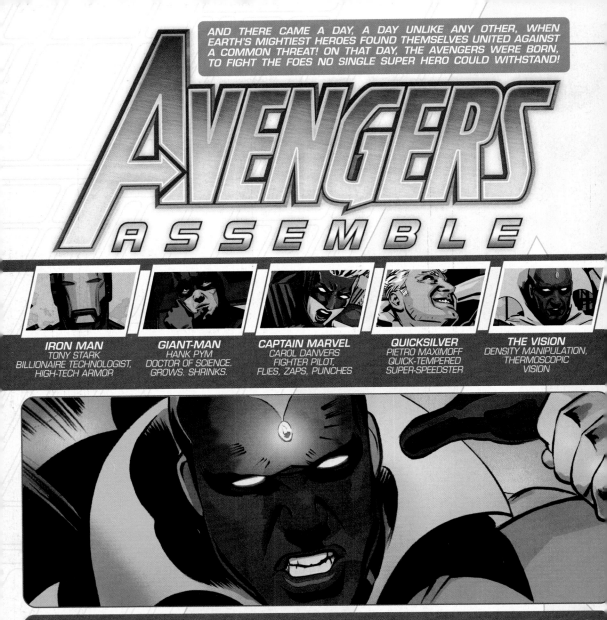

Created by The Avengers' nemesis Ultron as a being of destruction, the synthezoid known as the Vision overcame his villainous origins to become a force for good. Eventually he even joined the band of heroes he had been created to destroy.

As an Avenger, the Vision fell in love with his teammate, Wanda Maximoff. The two eventually married and had two children, Thomas and William. However, Thomas and William had been created through subconscious use of Wanda's magic powers. When the truth was revealed, the cyphers were no more and the marriage between Wanda and the Vision fell apart.

The loss of their children eventually drove Wanda mad, and in the fallout of her magic-enhanced delirium, the Vision was destroyed. After years of being disassembled, the Vision has returned. But though the pieces are all in the right place, whether or not the Vision is whole again remains to be seen...

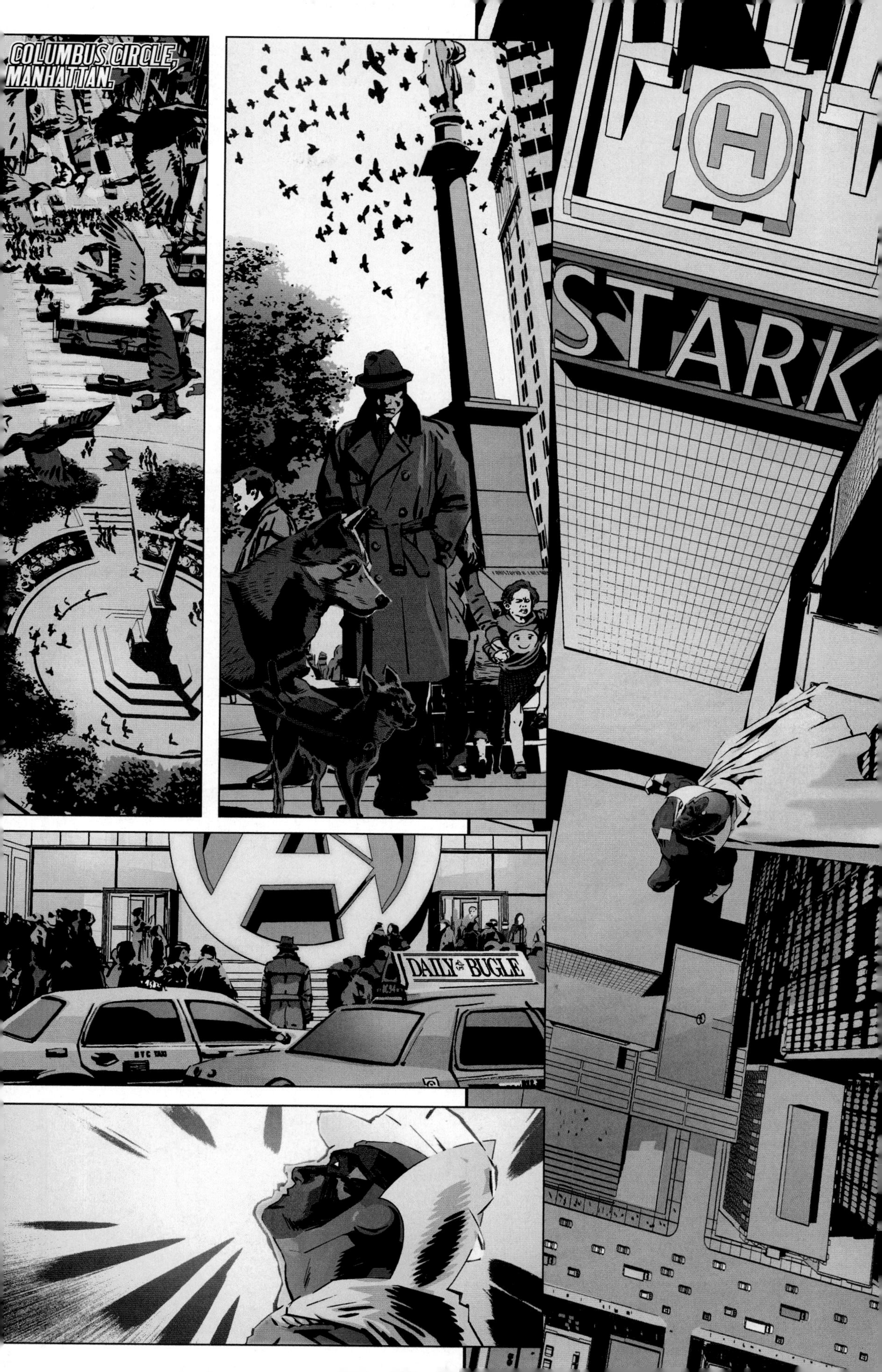
COLUMBUS CIRCLE, MANHATTAN.
STARK
DAILY BUGLE
NYC TAXI

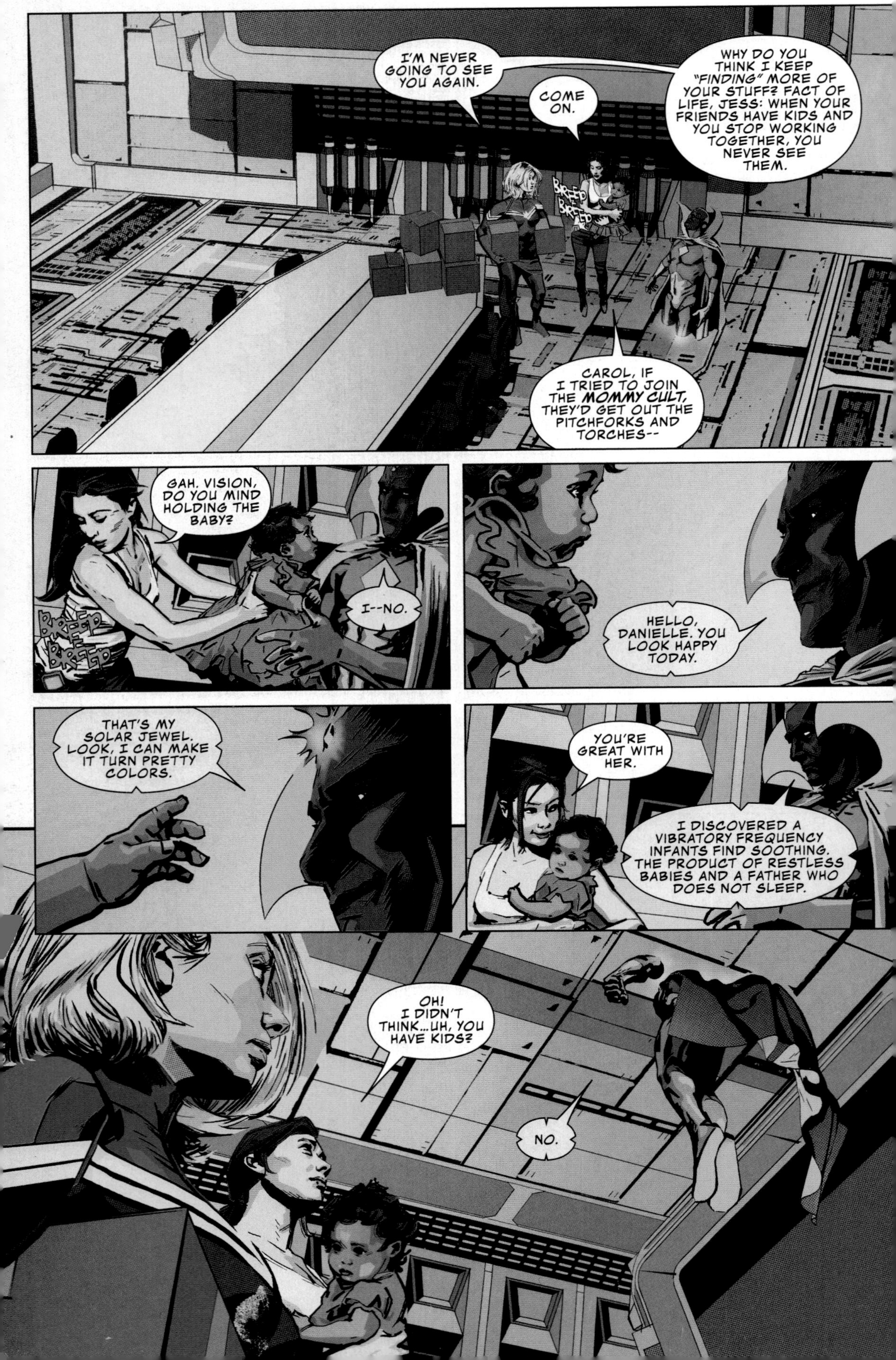
I'M NEVER GOING TO SEE YOU AGAIN.
COME ON.
WHY DO YOU THINK I KEEP "FINDING" MORE OF YOUR STUFF? FACT OF LIFE, JESS: WHEN YOUR FRIENDS HAVE KIDS AND YOU STOP WORKING TOGETHER, YOU NEVER SEE THEM.
BREEP BREEP
CAROL, IF I TRIED TO JOIN THE MOMMY CULT, THEY'D GET OUT THE PITCHFORKS AND TORCHES--
GAH. VISION, DO YOU MIND HOLDING THE BABY?
I--NO.
BREEP BREEP
HELLO, DANIELLE. YOU LOOK HAPPY TODAY.
THAT'S MY SOLAR JEWEL. LOOK, I CAN MAKE IT TURN PRETTY COLORS.
YOU'RE GREAT WITH HER.
I DISCOVERED A VIBRATORY FREQUENCY INFANTS FIND SOOTHING. THE PRODUCT OF RESTLESS BABIES AND A FATHER WHO DOES NOT SLEEP.
OH! I DIDN'T THINK...UH, YOU HAVE KIDS?
NO.

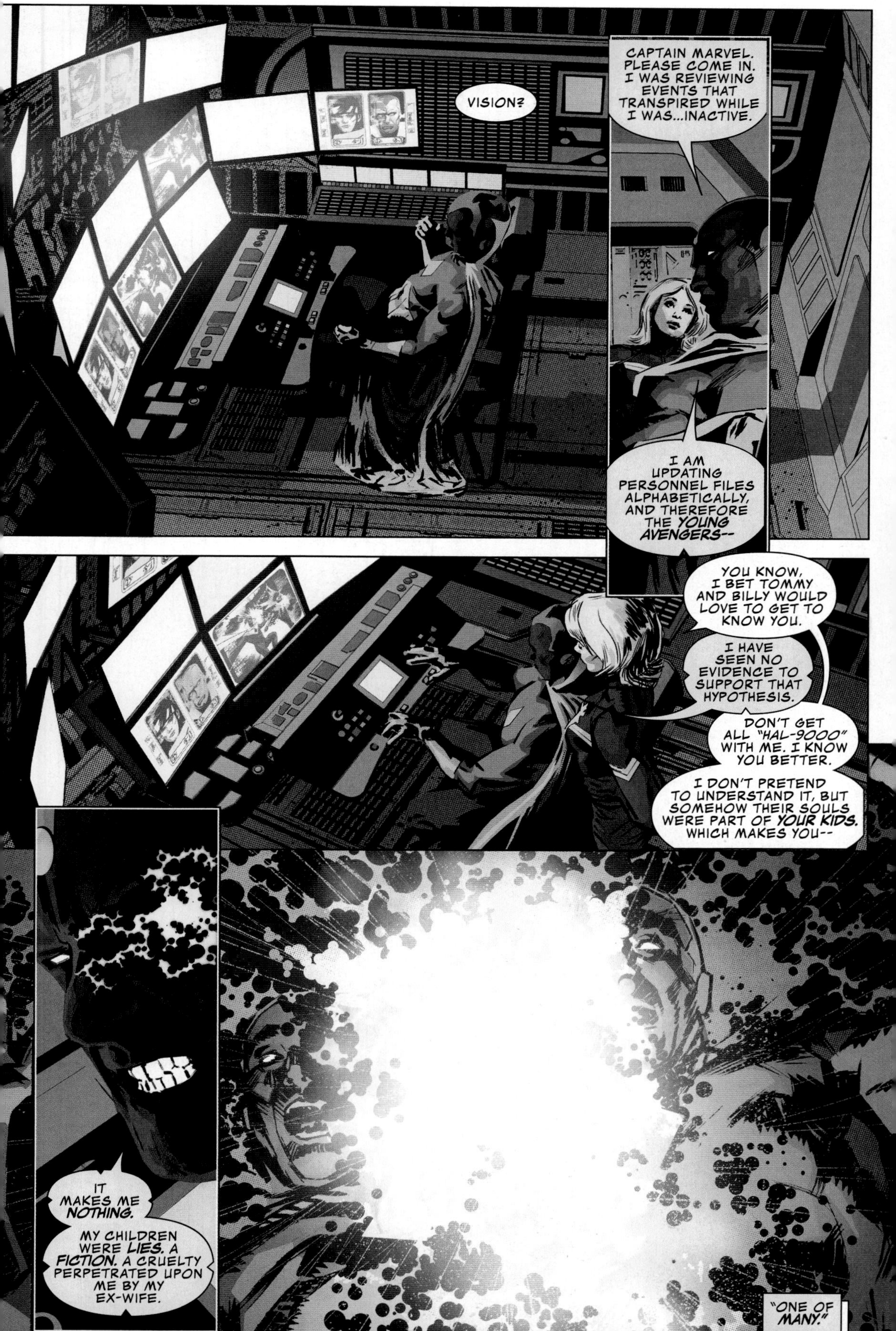
VISION?
CAPTAIN MARVEL. PLEASE COME IN. I WAS REVIEWING EVENTS THAT TRANSPIRED WHILE I WAS...INACTIVE.
I AM UPDATING PERSONNEL FILES ALPHABETICALLY, AND THEREFORE THE YOUNG AVENGERS--
YOU KNOW, I BET TOMMY AND BILLY WOULD LOVE TO GET TO KNOW YOU.
I HAVE SEEN NO EVIDENCE TO SUPPORT THAT HYPOTHESIS.
DON'T GET ALL "HAL-9000" WITH ME. I KNOW YOU BETTER.
I DON'T PRETEND TO UNDERSTAND IT, BUT SOMEHOW THEIR SOULS WERE PART OF YOUR KIDS. WHICH MAKES YOU--
IT MAKES ME NOTHING.
MY CHILDREN WERE LIES. A FICTION. A CRUELTY PERPETRATED UPON ME BY MY EX-WIFE.
"ONE OF MANY."

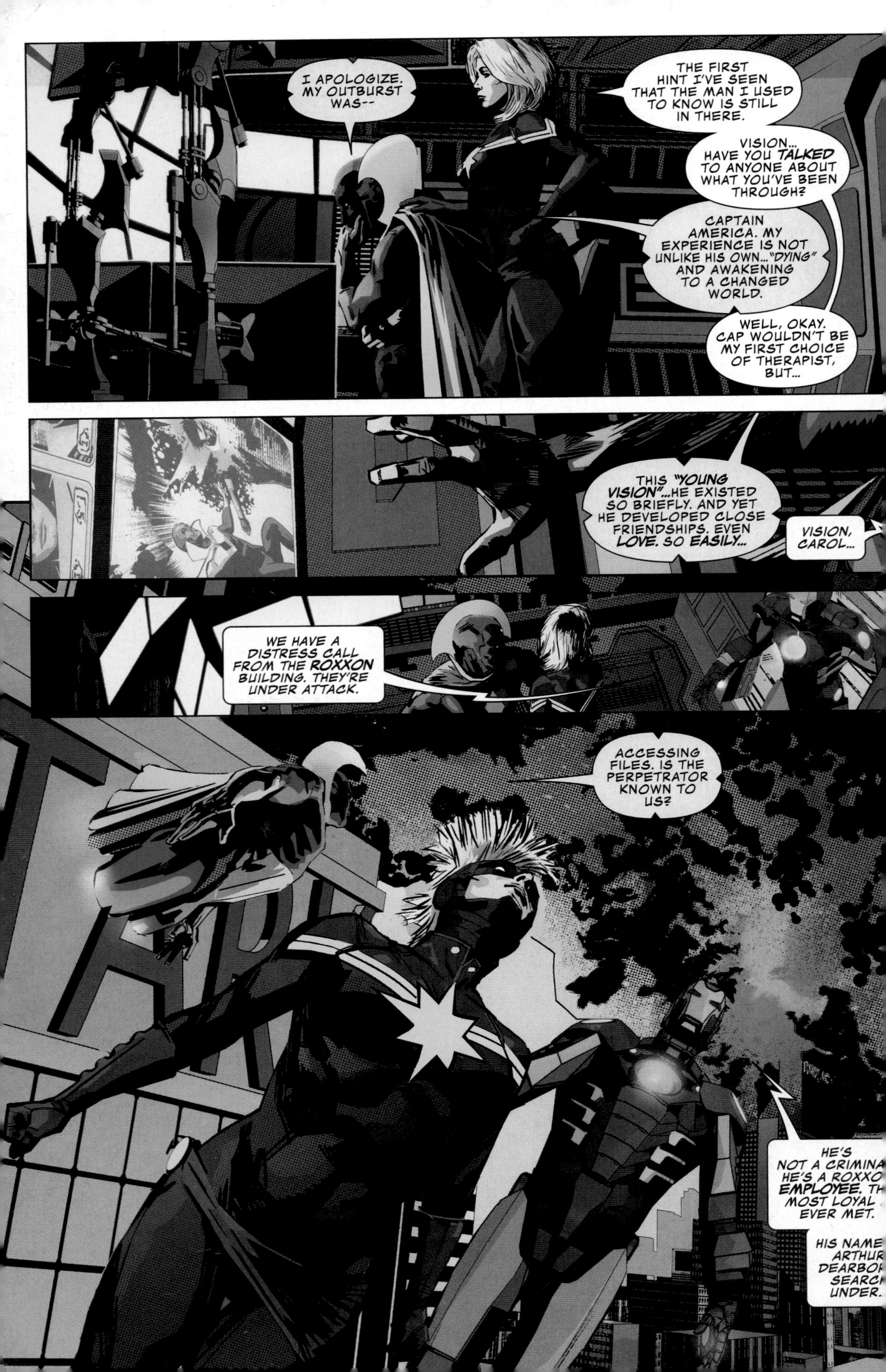
I APOLOGIZE. MY OUTBURST WAS--
THE FIRST HINT I'VE SEEN THAT THE MAN I USED TO KNOW IS STILL IN THERE.
VISION... HAVE YOU TALKED TO ANYONE ABOUT WHAT YOU'VE BEEN THROUGH?
CAPTAIN AMERICA. MY EXPERIENCE IS NOT UNLIKE HIS OWN..."DYING" AND AWAKENING TO A CHANGED WORLD.
WELL, OKAY. CAP WOULDN'T BE MY FIRST CHOICE OF THERAPIST, BUT...
THIS "YOUNG VISION"...HE EXISTED SO BRIEFLY. AND YET HE DEVELOPED CLOSE FRIENDSHIPS. EVEN LOVE. SO EASILY...
VISION, CAROL...
WE HAVE A DISTRESS CALL FROM THE ROXXON BUILDING. THEY'RE UNDER ATTACK.
ACCESSING FILES. IS THE PERPETRATOR KNOWN TO US?
HE'S NOT A CRIMINA HE'S A ROXXO EMPLOYEE. TH MOST LOYAL EVER MET.
HIS NAME ARTHUR DEARBOR SEARC UNDER.

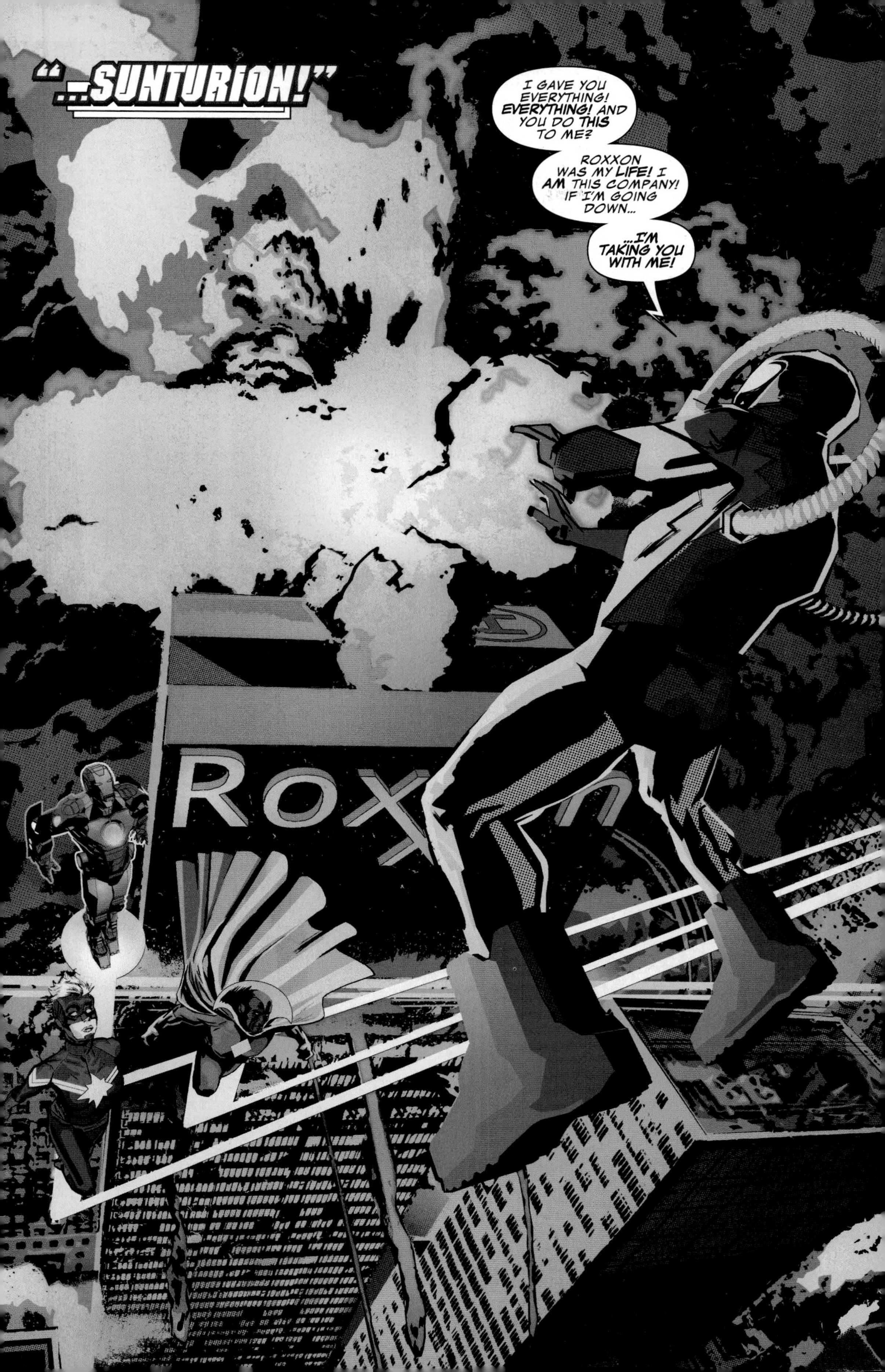
"...SUNTURION!"
I GAVE YOU EVERYTHING! EVERYTHING! AND YOU DO THIS TO ME?
ROXXON WAS MY LIFE! I AM THIS COMPANY! IF I'M GOING DOWN...
...I'M TAKING YOU WITH ME!
ROX

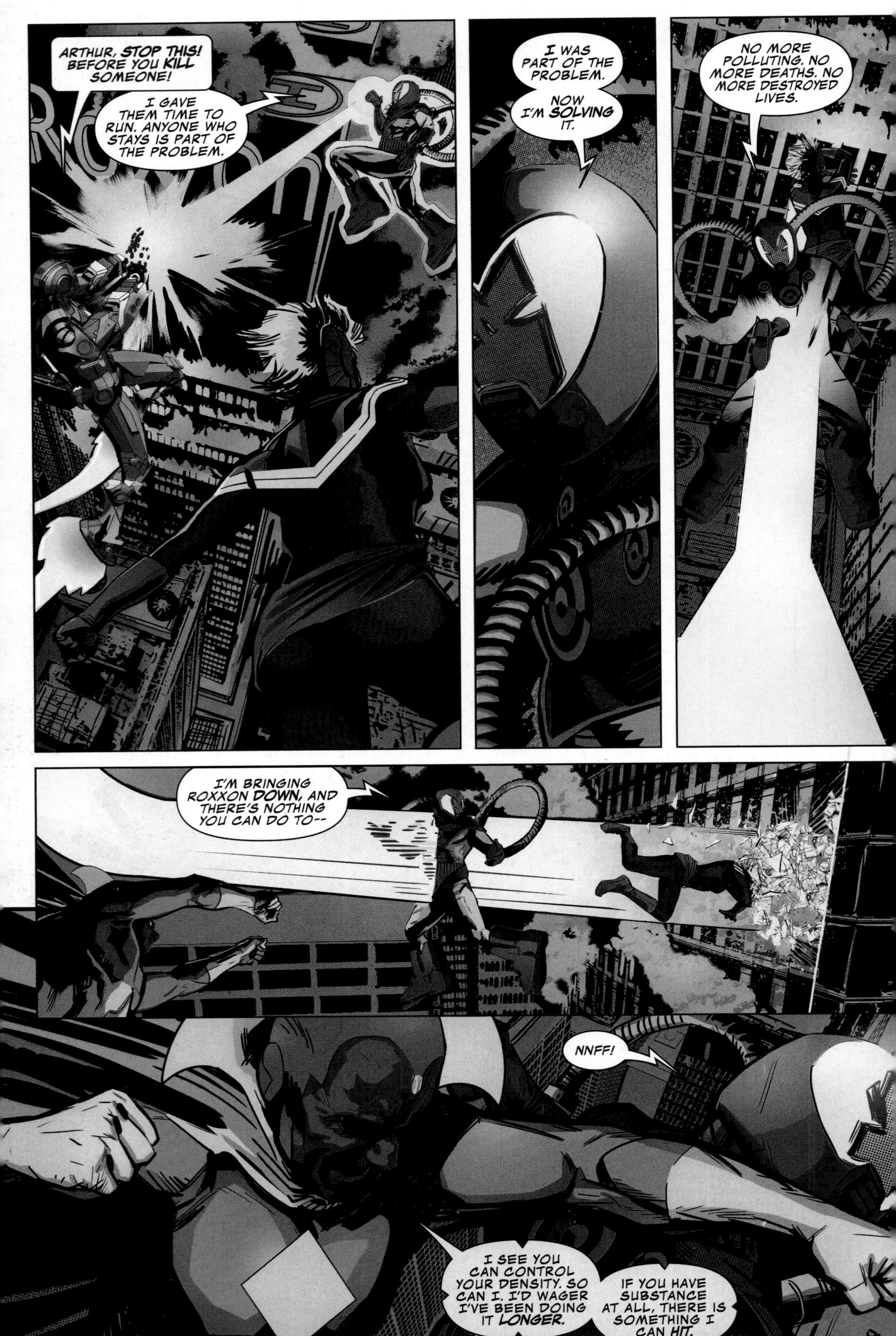
ARTHUR, STOP THIS! BEFORE YOU KILL SOMEONE!
I GAVE THEM TIME TO RUN. ANYONE WHO STAYS IS PART OF THE PROBLEM.
I WAS PART OF THE PROBLEM.
NOW I'M SOLVING IT.
NO MORE POLLUTING. NO MORE DEATHS. NO MORE DESTROYED LIVES.
I'M BRINGING ROXXON DOWN, AND THERE'S NOTHING YOU CAN DO TO--
NNFF!
I SEE YOU CAN CONTROL YOUR DENSITY. SO CAN I. I'D WAGER I'VE BEEN DOING IT LONGER.
IF YOU HAVE SUBSTANCE AT ALL, THERE IS SOMETHING I CAN HIT.

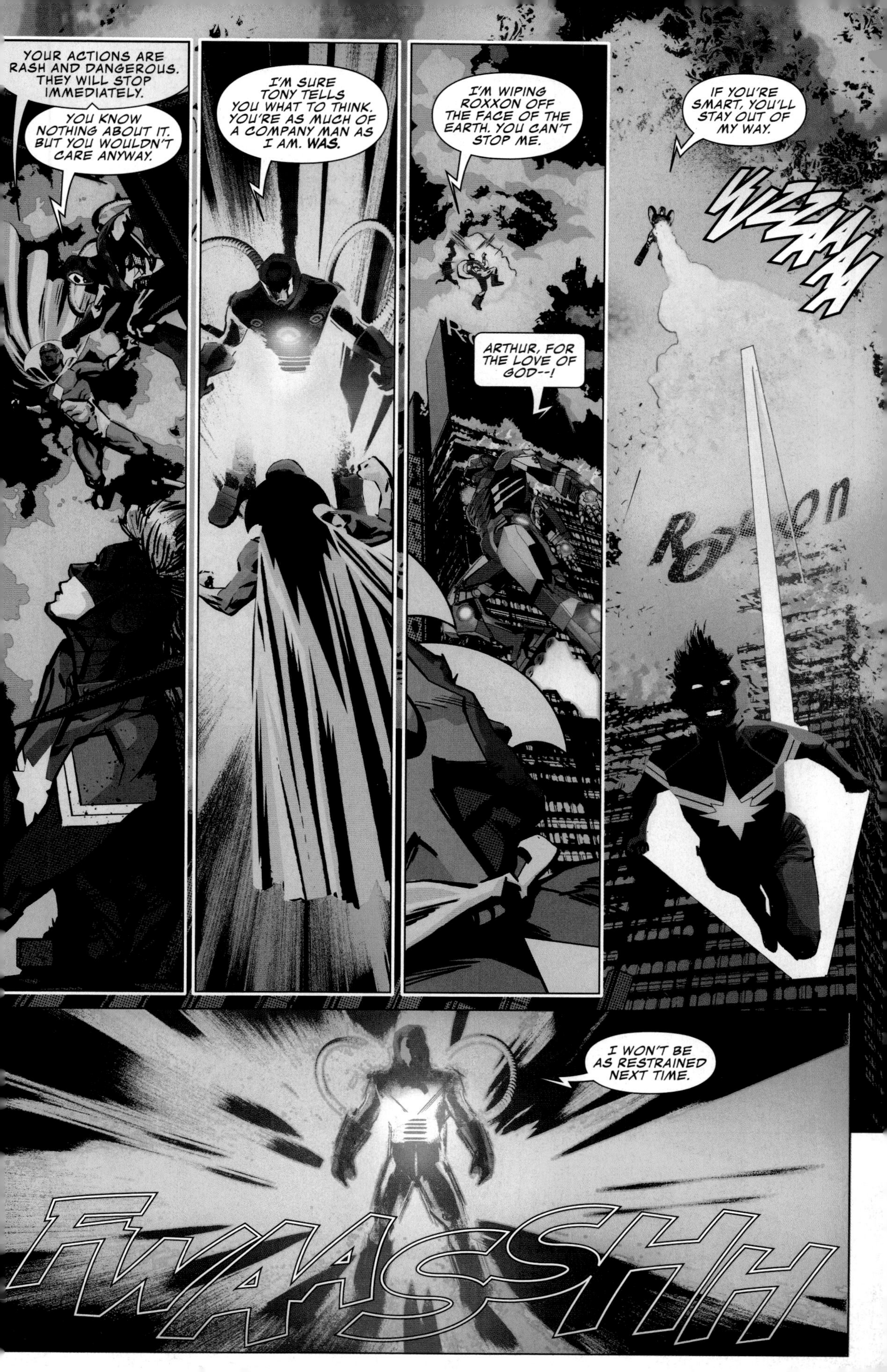
YOUR ACTIONS ARE RASH AND DANGEROUS. THEY WILL STOP IMMEDIATELY.
YOU KNOW NOTHING ABOUT IT. BUT YOU WOULDN'T CARE ANYWAY.
I'M SURE TONY TELLS YOU WHAT TO THINK. YOU'RE AS MUCH OF A COMPANY MAN AS I AM. WAS.
I'M WIPING ROXXON OFF THE FACE OF THE EARTH. YOU CAN'T STOP ME.
ARTHUR, FOR THE LOVE OF GOD--!
IF YOU'RE SMART, YOU'LL STAY OUT OF MY WAY.
VZZAAM
I WON'T BE AS RESTRAINED NEXT TIME.
FWASHH

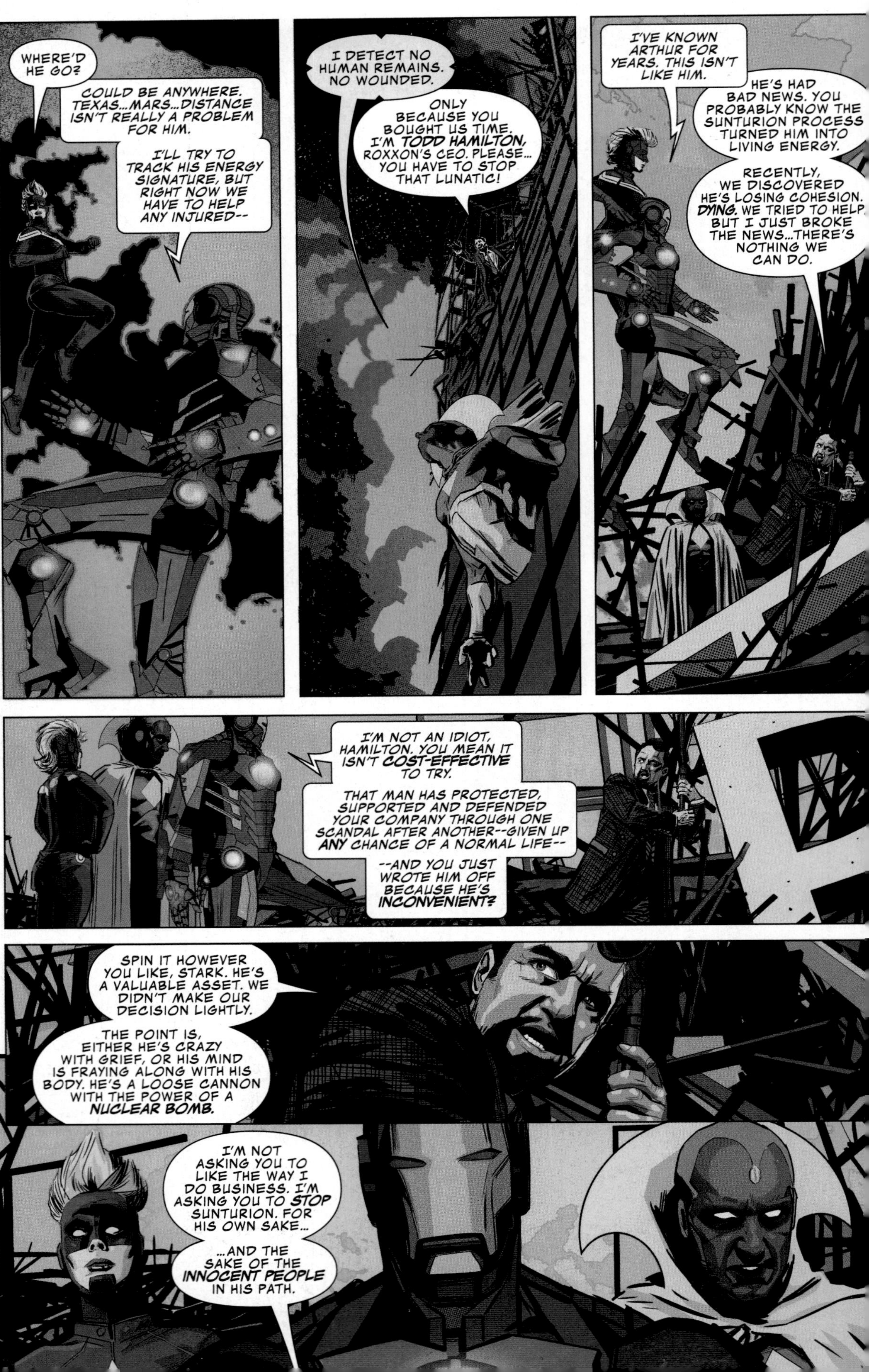
WHERE'D HE GO?
COULD BE ANYWHERE. TEXAS...MARS...DISTANCE ISN'T REALLY A PROBLEM FOR HIM.
I'LL TRY TO TRACK HIS ENERGY SIGNATURE, BUT RIGHT NOW WE HAVE TO HELP ANY INJURED--
I DETECT NO HUMAN REMAINS. NO WOUNDED.
ONLY BECAUSE YOU BOUGHT US TIME. I'M TODD HAMILTON, ROXXON'S CEO. PLEASE... YOU HAVE TO STOP THAT LUNATIC!
I'VE KNOWN ARTHUR FOR YEARS. THIS ISN'T LIKE HIM.
HE'S HAD BAD NEWS. YOU PROBABLY KNOW THE SUNTURION PROCESS TURNED HIM INTO LIVING ENERGY.
RECENTLY, WE DISCOVERED HE'S LOSING COHESION. DYING. WE TRIED TO HELP, BUT I JUST BROKE THE NEWS...THERE'S NOTHING WE CAN DO.
I'M NOT AN IDIOT, HAMILTON. YOU MEAN IT ISN'T COST-EFFECTIVE TO TRY.
THAT MAN HAS PROTECTED, SUPPORTED AND DEFENDED YOUR COMPANY THROUGH ONE SCANDAL AFTER ANOTHER--GIVEN UP ANY CHANCE OF A NORMAL LIFE--
--AND YOU JUST WROTE HIM OFF BECAUSE HE'S INCONVENIENT?
SPIN IT HOWEVER YOU LIKE, STARK. HE'S A VALUABLE ASSET. WE DIDN'T MAKE OUR DECISION LIGHTLY.
THE POINT IS, EITHER HE'S CRAZY WITH GRIEF, OR HIS MIND IS FRAYING ALONG WITH HIS BODY. HE'S A LOOSE CANNON WITH THE POWER OF A NUCLEAR BOMB.
I'M NOT ASKING YOU TO LIKE THE WAY I DO BUSINESS. I'M ASKING YOU TO STOP SUNTURION. FOR HIS OWN SAKE...
...AND THE SAKE OF THE INNOCENT PEOPLE IN HIS PATH.

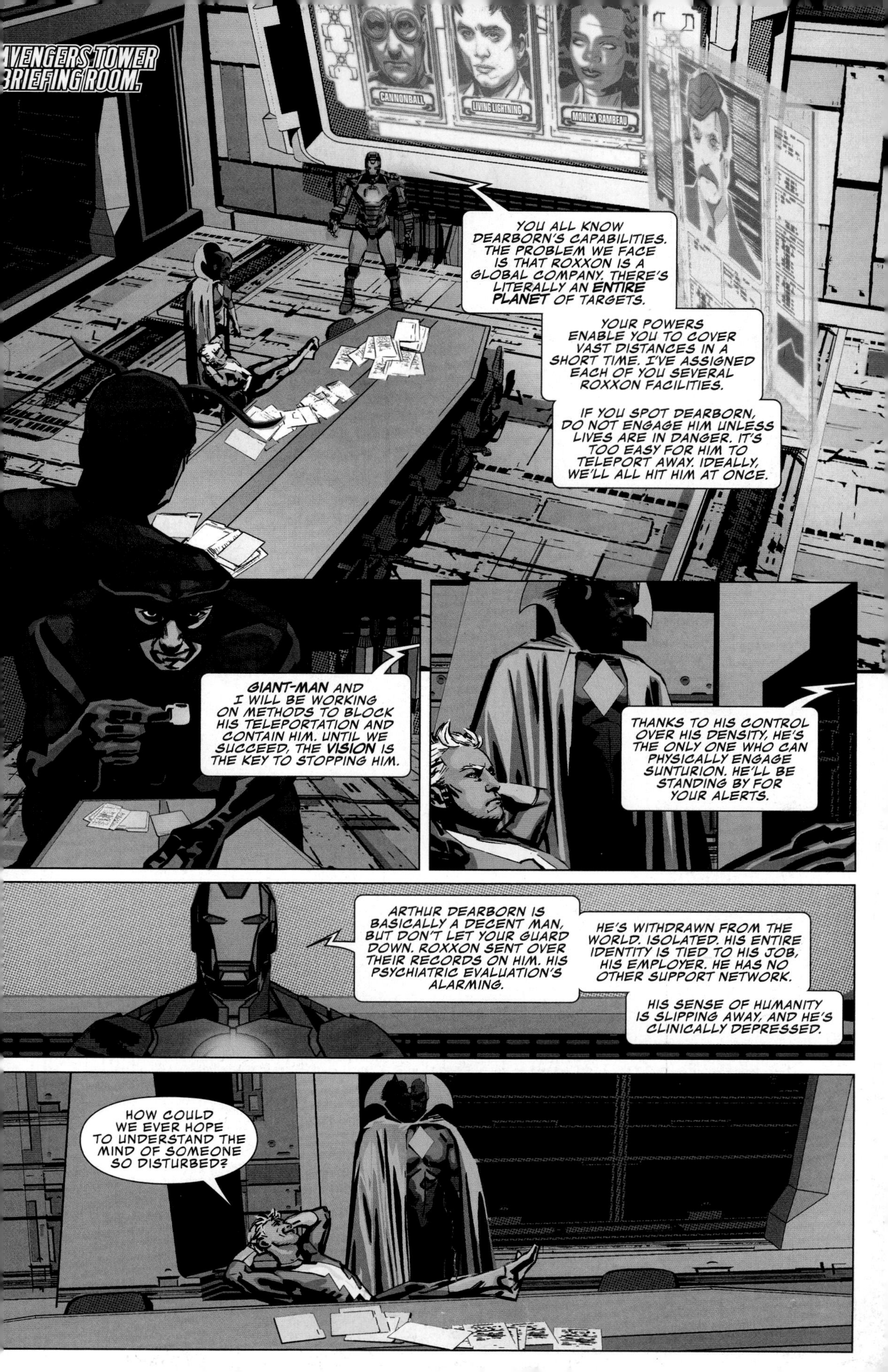
AVENGERS TOWER BRIEFING ROOM.
CANNONBALL
LIVING LIGHTNING
MONICA RAMBEAU
YOU ALL KNOW DEARBORN'S CAPABILITIES. THE PROBLEM WE FACE IS THAT ROXXON IS A GLOBAL COMPANY. THERE'S LITERALLY AN ENTIRE PLANET OF TARGETS.
YOUR POWERS ENABLE YOU TO COVER VAST DISTANCES IN A SHORT TIME. I'VE ASSIGNED EACH OF YOU SEVERAL ROXXON FACILITIES.
IF YOU SPOT DEARBORN, DO NOT ENGAGE HIM UNLESS LIVES ARE IN DANGER. IT'S TOO EASY FOR HIM TO TELEPORT AWAY. IDEALLY, WE'LL ALL HIT HIM AT ONCE.
GIANT-MAN AND I WILL BE WORKING ON METHODS TO BLOCK HIS TELEPORTATION AND CONTAIN HIM. UNTIL WE SUCCEED, THE VISION IS THE KEY TO STOPPING HIM.
THANKS TO HIS CONTROL OVER HIS DENSITY, HE'S THE ONLY ONE WHO CAN PHYSICALLY ENGAGE SUNTURION. HE'LL BE STANDING BY FOR YOUR ALERTS.
ARTHUR DEARBORN IS BASICALLY A DECENT MAN, BUT DON'T LET YOUR GUARD DOWN. ROXXON SENT OVER THEIR RECORDS ON HIM. HIS PSYCHIATRIC EVALUATION'S ALARMING.
HE'S WITHDRAWN FROM THE WORLD. ISOLATED. HIS ENTIRE IDENTITY IS TIED TO HIS JOB, HIS EMPLOYER. HE HAS NO OTHER SUPPORT NETWORK.
HIS SENSE OF HUMANITY IS SLIPPING AWAY, AND HE'S CLINICALLY DEPRESSED.
HOW COULD WE EVER HOPE TO UNDERSTAND THE MIND OF SOMEONE SO DISTURBED?

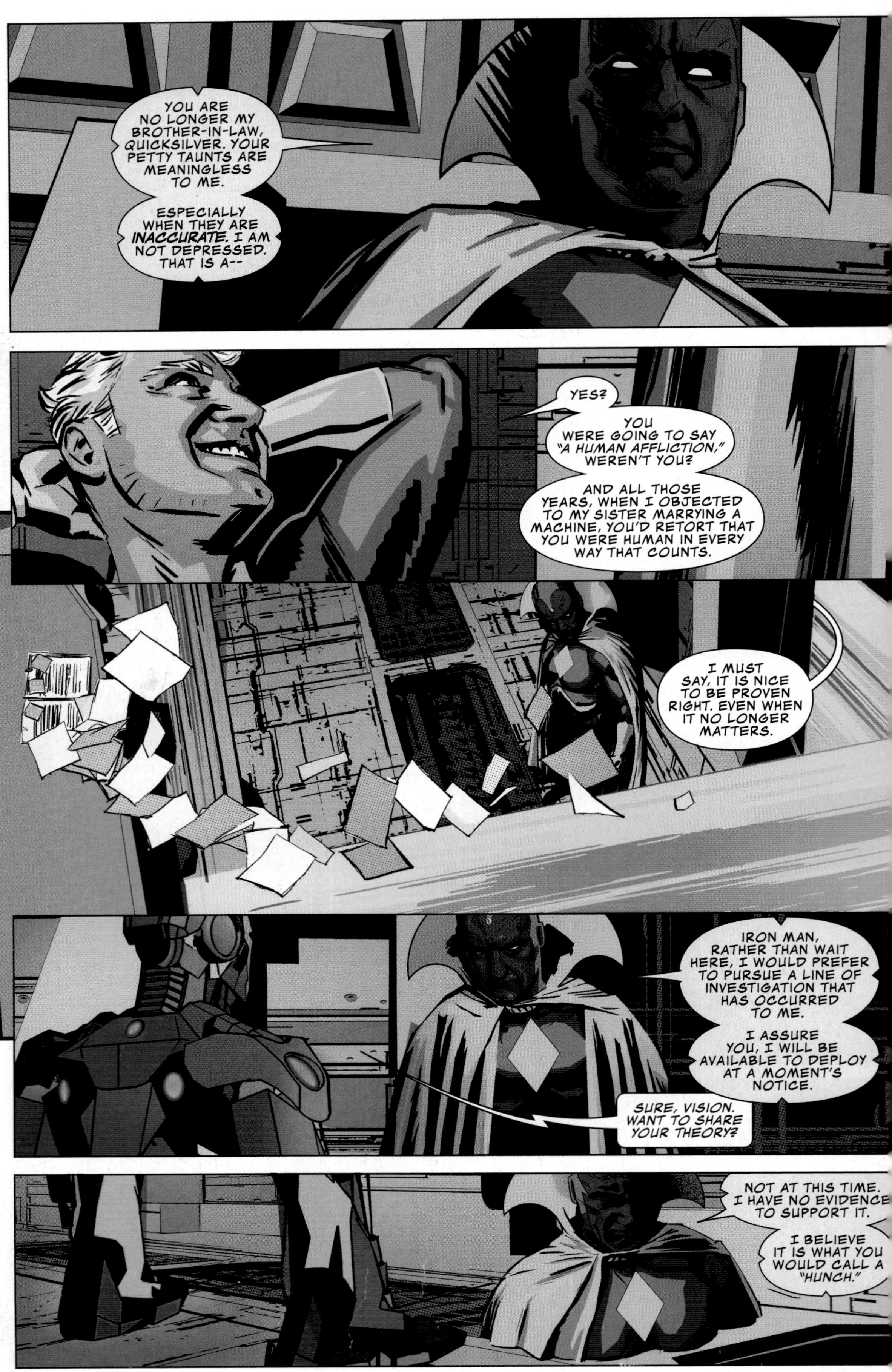
YOU ARE NO LONGER MY BROTHER-IN-LAW, QUICKSILVER. YOUR PETTY TAUNTS ARE MEANINGLESS TO ME.
ESPECIALLY WHEN THEY ARE INACCURATE. I AM NOT DEPRESSED. THAT IS A--
YES?
YOU WERE GOING TO SAY "A HUMAN AFFLICTION," WEREN'T YOU?
AND ALL THOSE YEARS, WHEN I OBJECTED TO MY SISTER MARRYING A MACHINE, YOU'D RETORT THAT YOU WERE HUMAN IN EVERY WAY THAT COUNTS.
I MUST SAY, IT IS NICE TO BE PROVEN RIGHT. EVEN WHEN IT NO LONGER MATTERS.
IRON MAN, RATHER THAN WAIT HERE, I WOULD PREFER TO PURSUE A LINE OF INVESTIGATION THAT HAS OCCURRED TO ME.
I ASSURE YOU, I WILL BE AVAILABLE TO DEPLOY AT A MOMENT'S NOTICE.
SURE, VISION. WANT TO SHARE YOUR THEORY?
NOT AT THIS TIME. I HAVE NO EVIDENCE TO SUPPORT IT.
I BELIEVE IT IS WHAT YOU WOULD CALL A "HUNCH."

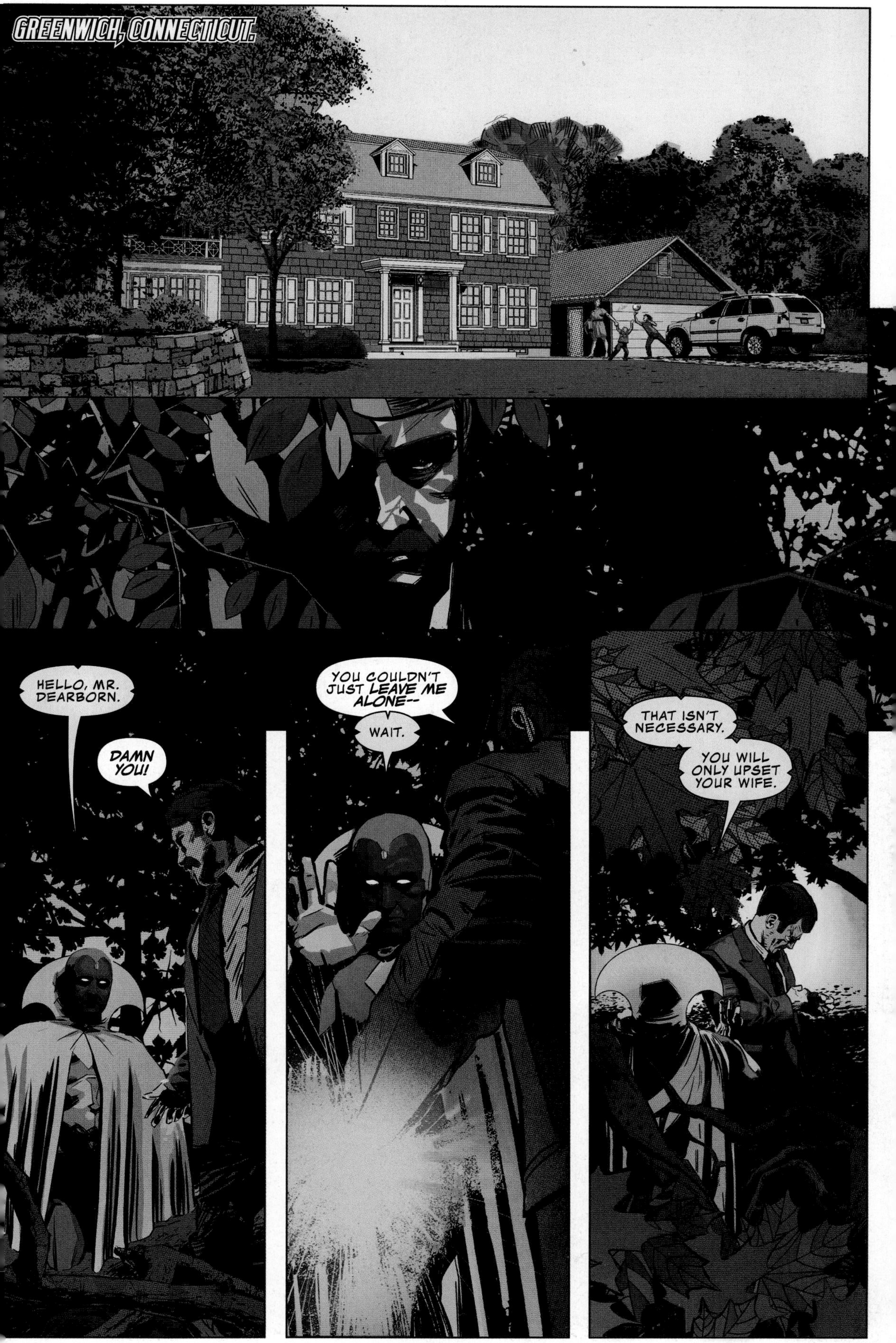
GREENWICH, CONNECTICUT.
HELLO, MR. DEARBORN.
DAMN YOU!
YOU COULDN'T JUST LEAVE ME ALONE--
WAIT.
THAT ISN'T NECESSARY.
YOU WILL ONLY UPSET YOUR WIFE.

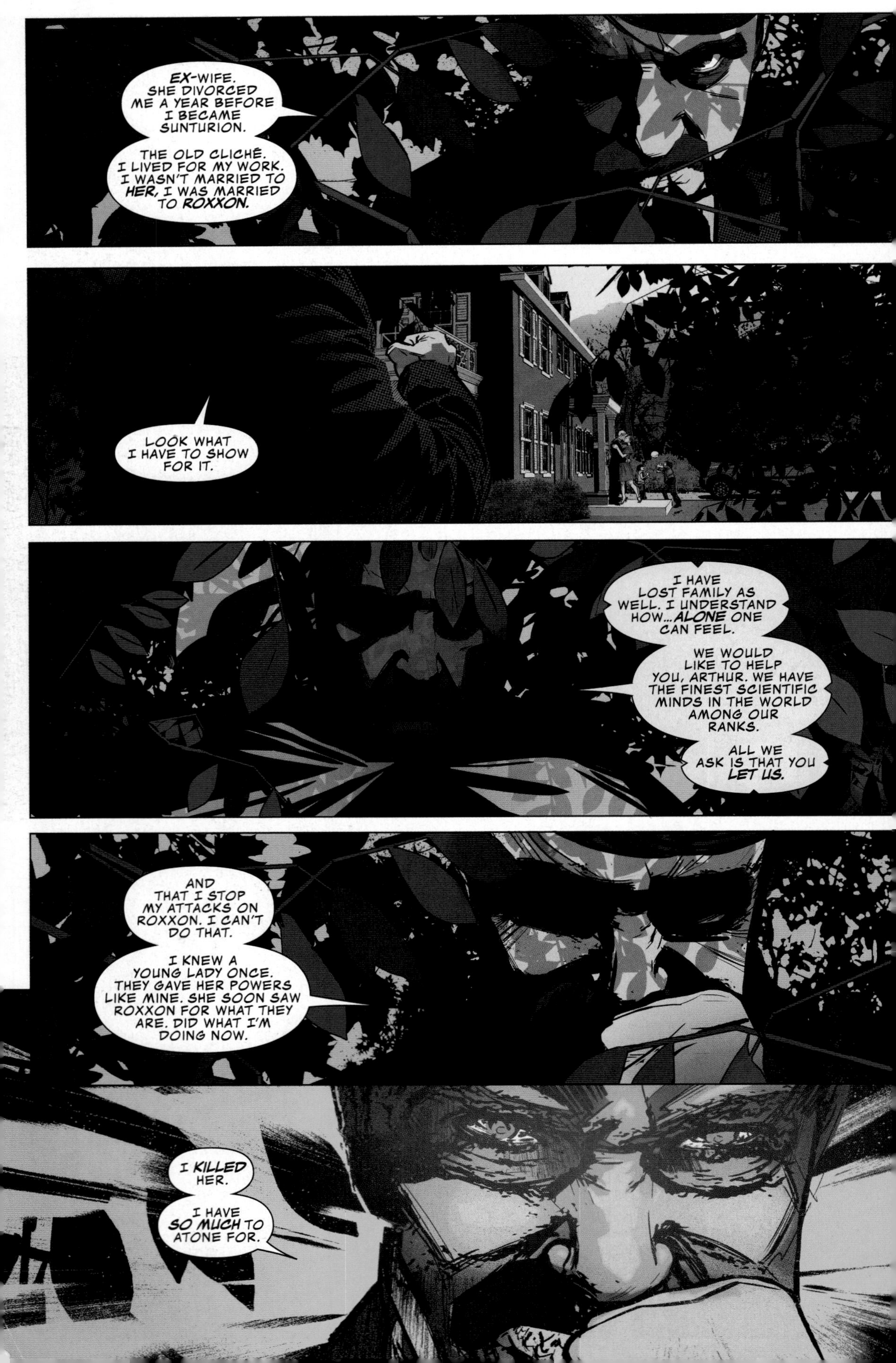
EX-WIFE. SHE DIVORCED ME A YEAR BEFORE I BECAME SUNTURION.
THE OLD CLICHÉ. I LIVED FOR MY WORK. I WASN'T MARRIED TO HER, I WAS MARRIED TO ROXXON.
LOOK WHAT I HAVE TO SHOW FOR IT.
I HAVE LOST FAMILY AS WELL. I UNDERSTAND HOW...ALONE ONE CAN FEEL.
WE WOULD LIKE TO HELP YOU, ARTHUR. WE HAVE THE FINEST SCIENTIFIC MINDS IN THE WORLD AMONG OUR RANKS.
ALL WE ASK IS THAT YOU LET US.
AND THAT I STOP MY ATTACKS ON ROXXON. I CAN'T DO THAT.
I KNEW A YOUNG LADY ONCE. THEY GAVE HER POWERS LIKE MINE. SHE SOON SAW ROXXON FOR WHAT THEY ARE. DID WHAT I'M DOING NOW.
I KILLED HER.
I HAVE SO MUCH TO ATONE FOR.

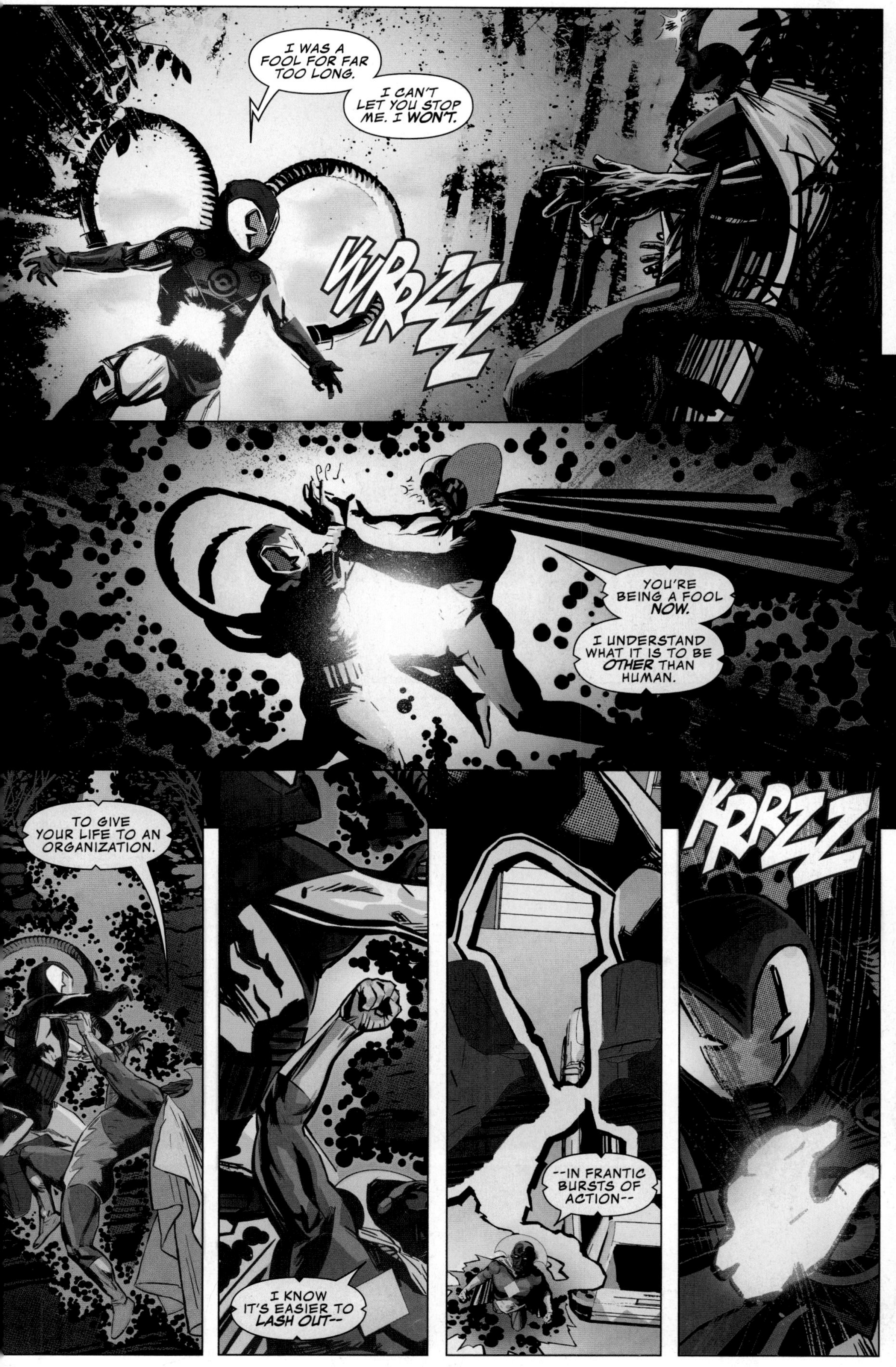
I WAS A FOOL FOR FAR TOO LONG.
I CAN'T LET YOU STOP ME. I WON'T.
VVRRZZZZ
YOU'RE BEING A FOOL NOW.
I UNDERSTAND WHAT IT IS TO BE OTHER THAN HUMAN.
TO GIVE YOUR LIFE TO AN ORGANIZATION.
I KNOW IT'S EASIER TO LASH OUT--
--IN FRANTIC BURSTS OF ACTION--
KRRZZ

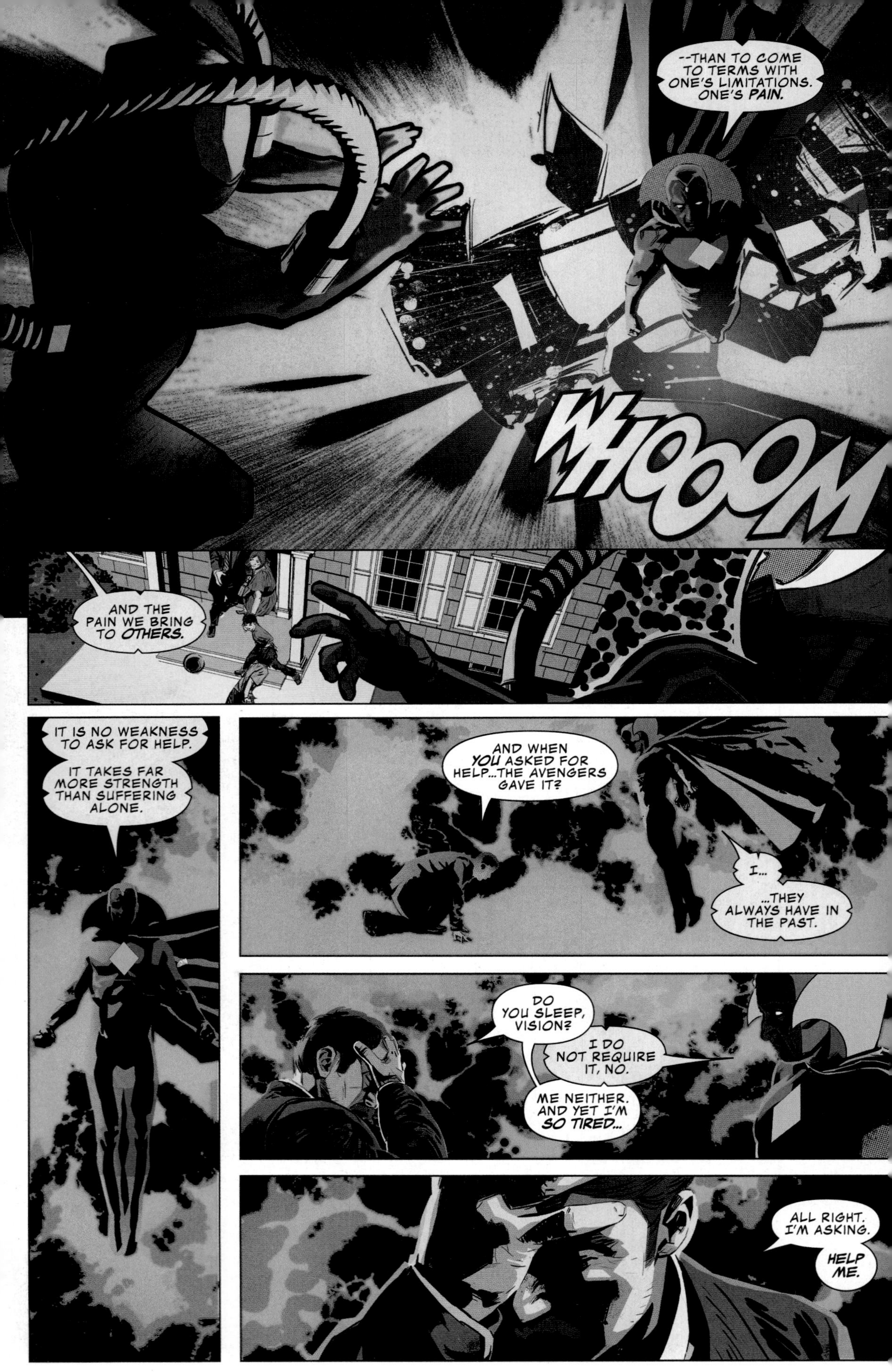
--THAN TO COME TO TERMS WITH ONE'S LIMITATIONS. ONE'S PAIN.
WHOOOM
AND THE PAIN WE BRING TO OTHERS.
IT IS NO WEAKNESS TO ASK FOR HELP.
IT TAKES FAR MORE STRENGTH THAN SUFFERING ALONE.
AND WHEN YOU ASKED FOR HELP...THE AVENGERS GAVE IT?
I...
...THEY ALWAYS HAVE IN THE PAST.
DO YOU SLEEP, VISION?
I DO NOT REQUIRE IT, NO.
ME NEITHER. AND YET I'M SO TIRED...
ALL RIGHT. I'M ASKING.
HELP ME.

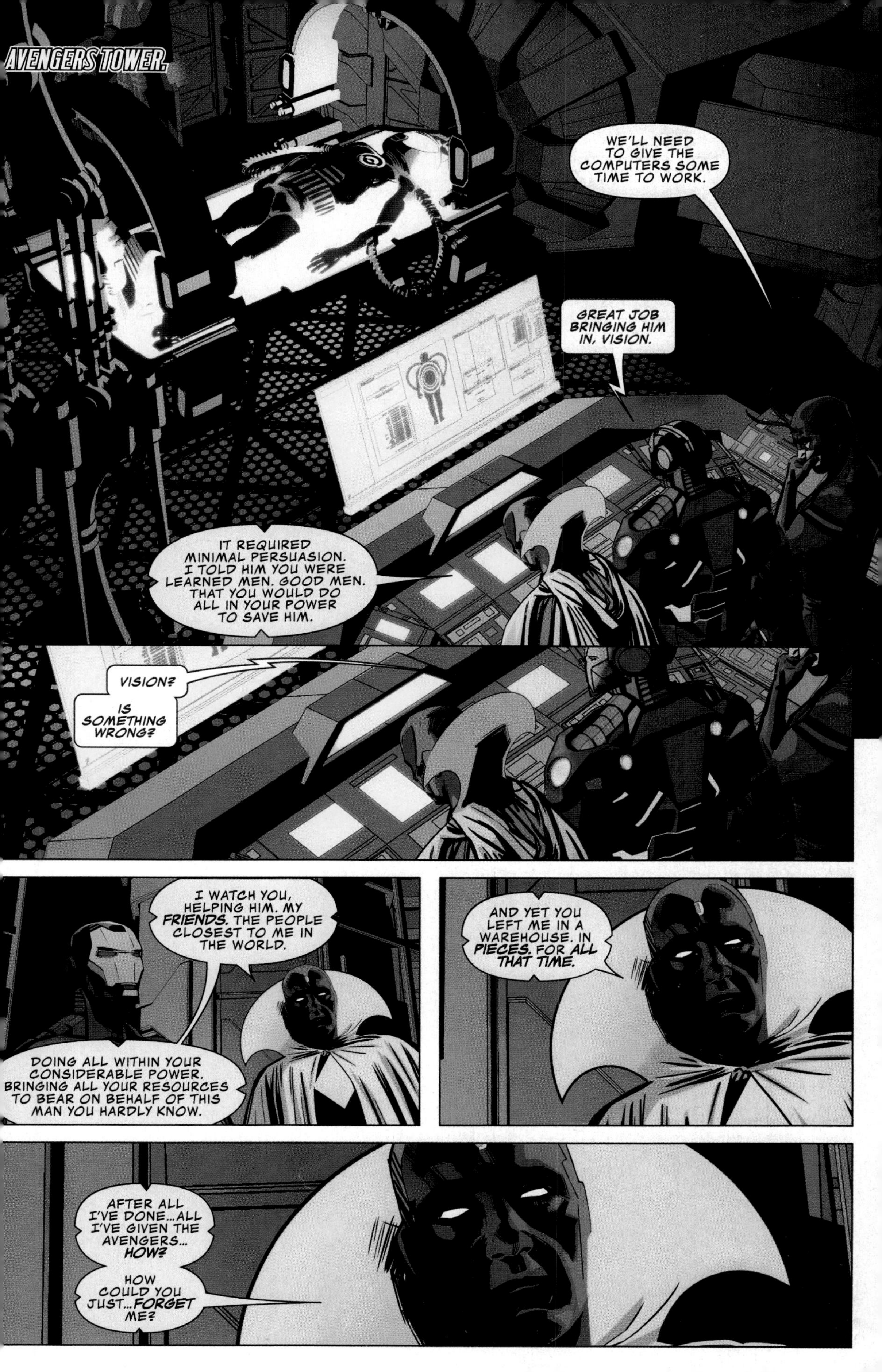
AVENGERS TOWER.
WE'LL NEED TO GIVE THE COMPUTERS SOME TIME TO WORK.
GREAT JOB BRINGING HIM IN, VISION.
IT REQUIRED MINIMAL PERSUASION. I TOLD HIM YOU WERE LEARNED MEN. GOOD MEN. THAT YOU WOULD DO ALL IN YOUR POWER TO SAVE HIM.
VISION?
IS SOMETHING WRONG?
I WATCH YOU, HELPING HIM. MY FRIENDS. THE PEOPLE CLOSEST TO ME IN THE WORLD.
DOING ALL WITHIN YOUR CONSIDERABLE POWER. BRINGING ALL YOUR RESOURCES TO BEAR ON BEHALF OF THIS MAN YOU HARDLY KNOW.
AND YET YOU LEFT ME IN A WAREHOUSE. IN PIECES. FOR ALL THAT TIME.
AFTER ALL I'VE DONE...ALL I'VE GIVEN THE AVENGERS... HOW?
HOW COULD YOU JUST...FORGET ME?

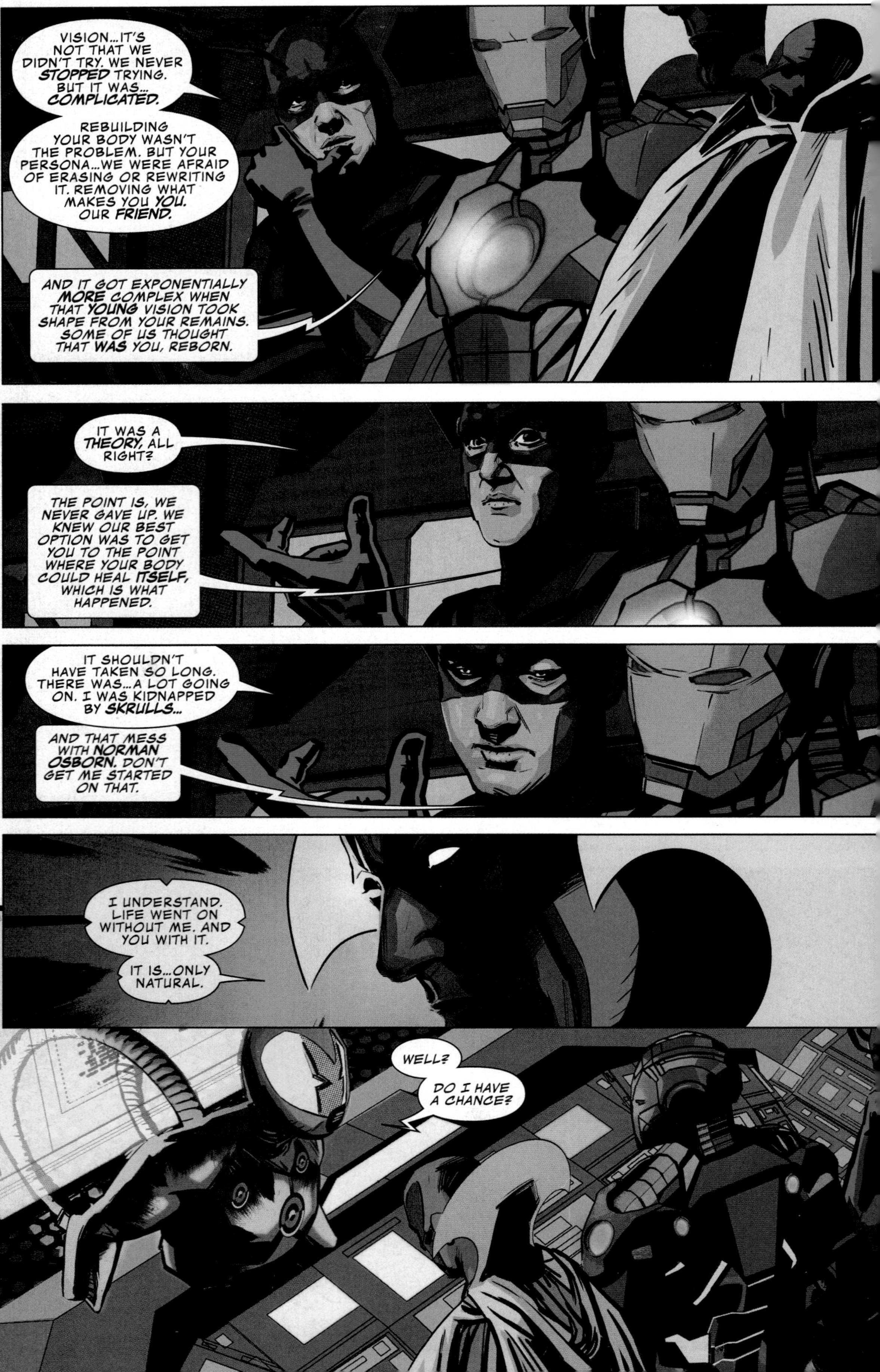
VISION...IT'S NOT THAT WE DIDN'T TRY. WE NEVER STOPPED TRYING. BUT IT WAS... COMPLICATED.
REBUILDING YOUR BODY WASN'T THE PROBLEM. BUT YOUR PERSONA...WE WERE AFRAID OF ERASING OR REWRITING IT. REMOVING WHAT MAKES YOU YOU. OUR FRIEND.
AND IT GOT EXPONENTIALLY MORE COMPLEX WHEN THAT YOUNG VISION TOOK SHAPE FROM YOUR REMAINS. SOME OF US THOUGHT THAT WAS YOU, REBORN.
IT WAS A THEORY, ALL RIGHT?
THE POINT IS, WE NEVER GAVE UP. WE KNEW OUR BEST OPTION WAS TO GET YOU TO THE POINT WHERE YOUR BODY COULD HEAL ITSELF, WHICH IS WHAT HAPPENED.
IT SHOULDN'T HAVE TAKEN SO LONG. THERE WAS...A LOT GOING ON. I WAS KIDNAPPED BY SKRULLS...
AND THAT MESS WITH NORMAN OSBORN. DON'T GET ME STARTED ON THAT.
I UNDERSTAND. LIFE WENT ON WITHOUT ME. AND YOU WITH IT.
IT IS...ONLY NATURAL.
WELL?
DO I HAVE A CHANCE?

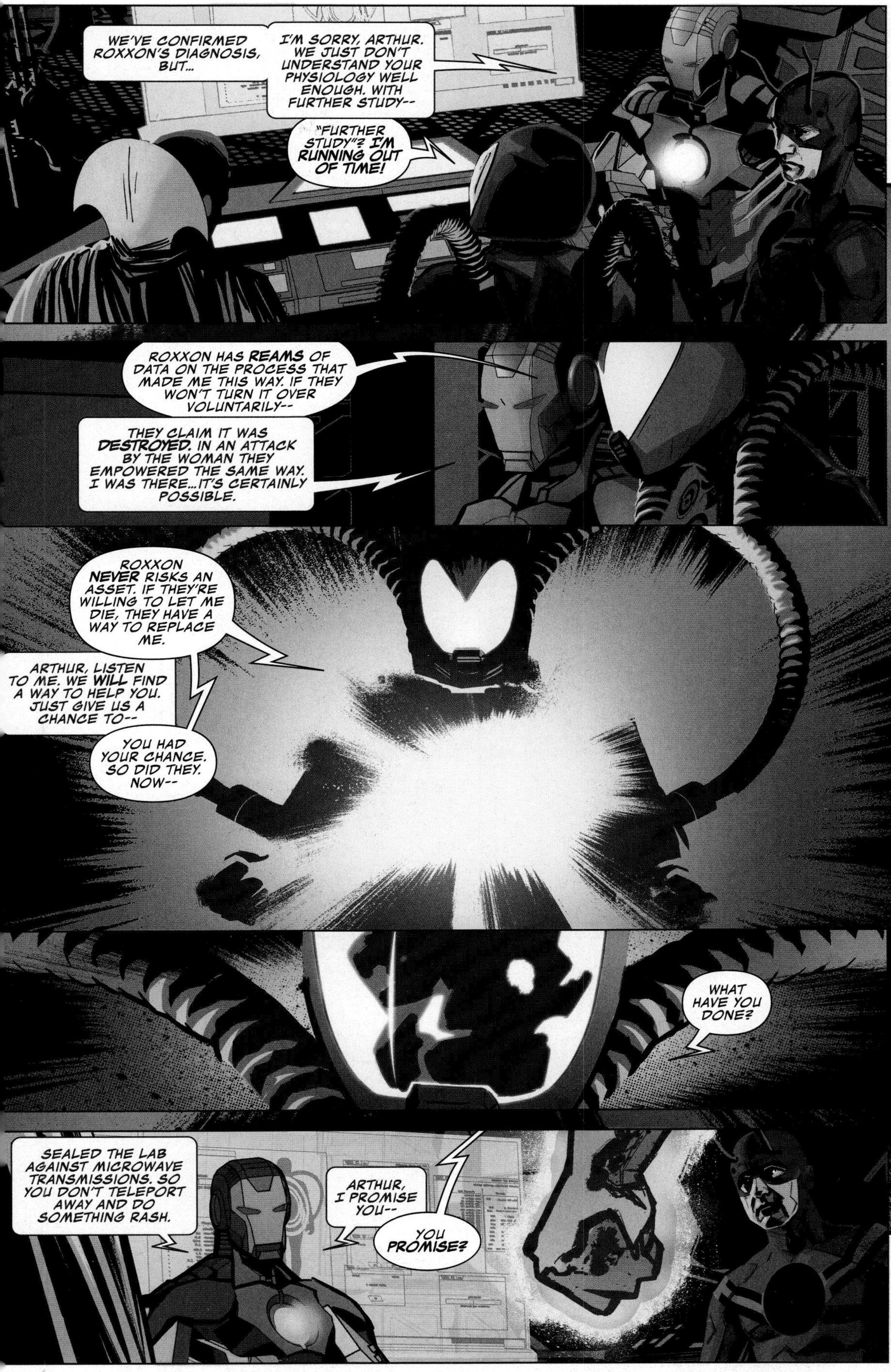
WE'VE CONFIRMED ROXXON'S DIAGNOSIS, BUT...
I'M SORRY, ARTHUR. WE JUST DON'T UNDERSTAND YOUR PHYSIOLOGY WELL ENOUGH. WITH FURTHER STUDY--
"FURTHER STUDY"? I'M RUNNING OUT OF TIME!
ROXXON HAS REAMS OF DATA ON THE PROCESS THAT MADE ME THIS WAY. IF THEY WON'T TURN IT OVER VOLUNTARILY--
THEY CLAIM IT WAS DESTROYED. IN AN ATTACK BY THE WOMAN THEY EMPOWERED THE SAME WAY. I WAS THERE...IT'S CERTAINLY POSSIBLE.
ROXXON NEVER RISKS AN ASSET. IF THEY'RE WILLING TO LET ME DIE, THEY HAVE A WAY TO REPLACE ME.
ARTHUR, LISTEN TO ME. WE WILL FIND A WAY TO HELP YOU. JUST GIVE US A CHANCE TO--
YOU HAD YOUR CHANCE. SO DID THEY. NOW--
WHAT HAVE YOU DONE?
SEALED THE LAB AGAINST MICROWAVE TRANSMISSIONS. SO YOU DON'T TELEPORT AWAY AND DO SOMETHING RASH.
ARTHUR, I PROMISE YOU--
YOU PROMISE?

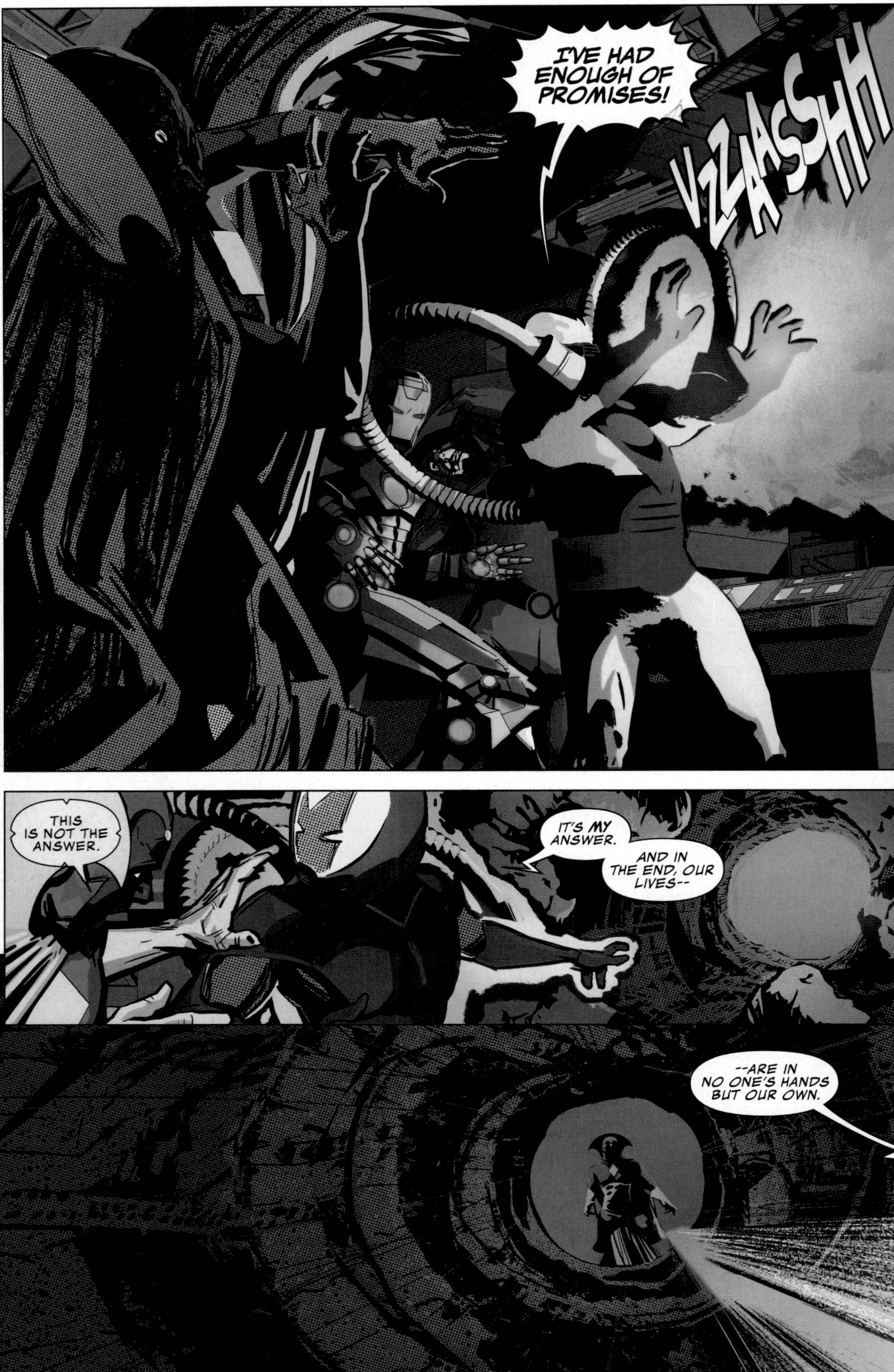
I'VE HAD ENOUGH OF PROMISES!
VZZAASSHH
THIS IS NOT THE ANSWER.
IT'S MY ANSWER.
AND IN THE END, OUR LIVES--
--ARE IN NO ONE'S HANDS BUT OUR OWN.

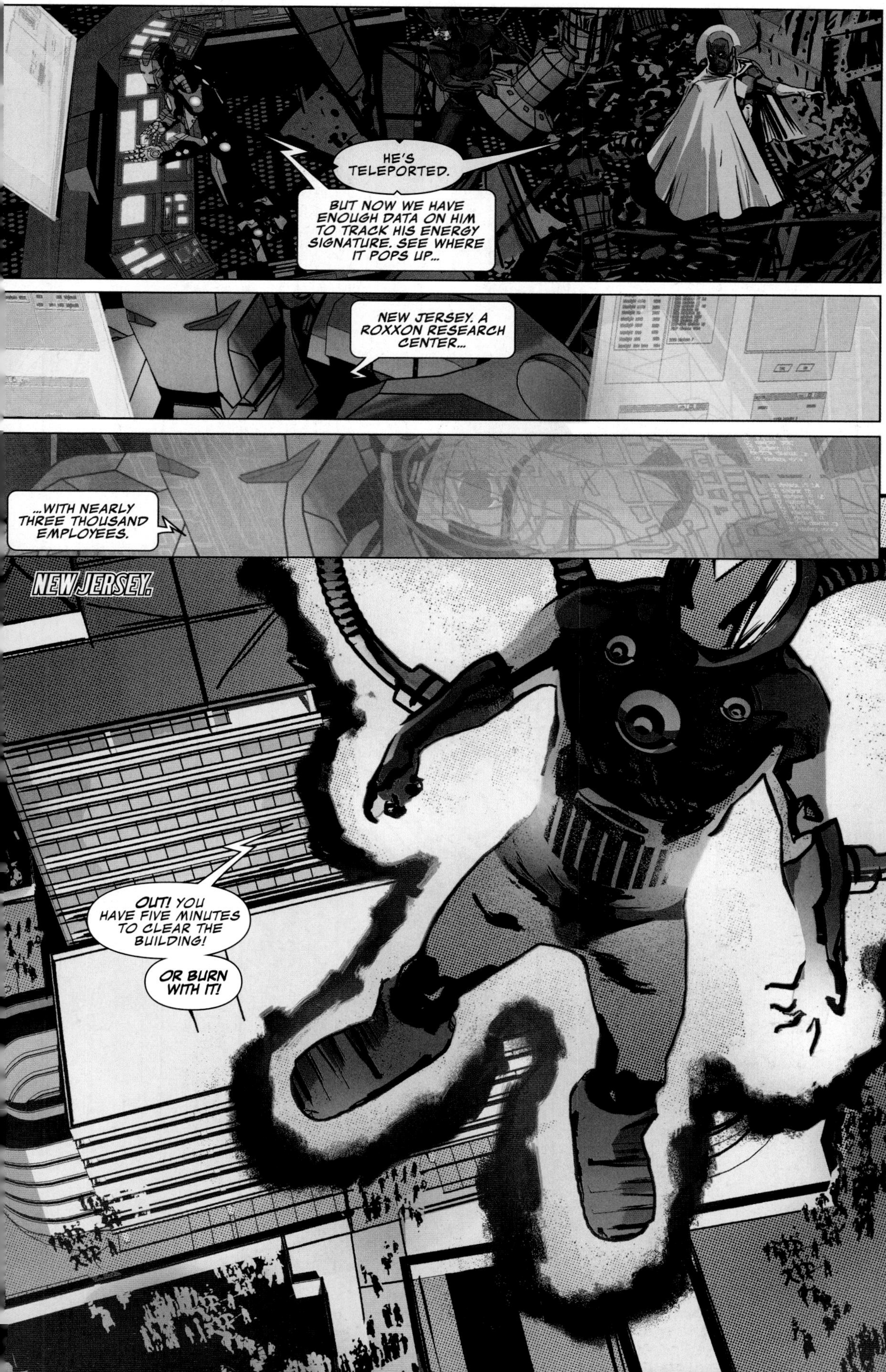
HE'S TELEPORTED.
BUT NOW WE HAVE ENOUGH DATA ON HIM TO TRACK HIS ENERGY SIGNATURE. SEE WHERE IT POPS UP...
NEW JERSEY. A ROXXON RESEARCH CENTER...
...WITH NEARLY THREE THOUSAND EMPLOYEES.
NEW JERSEY.
OUT! YOU HAVE FIVE MINUTES TO CLEAR THE BUILDING!
OR BURN WITH IT!

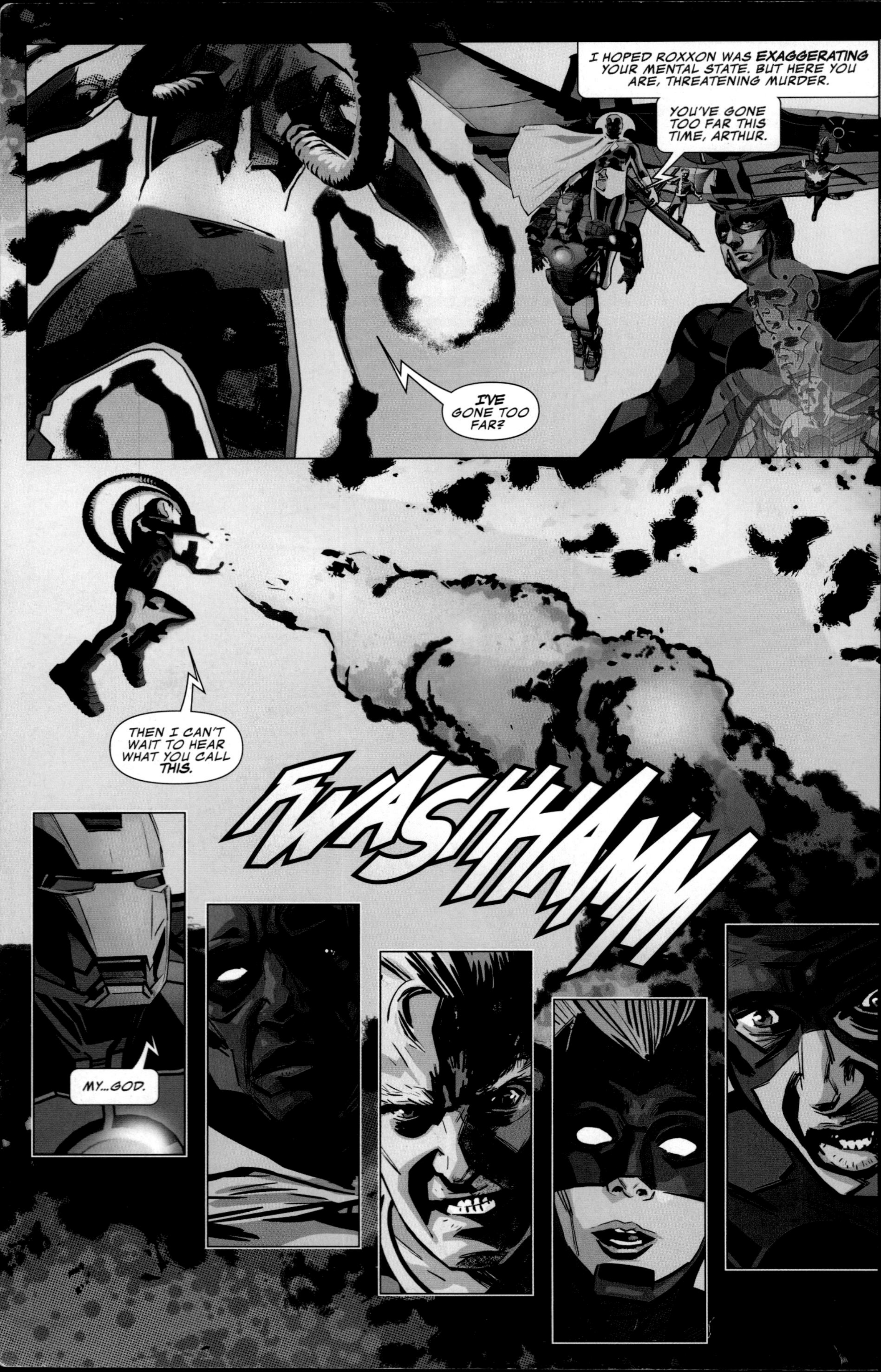
I HOPED ROXXON WAS EXAGGERATING YOUR MENTAL STATE. BUT HERE YOU ARE, THREATENING MURDER.
YOU'VE GONE TOO FAR THIS TIME, ARTHUR.
I'VE GONE TOO FAR?
THEN I CAN'T WAIT TO HEAR WHAT YOU CALL THIS.
FWASHHAMM
MY...GOD.

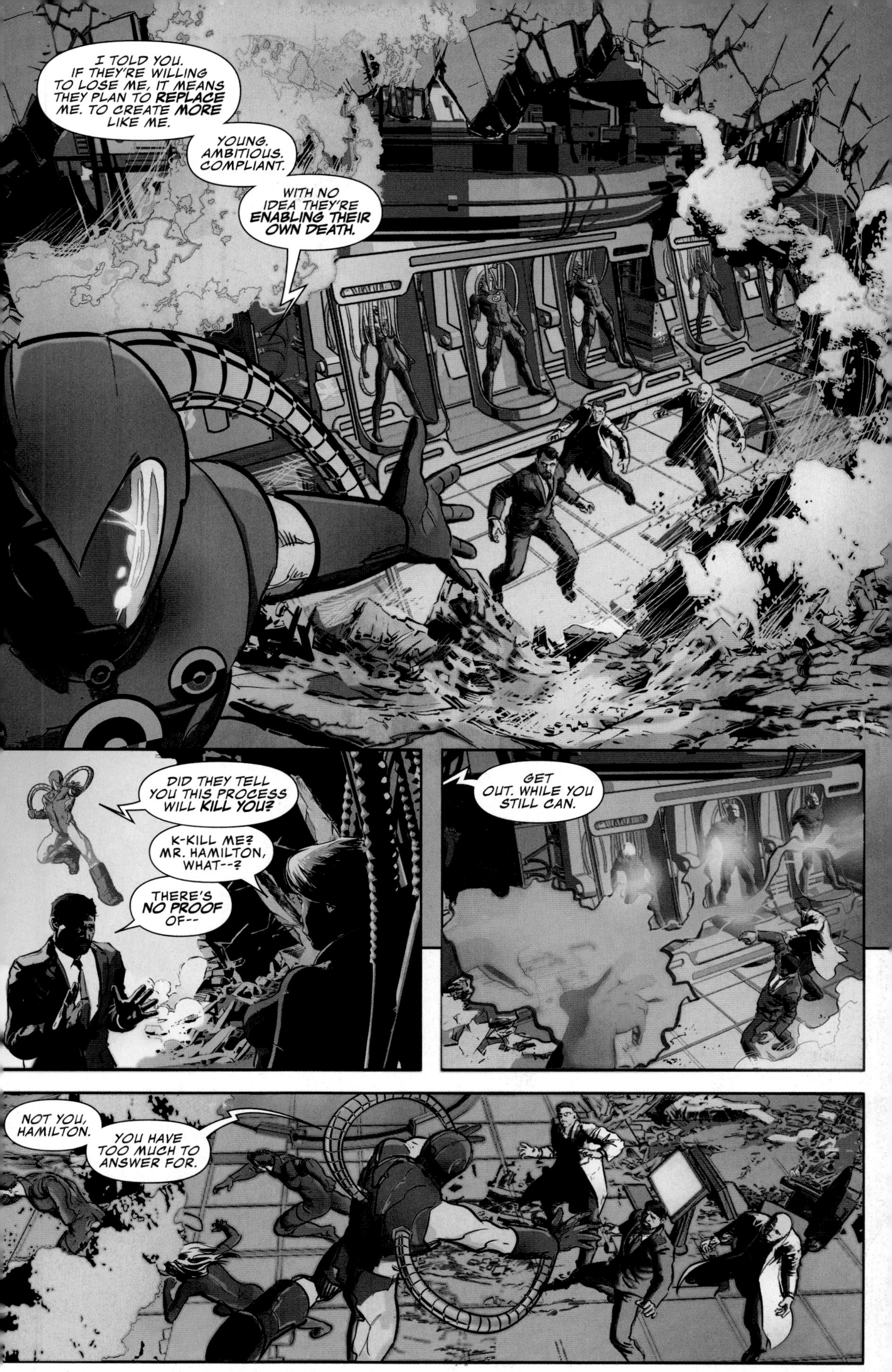
I TOLD YOU. IF THEY'RE WILLING TO LOSE ME, IT MEANS THEY PLAN TO **REPLACE** ME. TO CREATE **MORE** LIKE ME.
YOUNG. AMBITIOUS. COMPLIANT.
WITH NO IDEA THEY'RE **ENABLING THEIR OWN DEATH.**
DID THEY TELL YOU THIS PROCESS WILL **KILL YOU?**
K-KILL ME? MR. HAMILTON, WHAT--?
THERE'S **NO PROOF** OF--
GET OUT. WHILE YOU STILL CAN.
NOT YOU, HAMILTON.
YOU HAVE TOO MUCH TO ANSWER FOR.

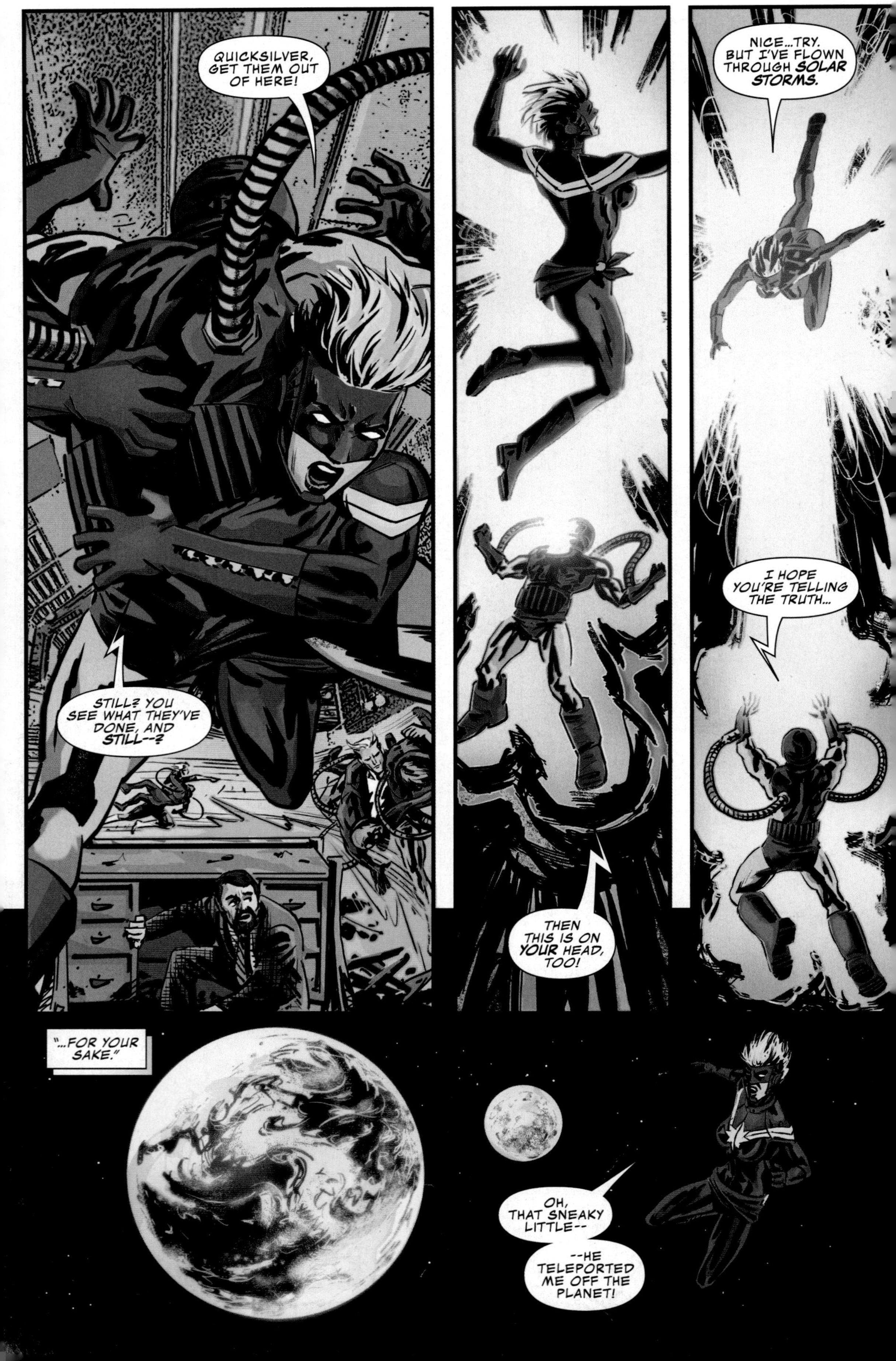
QUICKSILVER, GET THEM OUT OF HERE!
STILL? YOU SEE WHAT THEY'VE DONE, AND STILL--?
THEN THIS IS ON YOUR HEAD, TOO!
NICE...TRY. BUT I'VE FLOWN THROUGH SOLAR STORMS.
I HOPE YOU'RE TELLING THE TRUTH...
"...FOR YOUR SAKE."
OH, THAT SNEAKY LITTLE--
--HE TELEPORTED ME OFF THE PLANET!

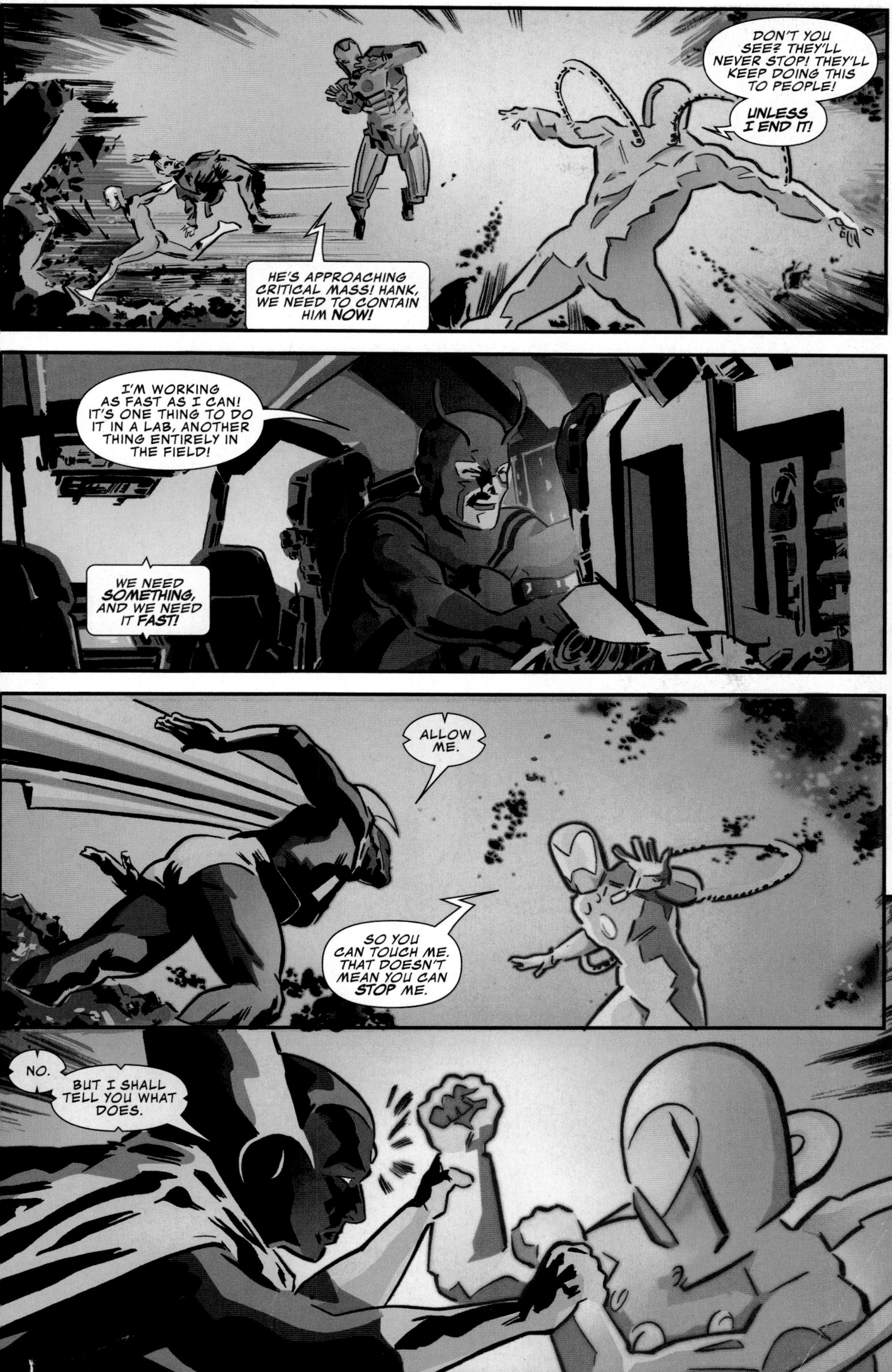
DON'T YOU SEE? THEY'LL NEVER STOP! THEY'LL KEEP DOING THIS TO PEOPLE!
UNLESS I END IT!
HE'S APPROACHING CRITICAL MASS! HANK, WE NEED TO CONTAIN HIM NOW!
I'M WORKING AS FAST AS I CAN! IT'S ONE THING TO DO IT IN A LAB, ANOTHER THING ENTIRELY IN THE FIELD!
WE NEED SOMETHING, AND WE NEED IT FAST!
ALLOW ME.
SO YOU CAN TOUCH ME. THAT DOESN'T MEAN YOU CAN STOP ME.
NO.
BUT I SHALL TELL YOU WHAT DOES.

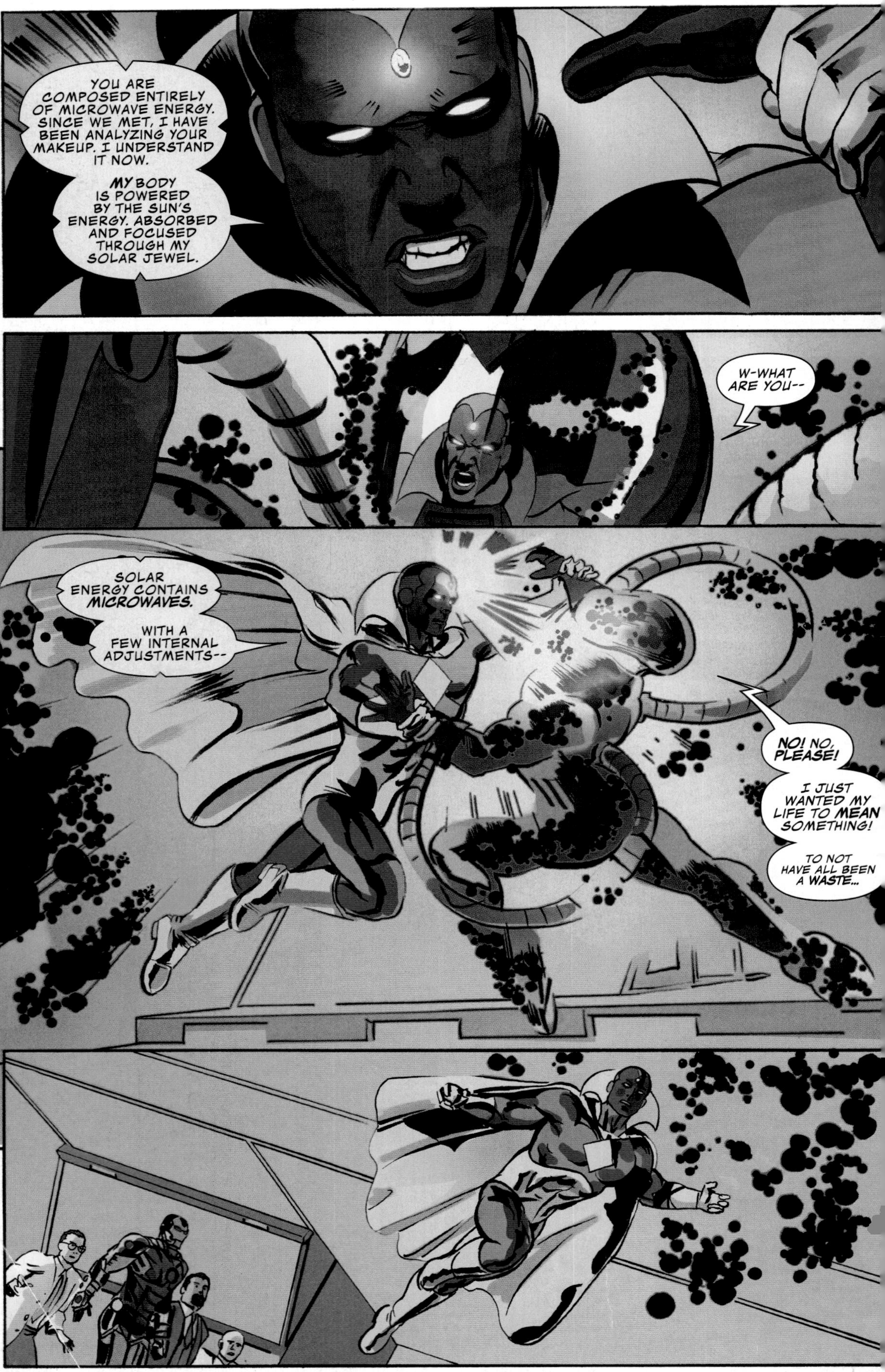
YOU ARE COMPOSED ENTIRELY OF MICROWAVE ENERGY. SINCE WE MET, I HAVE BEEN ANALYZING YOUR MAKEUP. I UNDERSTAND IT NOW.
MY BODY IS POWERED BY THE SUN'S ENERGY. ABSORBED AND FOCUSED THROUGH MY SOLAR JEWEL.
W-WHAT ARE YOU--
SOLAR ENERGY CONTAINS MICROWAVES.
WITH A FEW INTERNAL ADJUSTMENTS--
NO! NO, PLEASE!
I JUST WANTED MY LIFE TO MEAN SOMETHING!
TO NOT HAVE ALL BEEN A WASTE...

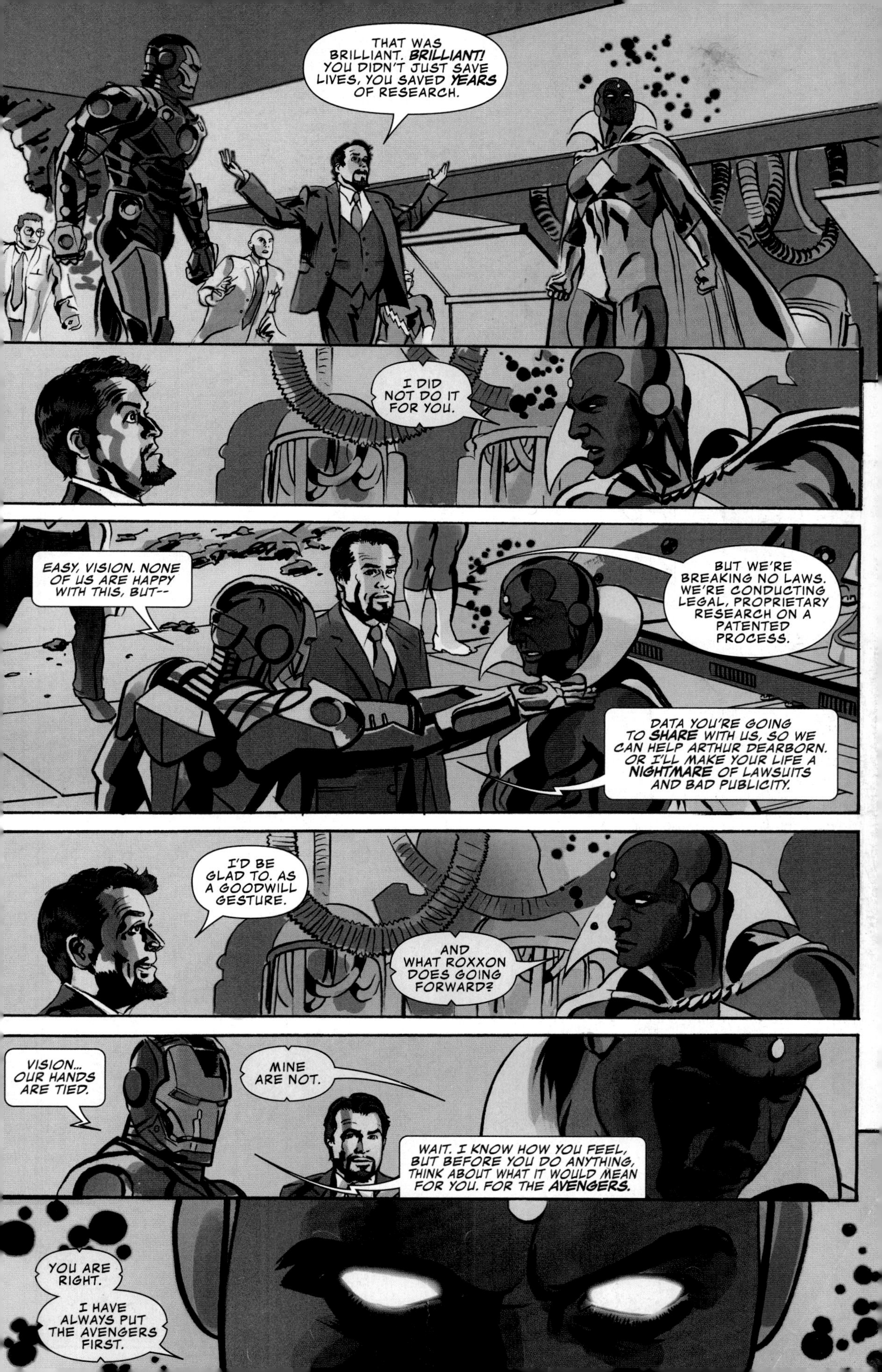
THAT WAS BRILLIANT. BRILLIANT! YOU DIDN'T JUST SAVE LIVES, YOU SAVED YEARS OF RESEARCH.
I DID NOT DO IT FOR YOU.
EASY, VISION. NONE OF US ARE HAPPY WITH THIS, BUT--
BUT WE'RE BREAKING NO LAWS. WE'RE CONDUCTING LEGAL, PROPRIETARY RESEARCH ON A PATENTED PROCESS.
DATA YOU'RE GOING TO SHARE WITH US, SO WE CAN HELP ARTHUR DEARBORN. OR I'LL MAKE YOUR LIFE A NIGHTMARE OF LAWSUITS AND BAD PUBLICITY.
I'D BE GLAD TO. AS A GOODWILL GESTURE.
AND WHAT ROXXON DOES GOING FORWARD?
VISION... OUR HANDS ARE TIED.
MINE ARE NOT.
WAIT. I KNOW HOW YOU FEEL, BUT BEFORE YOU DO ANYTHING, THINK ABOUT WHAT IT WOULD MEAN FOR YOU. FOR THE AVENGERS.
YOU ARE RIGHT.
I HAVE ALWAYS PUT THE AVENGERS FIRST.

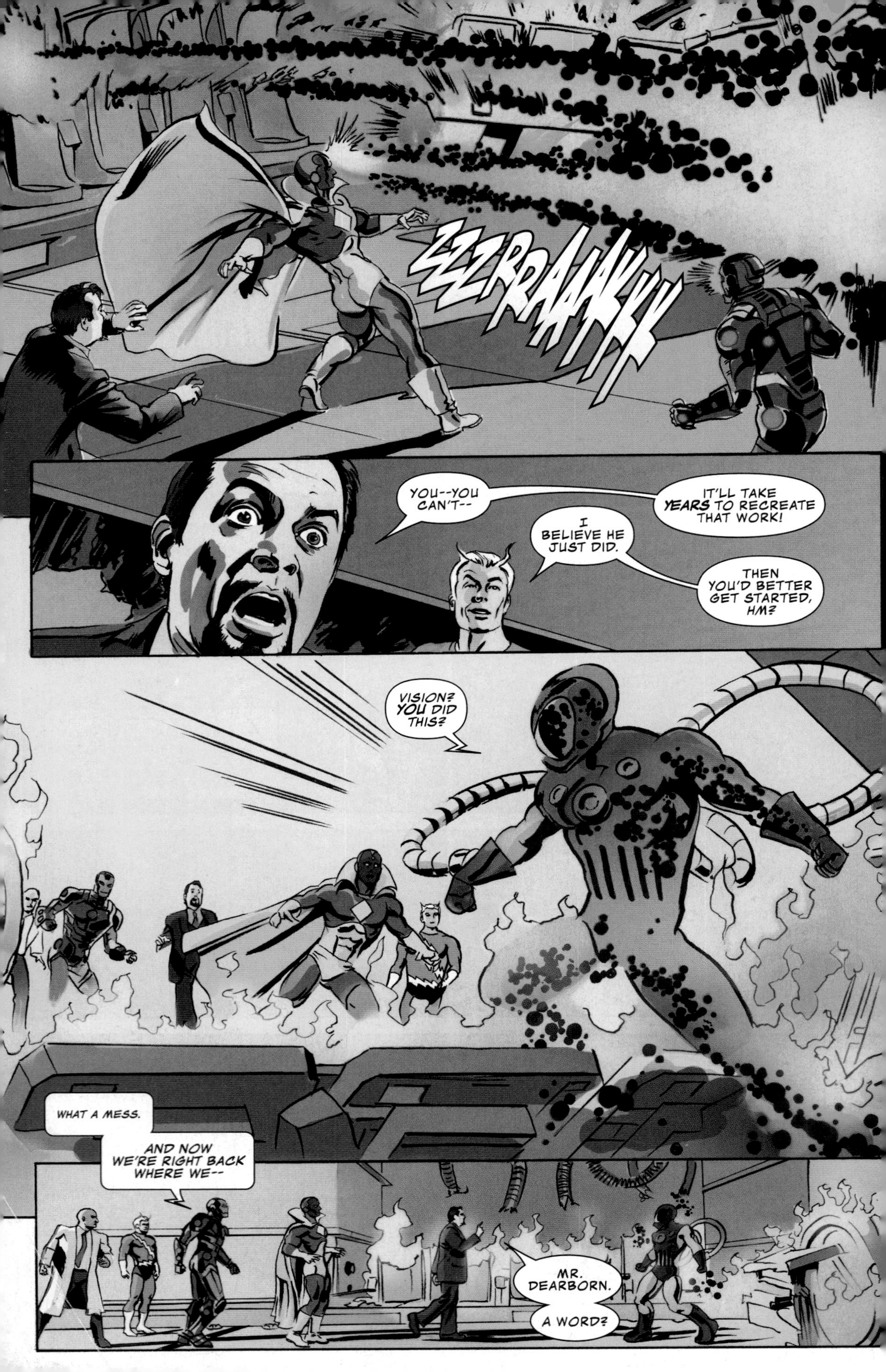

ZZZRRAAKKK
YOU--YOU CAN'T--
IT'LL TAKE YEARS TO RECREATE THAT WORK!
I BELIEVE HE JUST DID.
THEN YOU'D BETTER GET STARTED, HM?
VISION? YOU DID THIS?
WHAT A MESS.
AND NOW WE'RE RIGHT BACK WHERE WE--
MR. DEARBORN.
A WORD?

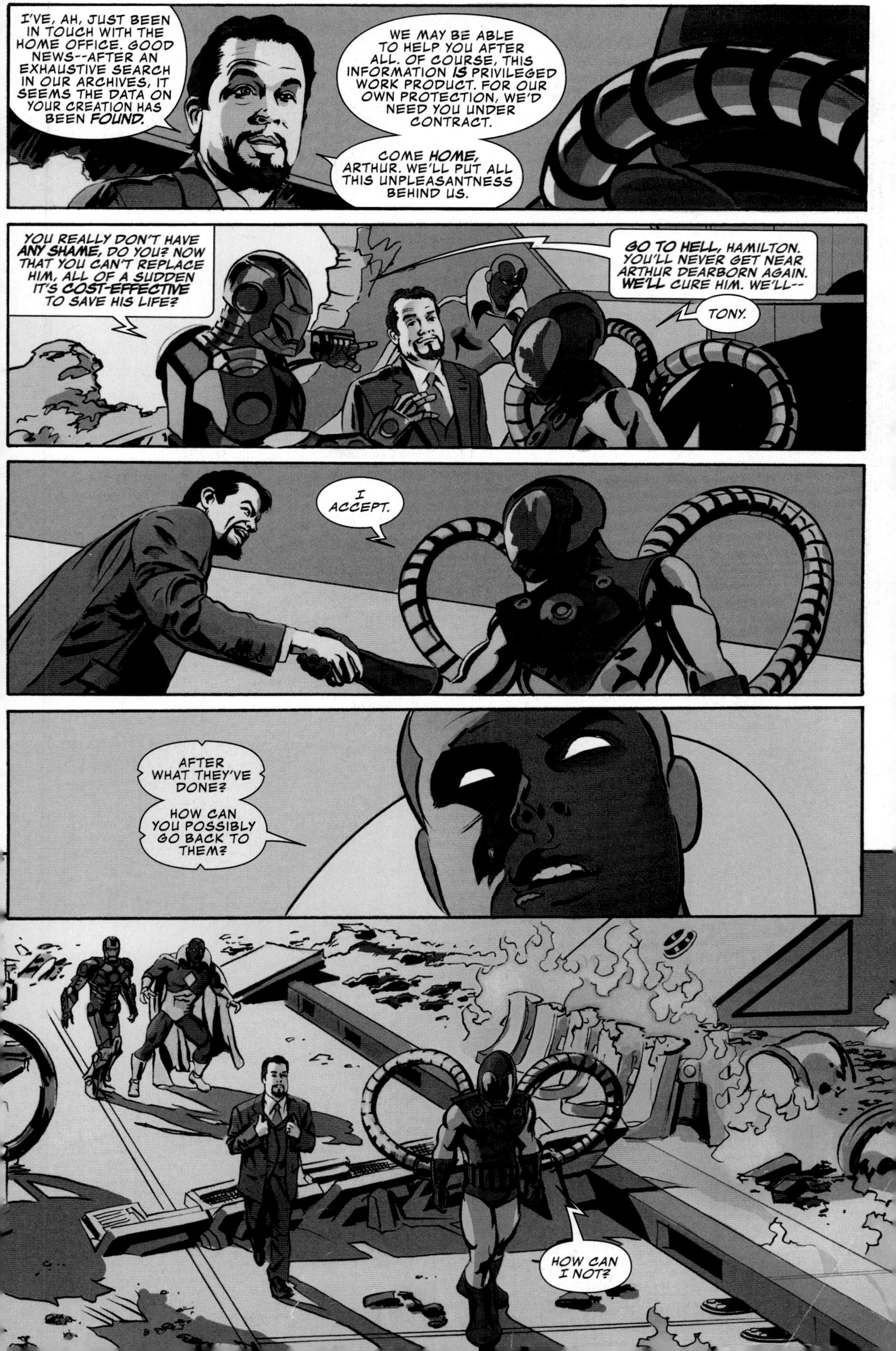
I'VE, AH, JUST BEEN IN TOUCH WITH THE HOME OFFICE. GOOD NEWS--AFTER AN EXHAUSTIVE SEARCH IN OUR ARCHIVES, IT SEEMS THE DATA ON YOUR CREATION HAS BEEN FOUND.
WE MAY BE ABLE TO HELP YOU AFTER ALL. OF COURSE, THIS INFORMATION IS PRIVILEGED WORK PRODUCT. FOR OUR OWN PROTECTION, WE'D NEED YOU UNDER CONTRACT.
COME HOME, ARTHUR. WE'LL PUT ALL THIS UNPLEASANTNESS BEHIND US.
YOU REALLY DON'T HAVE ANY SHAME, DO YOU? NOW THAT YOU CAN'T REPLACE HIM, ALL OF A SUDDEN IT'S COST-EFFECTIVE TO SAVE HIS LIFE?
GO TO HELL, HAMILTON. YOU'LL NEVER GET NEAR ARTHUR DEARBORN AGAIN. WE'LL CURE HIM. WE'LL--
TONY.
I ACCEPT.
AFTER WHAT THEY'VE DONE?
HOW CAN YOU POSSIBLY GO BACK TO THEM?
HOW CAN I NOT?

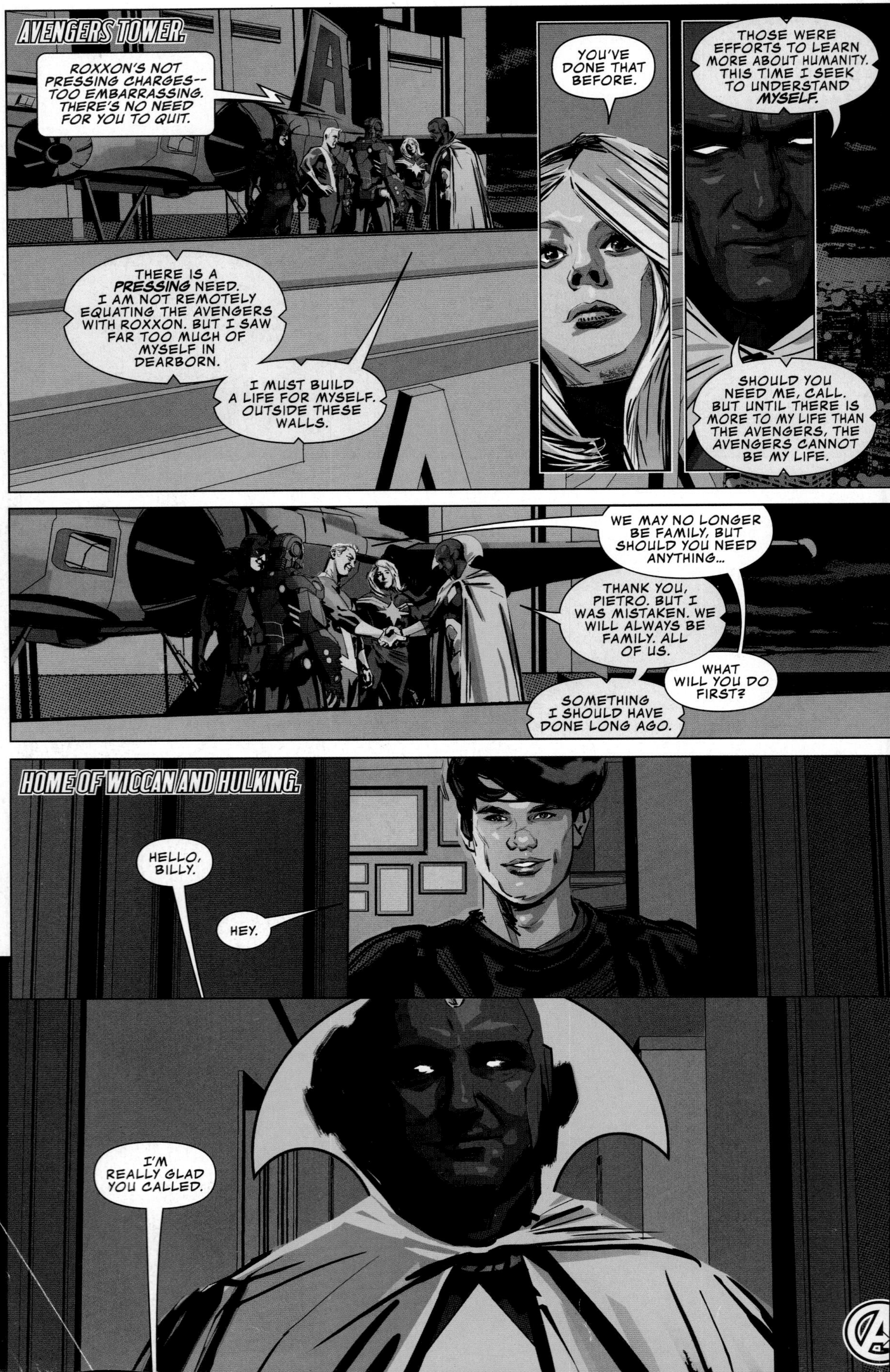
AVENGERS TOWER.
ROXXON'S NOT PRESSING CHARGES-- TOO EMBARRASSING. THERE'S NO NEED FOR YOU TO QUIT.
THERE IS A PRESSING NEED. I AM NOT REMOTELY EQUATING THE AVENGERS WITH ROXXON. BUT I SAW FAR TOO MUCH OF MYSELF IN DEARBORN.
I MUST BUILD A LIFE FOR MYSELF. OUTSIDE THESE WALLS.
YOU'VE DONE THAT BEFORE.
THOSE WERE EFFORTS TO LEARN MORE ABOUT HUMANITY. THIS TIME I SEEK TO UNDERSTAND MYSELF.
SHOULD YOU NEED ME, CALL. BUT UNTIL THERE IS MORE TO MY LIFE THAN THE AVENGERS, THE AVENGERS CANNOT BE MY LIFE.
WE MAY NO LONGER BE FAMILY, BUT SHOULD YOU NEED ANYTHING...
THANK YOU, PIETRO. BUT I WAS MISTAKEN. WE WILL ALWAYS BE FAMILY. ALL OF US.
WHAT WILL YOU DO FIRST?
SOMETHING I SHOULD HAVE DONE LONG AGO.
HOME OF WICCAN AND HULKING.
HELLO, BILLY.
HEY.
I'M REALLY GLAD YOU CALLED.

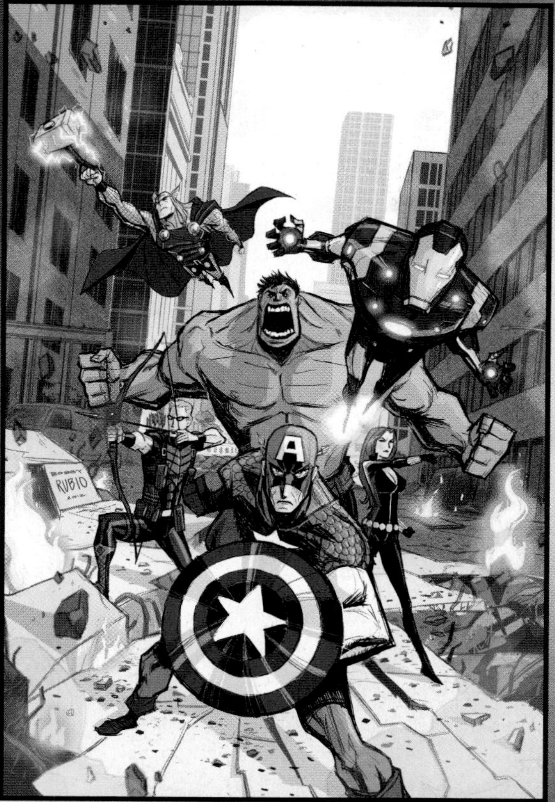
RUBIO

#9 VARIANT BY BOBBY RUBIO

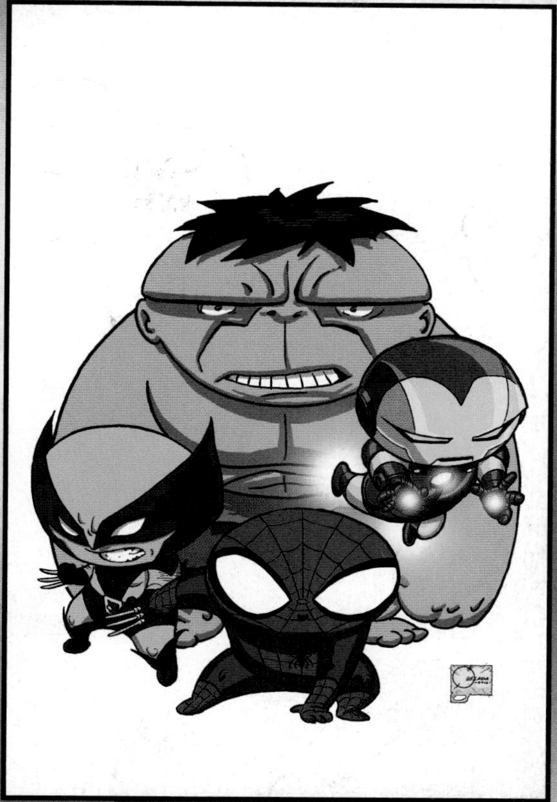

#9 VARIANT BY JOE QUESADA

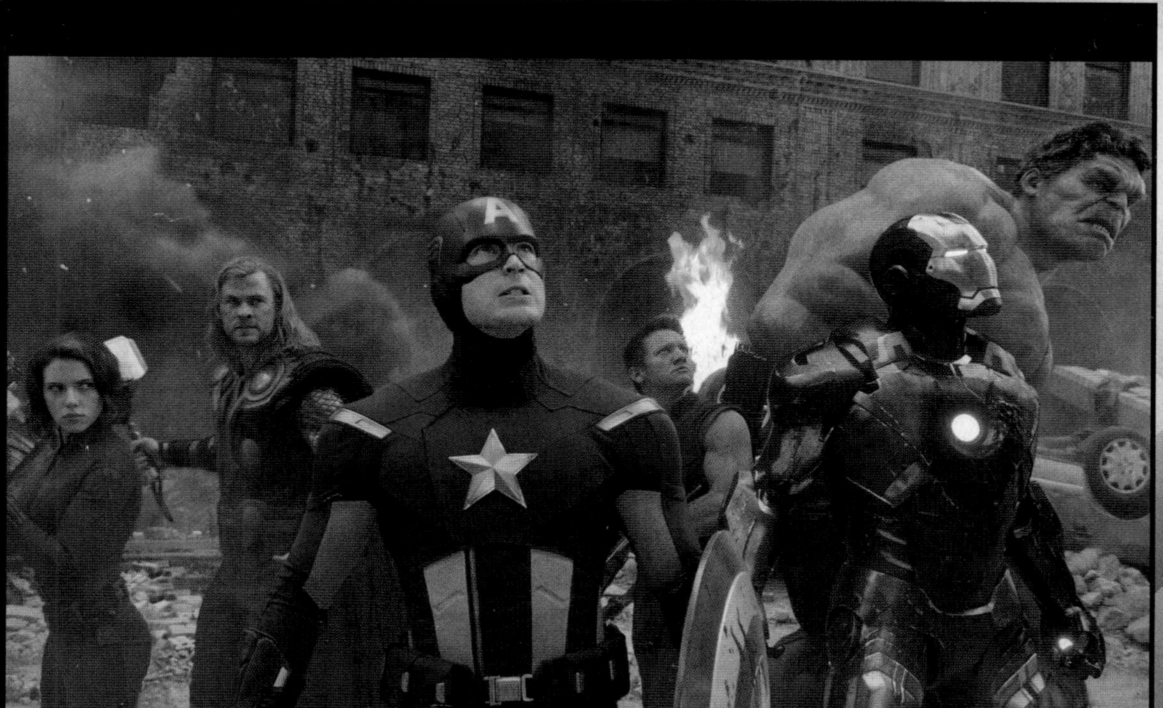

#9 WRAPAROUND VARIANT

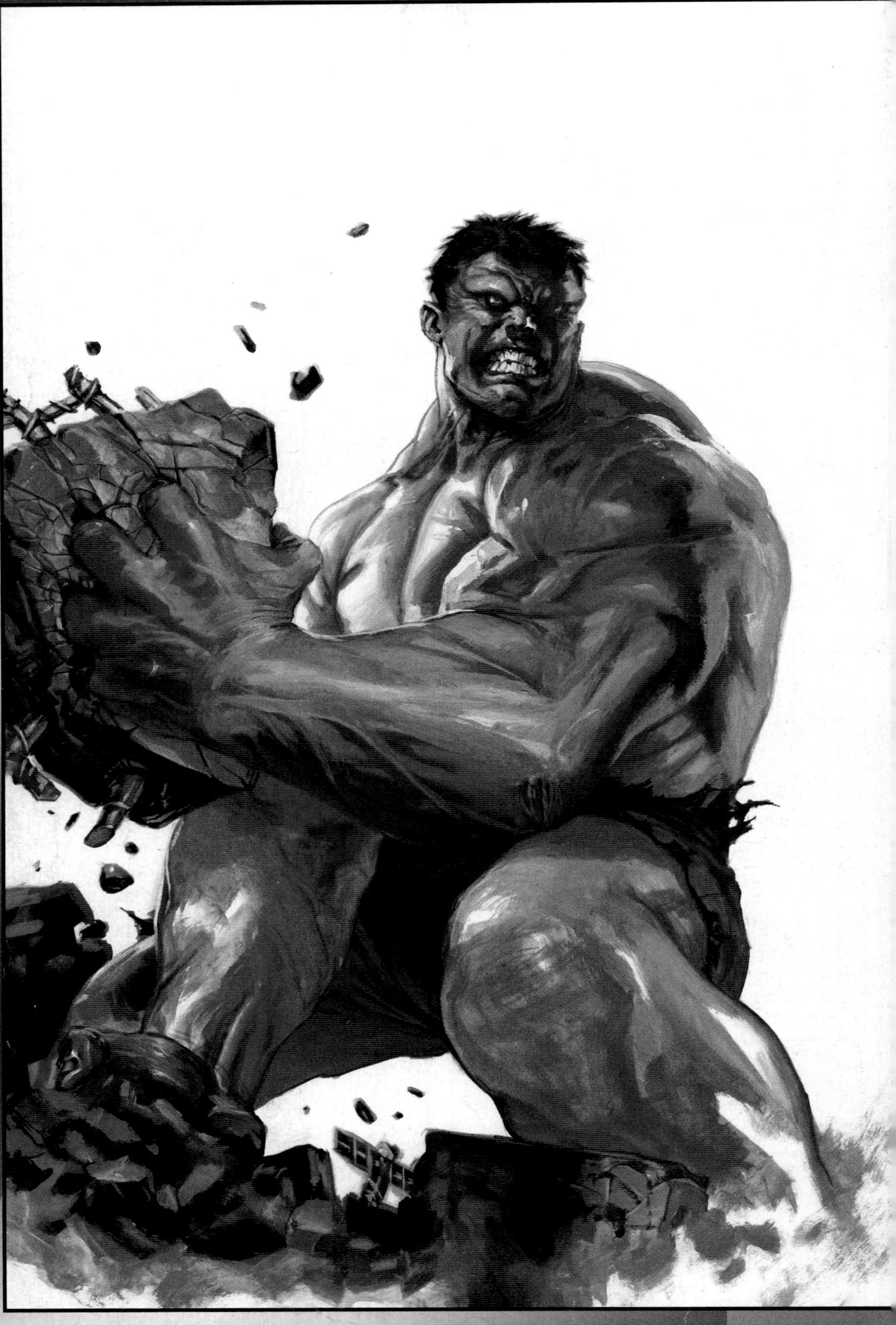

#10 VARIANT BY GABRIELE DELL'OTTO

#11 VARIANT BY STEPHANE PERGER

#13 VARIANT BY IN-HYUK LEE

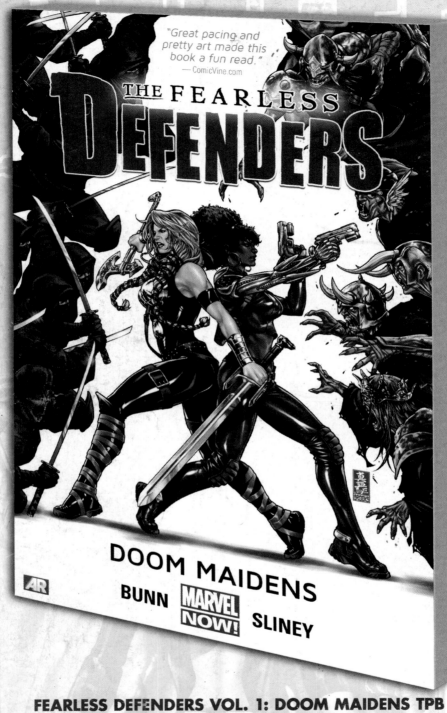